Consciousness and the Limits of Objectivity

Consciousness and the Limits of Objectivity

The Case for Subjective Physicalism

Robert J. Howell

OXFORD
UNIVERSITY PRESS

OXFORD
UNIVERSITY PRESS

Great Clarendon Street, Oxford, OX2 6DP,
United Kingdom

Oxford University Press is a department of the University of Oxford.
It furthers the University's objective of excellence in research, scholarship,
and education by publishing worldwide. Oxford is a registered trade mark of
Oxford University press in the UK and in certain other countries

First Edition published in 2013

Impression: 1

British Library Cataloguing in Publication Data

Data available

ISBN 978–0–19–965466–6

Printed and bound by CPI Group (UK) Ltd, Croydon, CR0 4YY

To Lanie

Contents

Acknowledgments

Several portions of this book have been adapted, often with significant changes, from previous publications. Parts of Chapter 1 were published in 2011 as "Physicalism, Old School," in *Consciousness and the Mind Body Problem: A Reader*. Eds. Torin Alter and Robert J. Howell, New York: Oxford University Press. Most of Chapter 2 was published in 2009 as "Emergentism and Supervenience Physicalism," *Australasian Journal of Philosophy*, 87:1. Portions of Chapters 3 and 4 involve arguments from "The Knowledge Argument and Objectivity," *Philosophical Studies*, September 2007. Chapter 5 is a revision of "The Ontology of Subjective Physicalism" *Nous*, 43:2, 2009.

Research on this book was aided in part by research leave granted by SMU in the Fall of 2009 during which I was a visiting scholar at the New York University department of philosophy as part of the NYU Consciousness Institute. My sincerest thanks to both SMU and NYU for their support. While in New York City, I received valuable support from the Ferris/Kennedy home for wayward philosophers, and I cannot thank Josh, Elizabeth, and Coop enough for their hospitality and friendship.

I have benefitted enormously from discussions with many individuals over the years. Though this book did not grow out of dissertation work, my advisors Jaegwon Kim and Ernest Sosa have continued to be very nurturing, and discussions with Jaegwon in particular have (quite obviously) continued to have a strong impact on my thinking about the topics in this book. I also benefitted greatly from an NEH Seminar in Mind and Metaphysics led by John Heil. John and the participants in that seminar were crucial in helping me get some of the key ideas into shape and I thank them all. Thanks to audiences at the University of Alabama, Brown University, and Washington University in St Louis, as well as audiences at the Tucson Consciousness Conference and several APA sessions. I am very grateful for, and have learned much from, discussions with Roberta Ballerin, Kati Balog, Jacob Berger, Ned Block, Richard Brown, Max Deutsch, Josh Dever, Carrie Figdor, Brie Gertler, Chris Hill, Cory Juhl, Amy Kind, Uriah Kriegel, William Lycan, Pete Mandik, Andrew Melnyk, Kevin Morris, Brendan Murday, Alyssa Ney, Brendan O'Sullivan, David

Papineau, Derk Pereboom, David Pitt, Jim Pryor, Ted Sider, Jon Simon, David Sosa, Jonathan Sutton, and Jessica Wilson. Special thanks go to Peter Momtchiloff for his continued editorial guidance.

I have the great fortune to be in an extremely collegial department filled with very strong philosophers. Everyone in the SMU department has helped me with this book in one way or another. I owe Doug Ehring a great debt for helping me become a better writer and philosopher during the past ten years, and the leadership and insights of Eric Barnes and Steve Sverdlik have been very important to me as well. I am particularly lucky to have as colleagues three excellent philosophers of mind who keep me honest and make me better: Philipe Chuard, Justin Fisher, and Brad Thompson. Philippe and Brad both read complete drafts of the book, prompting crucial revisions. Problems with the book remain—I know, because Philippe told me—but it would be a much weaker book indeed were it not for the BrainPains crew.

Ken Daley and Clayton Littlejohn deserve special mention not only for their insights in many a philosophical discussion, but for their friendship and support. I owe Torin Alter more than I can say, not only for being an inspiring co-author and for reading draft after draft of my own work, but for being one of my dearest friends. I doubt this book would exist without him.

Although it deserves a larger forum, I can't help but take space here to thank one of the angels of our discipline. David Chalmers is of course a philosopher of the highest order, but if he had never put pen to paper he would remain one of philosophy's MVPs. His willingness to help others, especially younger philosophers who have yet to achieve prominence, raises the bar for all of us. Though he didn't know me from Adam when I sent him my first paper on consciousness almost a decade ago, he read it and got back to me with comments in less than 12 hours . . . from Canberra. Again and again he has read my work, usually quickly finding the flaws that sent me back to the drawing board. Throughout, though, he has always been encouraging and has become a true mentor and friend.

Finally, I offer my greatest thanks to my wife Lanie, to whom this book is dedicated. Her support has been crucial to all of my work, and her love and friendship continues to make me a better person in all ways. As I finish this book, Lanie is just days away from giving birth to our first child. That's not only given me joy, but it's helped keep things in perspective. The book is done, but I eagerly await our next chapter.

Introduction

Writing a book about the philosophical problem of consciousness is a bit like opening a restaurant in New York City. Surely there are only so many ways to prepare a fish! When it comes to consciousness, positions have been staked out, mapped out, and the logical space seems to be getting pretty tight. The problem is by now familiar: conscious states, such as the state of seeing red or feeling pain, have natures that seem to be beyond the reach of physical explanation. While physics and the physical sciences can explain all the pushings and pullings of the world, and those pushings and pullings can explain a surprising amount, it is difficult to imagine how they might fully explain what it's like to taste chocolate. These features of experiences can only be known "from the inside" by actually having the experiences. Faced with this difficulty, most philosophers have divided into three factions:

The hardliners: The hardliners deny the initial intuition, or at least its value in thinking about consciousness. Consciousness can be fully explained and understood by the physical sciences, and actually experiencing those states will add nothing to that understanding.

The epistemicists: The epistemicists maintain that though there is something one can learn by actually having an experience, this does not imply that physicalism is false. There is an epistemic gap between our understanding of physical states and our understanding of conscious phenomenal states, but there is no corresponding metaphysical gap.

The non-physicalists: The non-physicalists—who include dualists, panpsychists, proto-panpsychists, and the like—claim that this gap between our understanding of the physical world and our grasp of phenomenal consciousness does warrant a metaphysical conclusion. Physicalism must be false.

While there are ways of carving things up into thinner slices, this threefold division captures the major positions. One group denies the datum (or at least its importance as datum), another group accepts the datum and denies the inference from it, and the last group accepts both. Unless everyone has the basic dialectic incorrect, these positions seem to exhaust logical space. Each space is well populated by individuals with subtly different views, and excepting a few conversions, once philosophers choose a place to camp they rarely feel the need to move.

The majority of philosophers, it seems, are satisfied with the epistemicist position in one form or another, pleased to be able to have their cake and eat it too. While I will ultimately embrace a version of epistemicism, it is one of the main themes of this book that current epistemicists have not yet earned their peace of mind.[1] When subjected to scrutiny their view has a distinctly non-physicalist fragrance. In particular, I will argue that maintaining their view requires them to believe in a special epistemic relation, the relation of acquaintance, which is not easily squared with a purely physicalistic outlook. What's more, this commitment in turn forces them to deny that any objective depiction of the world can be complete. That is, physics must in some sense prove incomplete.

I suspect that if convinced of my arguments, many current epistemicists will find themselves sliding to a hardline stance. Denying "objectivism" will seem far too close to denying physicalism for most physicalists. I think this worry is real, and it should be recognized, but that there is ultimately a way to save the epistemicist project from complete collapse. It is to embrace a "subjective physicalism." Doing so, however, will require a bit more metaphysical spadework than most epistemicists have done. Even making sense of subjective physicalism takes a little doing, much less making it palatable.

This book attempts to show a way forward for the dedicated physicalist who is gripped by the problem of consciousness and wants to give the basic data their full due. It does so in part by developing a truly metaphysical definition of physicalism, untainted by epistemic elements, and it argues that only by questioning the non-physicalist's metaphysical arguments "upstream" of his position that the anti-physicalist arguments can be

---

[1] It is instructive, I think, that one of the earliest epistemicists—Terry Horgan (1984) —doesn't seem to have this peace of mind. The worries expressed in Horgan and Tienson (2001), for example, are of the sort that must still be dealt with.

resisted. It also attempts to explain the role of acquaintance in our appre-
hension of phenomenal properties, and to explain how the introduction of
this relation solves problems without introducing worse ones. In my view,
subjective physicalism is not so much an alternative to epistemicism as it is
a more honest and more complete form of it. It is more honest, I claim,
because it acknowledges its dependence on acquaintance and the loss of
objectivism. It is more complete because it recognizes that simply "going
epistemic," even to the point of embracing acquaintance, doesn't get one
out of the anti-physicalist arguments unless some further ontological work
is done.

Subjective physicalism occupies an admittedly uncomfortable space
between traditional epistemicism and non-physicalism. It can seem so
uncomfortable—a fact I discuss in the final chapter—that one wonders
why one shouldn't just give up the game and become a dualist or some
other flavor of non-physicalist! The reason is simple: these views, far from
bringing phenomenal experience to the fore, unintentionally relegate
them to irrelevance.

Although the problem of mental causation is well rehearsed, it is worth
reviewing. This problem provides a significant part of the motivation for a
physicalistic account of the puzzle of conscious experience, and it will
occupy the background of much of the discussion to come. The problem
of mental causation is a result of the apparent inconsistency of the
following independently plausible theses:

1. *Mental distinctness*: The mental is not identical with the physical.
2. *Physical adequacy*: Physical events have sufficient physical causes if
   they are caused at all.[2]
3. *Mental causation*: Some physical events are caused by mental events.
4. *Non-overdetermination*: Not every case of mental causation is a case of
   overdetermination.

If these theses are in fact inconsistent, any three of them constitutes a valid
argument against the fourth. It is not unusual for physicalists to argue

---

[2] I prefer speaking of physical adequacy instead of "the causal closure of the physical" since
the latter, but not the former, seems to imply that physical events only cause physical events.
This problem arises, however, from the plausible view that a physical account can be provided
for why physical events happen.

against mental distinctness by appealing to theses 2 through 4. Papineau puts the case succinctly:

> Many effects that we attribute to conscious causes have full physical causes. But it would be absurd to suppose that these effects are caused twice over. So, the conscious causes must be identical to some part of those physical causes.[3]

It is somewhat ironic that the physicalist is in a better position than the dualist to acknowledge the centrality of conscious thought in our lives. In fact, the dualist faces a painful choice between isolation and infection: either conscious states exist in causal isolation without contributing anything new to the physical world (which is a consequence of rejecting either mental causation or non-overdetermination) or there are physical events that cannot be explained by the physical sciences. In the latter case consciousness is not simply a benign addition to the physical system but infects causal claims within the domain of physics.

It is important not to underestimate the significance of either isolation or infection. It is tempting to think that the epiphenomenality of consciousness might not be such a disaster. It might even be thought that contemporary science is showing us that consciousness does not play the causal role we think it does, and so the epiphenomenality of consciousness actually receives empirical support.[4] This cannot be the case. Even if it turns out that conscious experiences do not play the roles in behavior that we think they do, the idea that they play no role at all is absurd. At the very least conscious states had better play a causal role in our knowledge of them and in our talk about them. The empirical tests, in fact, assume as much since they rely upon physical signs (such as verbal reports) to tell the experimenter when the conscious experience is present. Surely if we have to give up on the idea that our reports and descriptions of our conscious experiences are not in fact caused by them we should second guess our resistance to eliminativism. After all, it would be hard to explain how we are in epistemic contact with them at all!

The infection that would come with interactionist dualism is probably to be preferred to epiphenomenalism, but the consequences are pretty undesirable here as well. Consider the prospects for neuroscience.

---

[3] Papineau (2002, p.17).

[4] I have in mind experiments by Libet et al. (1983), Milner and Goodale (1995), and claims made in Ramachandran and Blakeslee (1998) and Wegner (2002). See Blackmore (2004) for an accessible presentation of some of this research.

Presumably many of the psycho-physical causal interactions would be between conscious events and neural events. Neuroscience only talks about the latter. Take a particular neural event N1 that has a non-physical cause C1. Since C1 falls outside of the domain of neuroscience and cannot be detected by its method, either the neuroscientist will think that N1 is uncaused, or she will claim that N1 is directly caused by some previous physical (probably neural) event N*. Either way, the neuroscientist is wrong. The greater the number of psycho-physical interactions, the worse off neuroscience is. The best we could hope for would be a model that allows us to make predictions about neural events, but we would have to give up on any claim that neuroscience was giving us the correct picture of things. The infection does not stop at neurons, however. Neurons are made of physical particles which are themselves made of physical particles. Neurons fire because of charge inequalities which are the result of the movement of ions across the cell membrane. This should be completely determined by facts such as the presence of positively charged sodium and potassium ions, the gating of ion channels, etc. All of these things should be governed by electro-chemical and physical laws, but if N1 really fires because of a non-physical conscious event, and there is no overdetermination, they simply can't be. Somewhere along the line there will have to be an event that either appears uncaused or appears to be caused by something that does not in fact cause it. This means that there is unlawful behavior somewhere, either in the activity of the potassium ions, or in the ion gates, etc. In any case, it will turn out that the electro-chemical laws are falsified by some chemical reactions in the brain. And of course the infection goes deeper, since chemical reactions are governed by physical laws.

The resulting infection is not only troubling because it goes all the way down to the basic sciences. It is most troubling, perhaps, because the infection would not be local. The potassium in our neurons is just like potassium elsewhere, and the atoms that make up that potassium are just like atoms elsewhere. It is not as if the chemical and physical laws hold for all atoms except for the ones in brains. If they do not hold of the atoms in brains, they do not hold of atoms at all. If interactionist dualism is true, our best picture of the world is fundamentally flawed.

The fact that non-physicalist views give us isolation of infection means that we should avoid them if we can. Subjective physicalism offers a way to do this, even as it gives up on a few other physicalist goals such as the completeness of objective theories such as physics. Objective theories are only incomplete in a limited, epistemic sense, however. Put simply, subjective physicalism is the view that ontologically the world is entirely physical. Everything that there is supervenes upon the basic physical particles and properties. Nevertheless, not every feature of the world can be completely grasped by objective theorizing. This is not because there are ghostly features of the world at the bottom level, as panpsychism might have it, or that there are emergent phenomena at the more sophisticated level of minds. Both of these would be ontological conclusions. The claim is rather that at certain levels of complexity, at the level of knowers, there are ways of grasping the world that are different than those given by objective theorizing and that cannot be attained by such theorizing.

This book divides into three parts. The first, "Defining Physicalism," sets the stage for the debate. This is important to do from the outset, since many definitions confuse issues of epistemology and the successes of science with the ontological doctrine of physicalism. By doing so, they can make logical space look smaller than it is. The problem of defining the physical has two parts. One is to define what it is for basic properties to be physical, and the other is to establish the relation everything else must bear to those properties if the doctrine of physicalism is true. I address these issue in Chapters 1 and 2. The second part of the book, The Threat of the Subjective, argues that all of the ways to resist the knowledge argument against physicalism without becoming a hardliner require denying object-ivism. The discussion of the knowledge argument and our surprisingly limited devices in responding to it occurs in Chapter 3, and Chapter 5 teases out the implications for and the proper understanding of "objectiv-ism." It would seem that embracing objectivism leads rather quickly to the denial of physicalism. The third part of the book argues that this is not in fact the case by discussing several arguments which push in that direction. In Chapter 5, I discuss the conceivability argument and Max Black's "presentation argument," exposing along the way the optional metaphys-ical commitments that make those arguments plausible. In Chapter 6, I return to the knowledge argument—highlighting its common premise with the conceivability argument—and describe how acquaintance can be used to defuse those arguments without that relation itself falling prey to the anti-physicalist arguments. In Chapter 7, the final chapter, I take a look back, considering the costs and benefits of subjective physicalism, and comparing it to other views on the table.

Although I do tend to view everything here as a package, from the definition of physicalism to the role of acquaintance, it should be said that many of the different positions and arguments of the book can stand alone. Those philosophers who are either unbothered by the problem of defining physicalism, or are perfectly satisfied deferring to the science of physics, might have little interest in Part I of the book, for example. It is, I hope, a virtue of my defense of physicalism that it does not depend on anything particularly idiosyncratic about my definitions of that notion. Nothing, so far as I can tell, is hidden in these definitions that allows physicalism too easy a defense. Similarly, though my defense of the acquaintance strategy is couched in a two-dimensional semantics, philosophers averse to such views can probably *mutatis mutandis* preserve the central idea of the acquaintance theory in the semantics of their choosing. The account in this book tends to stay close to the definitions and semantics invoked by the anti-physicalists, not only because I find myself in sympathy with them, but because I am interested in a defense of physicalism that cannot be accused of changing the topic or of ignoring the dualist's insights. Perhaps some will find this too concessive, but if physicalism can be defended while still in a concessive mood, all the better.

PART I

Defining Physicalism

Why worry about defining "physicalism?" Many philosophers discussing the problem of consciousness don't bother with the issue, but being clear about what this problem really is requires that we do. The problem of consciousness, in philosophy anyway, is raised by a group of arguments claiming that the existence of consciousness is not compatible with physicalism. If we are interested in whether or not these arguments succeed, indeed if we are interested in understanding what the arguments claim, we should become as clear as possible about what they mean by "consciousness" as well as what is involved in physicalism.

What should we look for in such a definition? If it is to serve our purposes—in evaluating the anti-physicalist arguments—it must at the very least divide the terrain in the way the arguments seem to presuppose. It would be silly to equate "the physical" with "the real," for example, since the conclusion of these arguments would be self-contradictory. So, we will let our definition be guided by the arguments. Furthermore, if possible our definition should make it as easy as possible to evaluate the premises of the arguments. If the arguments claim that we can imagine a physical duplicate of our world which lacks consciousness, we should know what we are being asked to imagine, and ideally we should have some sense of how to imagine it in the detail required by the arguments. Vague definitions, therefore, which define the physical in terms of the conclusion of a future physics, are of no help. Our definitions should also help to contextualize the concerns of the anti-physicalists in a greater tradition of arguments. They are asking of consciousness, for example, what some philosophers and scientists once asked about life. So though we should let our definition be guided by the arguments, it should not ignore the fact that the questions they are raising are parts of a larger question.

For these reasons and others, we cannot simply rest with the view that physicalism maintains that everything is physical. Such a flat-footed definition has two shortcomings. One failing is that it is not particularly informative, since it employs one of the notions most in need of clarification. The problem with understanding physicalism isn't really the "-ism," but the "physical." What does it mean for a property or thing to be physical? Many theorists think there is a further problem with this simple definition. Even if we could pin down what it meant to be physical, do we really want it to claim that everything—as in every property or object—is physical? Need it claim that numbers are physical objects, or that the property of being jovial is a physical property? Perhaps, but perhaps not. This will partly depend on how one defines physical, and just how strict one's notion of physicalism is. At the very least, this concern should lead us to be a bit more cautious in advancing our definition.

The problem of defining "physicalism" divides into three parts. First, the definition should specify the domain of physicalism. Should it cover numbers and other abstracta? Should it cover supernatural divine entities or simply concrete things of the sort we discover in scientific investigations? Call this the *domain problem*. Second, it should provide a precise characterization of what it takes for something to be physical in a narrow sense. Call this the *base problem*. Third, it should indicate a relation things must hold to the objects or properties described by the base notion if they are to be called physical in a more general sense. Call this the *relation problem*. So, for example, one could define physicalism as the view that every contingent property is identical with a property posited by current physics. The domain of this thesis is "contingent properties," the base notion is "properties posited by current physics" and the relation is "identity."[1]

To see how each of these three parts can raise issues, we can look at some problems with this straw-man definition. First, suppose one were engaged in a debate about the physicality of numbers. This definition would essentially be useless, since it doesn't concern things like numbers. So, the domain one is interested in studying might well affect what is

---

[1] See Stoljar (2010).

appropriate for the domain of the definition.[2] The base problem is more philosophically interesting. In the straw-man definition, for example, the base looks to be far too restrictive. Physics will surely discover new particles and properties as it progresses. If it does, they will be non-physical by this definition even if they are simply new sorts of spin or charge. Furthermore, what should we say about other possible worlds with different items? Are they of necessity not physical? It would seem so according to this definition. As we'll see, such a definition doesn't seem to be of much value in philosophical debates about the truth of physicalism. Even overlooking this problem however, there is a further issue with the relation in the definition. Are cars posited by physics? Are cells? Is joviality? Doubtful. Physics just doesn't talk about such things, at least explicitly. But there are cars, cells, and jovial creatures and since they are not identical with the basic posits of physics, this straw definition would make physicalism false.[3] This is fine for some purposes, but it doesn't seem to get at the question we are asking in the philosophy of mind—if it did, we wouldn't need such complicated arguments. There is another question we are asking, and to be precise about what this question is, we must be clear about our definition of physicalism.

When defining physicalism, at least in the context of the mind/body debate, philosophers tend to agree that the domain should be the concrete things and properties in this world. As philosophers of mind, we are not particularly interested in the physicality of numbers or sets. We are also not necessarily interested in whether or not ghosts or souls are possible. Some physicalists think they are possible, some don't.[4] Those who believe ghosts are possible are still physicalists because they think that this world lacks things like ghosts. Since there is not much controversy on these matters, I will go along with the crowd on the domain problem.[5]

There is quite a bit of controversy, on the other hand, surrounding both the base problem and the relation problem. Some philosophers think there

---

[2] In other words, what counts as "physical" might well be interest relative. Thus debates, say, about the proper province of physics might invite different definitions than debates about the physicality of consciousness. There is some question as to whether or not physics posits numbers as they are indispensible to the science. I have some doubts about whether their use implies that they are posited, but if so another example would be preferable.

[3] Stoljar (2010).

[4] See Jackson (1998), Lewis (1999b), and Levine and Trogden (2009).

[5] The contingency intuition will raise issues for supervenience, however, and so it will be discussed further in a later section.

is no good way to define the base set of physical properties. Traditional definitions in terms of spatio-temporality face counterexamples, and other proposals have their own serious shortcomings. If these philosophers are right, definitions of physicalism in terms of such a base don't get off the ground. Philosophers also disagree about the relation all things must hold to the base properties. It was long popular to describe physicalism in terms of a supervenience relation, but many philosophers have found such formulations inadequate. In their place some favor a "realization" relation, others a relation of "causal inheritance."[6]

In the following two chapters I defend versions of the more traditional views on these problems. In the first, I characterize the base in a somewhat Cartesian manner, in terms of spatio-temporality. In the second, I will defend a supervenience version of physicalism.

[6] See Melnyk (1997) for the first, Wilson (2002) for the second.

1

The Base Problem

What does it mean for a property to be physical? I will attempt to answer this question in what follows, but first a word of clarification. Quite obviously, philosophers don't own words and none can prevent others from using their words as they please. "Physical" and "physicalism" mean different things to different people, and even different philosophers have different things in mind.[1] In circumstances like this neither a tyrannical insistence on one definition nor a *laissez faire* egalitarianism is appropriate. Sometimes people are talking past one another, but at other times there is real disagreement. To determine which case is which, we need to be clear about our definitions.

At least two quite different questions can be guiding us in a definition of the physical. One is about the appropriate domain for the science of physics. Philosophers and scientists in that discussion would be debating what physicists could properly incorporate in their theories, and this might be guided by methodological considerations and meta-scientific considerations. There is another question, however, which is about whether consciousness is fundamentally new to the world or whether it ultimately should count as "physical." Philosophers and scientists answering this question might not have any interest in delimiting the proper domain of physics. They might think, for example, that physicists should do whatever they want as they are the masters of a certain notion of "physical." These philosophers are interested, however, in crystallizing the positions in an ontological debate. As such, they will be guided more by considerations that should govern that debate. It might turn out that these two projects yield the same notion of "physical," perhaps because the considerations that should govern the ontological debate are dominated by the desire to

---

[1] I thank my referees for helping me see the need for this clarification.

ground consciousness in whatever it is that physicists wind up talking about. But it might not.

I am interested in the notions of "physical" and "physicalism" that should govern the ontological debate surrounding the mind–body problem. It is quite possible that this should not yield the same definition of "physical" as the debate about the domain of physics for the simple reason that scientists should want to include epistemological and methodological constraints on their definition that have no place in a purely ontological debate. So though I will be sensitive to considerations that arise in the debate about physics, because they will at times be relevant, I will feel few pangs admitting that physics might well wind up concerning itself (quite properly) with that which is not physical in my sense.[2] Understood correctly this is not incoherent. It is, in fact, not unlike the stance of those who believe that that physics concerns itself with things that are not "material." Though my notion of the physical embraces more than the things typically counted as "material," someone who insisted on giving all uses of "physical" to the physicists are welcome to see me as defining a closely related term which is of more direct interest in the mind–body debates.

The Base Problem: Definitions and Despair

The Cartesian proposal

Modern history in this debate begins with Descartes. Descartes famously held that to be material is to be extended in space. This forms a stark contrast to mental things which, according to him, cannot be divided and are not extended.[3] This influential proposal has a great deal of plausibility. Paradigmatic physical objects such as chairs are spatial and things like souls are not.[4] There are, however, at least two problems with limiting the physical to things that are extended in space. First, it is not obvious how to widen this definition to include physical properties as well as things.

---

[2] Galen Strawson (2008, p.54) adopts the notion of physicsalism to refer to the view that "the nature or essence of all concrete reality can in principle be fully captured in the terms of physics." I embrace his distinction between this and physicalism, despite trying in a way he does not to hew close to what traditional materialists have meant by the physical.

[3] Descartes (1642, p.17, as well as p.59).

[4] I use "materialism" and "physicalism" interchangeably.

A physical property cannot simply be a property of a physical thing, since many property dualists—who believe that non-physical properties, like qualia, are properties of physical brains—would thereby be counted as physicalists. Nor can we define a physical property as that which requires its bearer to be extended, because it is not obvious that all physical properties require that their bearers be extended in space. Properties such as being curved might, but it is less clear for cases like charge. As a matter of fact, many think that electrons, which posses charge, are not extended.[5] This leads naturally to the second problem. After several centuries of science, we are willing to embrace things as physical that are, at least arguably, not extended. Electrons constitute one example, but forces, perhaps, constitute another. These things are, of course, *located* in space even if they are not extended, so it might seem the Cartesian can retreat and claim that something is physical if and only if it is located in space, but this seems too permissive. A dualist might well maintain that souls or thoughts are located in space because of the bodies they are connected to. Such a dualist would not thereby be a physicalist.

There are, perhaps, other moves for the Cartesian to make but the traditional Cartesian proposal is in trouble.

Definitions in terms of physics

The Cartesian definition of the physical failed in part because the progress of the physical sciences led us to see that very strange things, such as electrons, quarks, and fields, make up the physical world. This makes one pessimistic that anything substantial can be determined a priori about what all physical things and properties will have in common. This is one reason why it has proven very popular to define the physical in terms of physics itself: to be a physical property is to be a property that is expressed by a predicate in physics.

---

[5] Whether or not one considers an electron to have "size" apparently depends on how one asks the question. On the one hand, scientists speak of an "electron radius" and the perfectly spherical shape of the electron—as in Hudson et al. (2011). On the other hand, they maintain it has no size. While this is decidedly out of my depth, the idea appears to be that there is no way to measure an electron size, though one can measure its interactions with electrical fields. This interaction produces perfectly spherical distortions, but the electron is not necessarily identical to this effect. See Leanhardt (2011).

This definition faces a notorious difficulty often attributed to Carl Hempel.[6] Either the definition proceeds in terms of what is countenanced by current physics or it proceeds in terms of what would be acknowledged by some future, perhaps completed physics. If the former, physicalism is surely false since current physics is almost certainly incomplete.[7] If the latter, however, it is hard to give content to the notion since no one knows what a future physics will look like. What's more, we can't be sure that the standards and methods of a future physics won't be perverse and incorrect, perhaps allowing things we do not wish to allow and excluding things we do not wish to exclude.[8] One could prohibit such perversities by insisting upon an ideal physics, but the content of this notion is far too vague to be of much use, and one suspects it is essentially circular: an ideal physics will include all and only the physical.

Perhaps the most compelling criticism of the definitions in terms of physics, to my mind, is that it ultimately characterizes the ontological thesis of physicalism in terms of something epistemological—in particular, our ways of knowing and theorizing about fundamental entities.[9] There is a sort of "Euthyphro" question here: "Are physical things physical because physics studies them, or does physics study them because they have certain features?" If the former was the case, what reason would a physicist have to add something (or eliminate something) from his field of study? The posits of physics would seem to have an air of arbitrariness. If the latter, and there is some feature that makes things the appropriate study of physics, then that looks to be the sort of feature that should figure into a definition of physicalism.

---

[6] Hempel (1969).

[7] See Melnyk (1997 and 2003) for a heroic attempt to defend such definitions by defining physicalism in terms of current physics. See Wilson (2006) for persuasive criticisms.

[8] See Chomsky (1968, pp.83–4) for a similar concern. Wilson (2006) argues for a combination of the definition in terms of physics and a *via negativa* definition. That would solve this Chomskian problem, but it would introduce the problems we will see with the *via negativa*, and it would still have the "Euthyphro" problem.

[9] Talk of things or properties as "fundamental" is pervasive, but it isn't always clear what is meant. To say that something is fundamental can mean it is indispensible, or that it is explanatorily basic, or that it is that upon which all else supervenes, etc. While I would be happier to have a clearer notion, what I intend is roughly that a property is fundamental iff it cannot be explained in terms of other, simpler properties. If there is no fundamental level (as suggested by Schaffer (2003)) most talk about fundamentality can be reconstrued in terms of relative fundamentality, as done in Wilson (2012, p.2).

This question can be pressed by thinking about things in another world that are not studied by our physics, present, or future, but have the basic earmarks of physicality and are similar to things in our world.[10] Are they physical? It seems perverse to deny it. Suppose at some point in the past physics had taken a different turn, perhaps refusing to acknowledge non-deterministic phenomena. Would physicalism be false in that world because there were phenomena physicists refused to acknowledge as governed by what they considered physical laws? Surely not. It is not the science that makes for the type of thing, but the type of thing that makes it the proper study of a science.

To put yet another spin on the point, take the statement: "Every (possible) physical thing will (or could) be discovered by a science either identical to or relevantly similar to our physics." This sounds like hubris! Why should we think such a thing? If "physical" is defined in terms of physics, this statement is an a priori truth! This doesn't seem to be the sort of thing that should be a priori —or at the very least it shouldn't just be definitional. Granted, we do have confidence in our physical sciences, but couldn't they be limited with respect to their own intended domain? To suppose this is not to suppose some far out skeptical scenario. There can be, I think, good reasons for being confident in the path of our sciences. But our confidence that our physical sciences (or sciences relevantly similar) can discover (or posit, or explain, etc.) every physical thing should stem from the fact that we know that physical things have certain characteristics which make them extremely likely to be discovered by physical sciences. Our confidence shouldn't be justified by our definitions.

One interesting possibility is to claim that "posited by physics" (or whatever the relevant condition for physicality would be according to these sorts of views) is not meant to be a definition of the physical, but is instead a reference fixing description that picks out the essence of physicality.[11] This would allay the Euthyphro concerns and would make the essence of physicality non-epistemic since it is because of this independent nature of physical things that they are physical; we just describe that nature in terms of our scientific project. (The fact that the science posited it would not be what made it physical, though it might be what enabled our

---

[10] This is a development of a line of thought started in Stoljar (2001).

[11] This possibility is developed by Braddon-Mitchell and Jackson (2006) but was brought to my attention by Philippe Chuard.

reference to it.) This strategy would also take care of cross-world comparisons. If there are intuitively physical things in other worlds which our science does not and will not posit, they can still be physical because they share a nature with the things physics discovers in our world.

Though this interesting suggestion does take care of some of our concerns, it worsens others. Again there is a question of whether we are talking about current or future physics. If it is future physics, we again have a serious vagueness problem and a worry that physics could go off the rails. The present physics version does not have this problem, and it doesn't have the problem that it will necessarily be falsified by future physics. The problem is that it is extremely vague. What is this nature supposed to be? What guarantee do we have that there is such a nature? What will it be like, and how are we to assess the question of whether or not it gives rise to mentality? It would be preferable to come up with a plausible story of that nature, that which appears to be picked out by physical sciences, and use that as our working—though perhaps defeasible—definition of "physical." This, though, is to seek a positive definition independent of the definitions in terms of physics.

Methodological definitions

Instead of speaking of a future physics, which might go terribly wrong, or an ideal physics, which remains vague, perhaps we can define physicalism in terms of the methodology of physics and the physical sciences. This sort of approach faces a cousin of Hempel's dilemma. The methodology of physics has changed quite a bit since the time of Newton, and there is reason to believe that it will continue to change. Is it the methodology of current physics, or future physics that should figure into a definition of the physical? Familiar problems arise with either option.

Perhaps, though, there is something methodologically central that would figure into anything that we would be willing to recognize as physics. Perhaps intersubjective verification of experimental results or law based explanations are central to anything we would be willing to call a physics. There is probably something to this.[12] But once again, we seem to face the Euthyphro question, and once again something epistemic seems to be inserted into something which should be metaphysical. Is it

---

[12] See Dowell (2006).

really a necessary truth that our methods will discover (or explain, etc.) all and only physical things? Shouldn't we at least allow for the possibility that there are physical things beyond the reach of our methods or that our methods will rope in things that are not properly physical? It seems we craft our methodology in such a way that it will do a good job of discovering and explaining a certain type of thing, and our confidence that it will be successful stems in part from what we think characterizes that sort of thing. A definition that justifies our optimism on this front has something going for it. But a definition that makes our optimism definitionally warranted seems to lack an appropriate realism about the physical.[13]

Demonstrative definitions

One might be inclined to say that things are physical if they are sufficiently similar to "that stuff" where a sufficiently comprehensive sample of dirt, tables, chairs, and unequivocally physical things are demonstrated.[14] One suspects real problems will emerge with both of the "sufficient" qualifiers in this definition. It is not at all obvious that one could specify what constitutes sufficient similarity or what constitutes a sufficiently comprehensive (but not too comprehensive) sample without characterizing the respect of similarity, and this would seem to be in the neighborhood of a non-demonstrative definition of the physical. Relatedly, the fundamental physical properties of the universe probably bear little salient resemblance to paradigmatic physical objects. A quark is not much like a chair. So the demonstrative definitions are likely to result in the fundamentals of physics not being physical.[15] Additionally, if panpsychism is true, the demonstrative definitions would count panpsychism as a form of physicalism. This would get the intuitive extension of "physical" incorrect, so demonstrative definitions should be rejected.[16] We might be inclined to amend the

---

[13] This objection is one that probably shouldn't work against an attempt to define physicsalism, or the types of things that should be posited by physicists. For physics success is defined (in part) by predictive power and so it is quite appropriate that there be an epistemic element in what it might take to be physical in this sense.

[14] See Snowdon (1989).

[15] The way to solve this problem is probably to say that things are physical only if they include nothing that is not involved in the existence of things like "this." Since quarks are involved, they will be included. The next problem still arises, however.

[16] Montero (1999). Really what should be said is that demonstrative definitions *might* fail, because if this world is panpsychist, paradigmatically non-physical properties will be counted

demonstrative proposal, to say that the physical is the stuff that is like "this stuff—assuming that this stuff is as we think it is." But now it looks as though the real substance of the demonstrative definition is in its proviso. The question of what is physical becomes the question of what we think characterizes paradigmatically physical things, and answering this question requires that we move beyond demonstratives and actually give some conditions for physicality. This is precisely what the non-demonstrative theories—including my own—try to do.

Negative definitions

At least in the context of the mind–body problem, it is very tempting to define physical properties negatively, in terms of what they are not. Philosophers are inclined to reject other attempts at definition because they wind up counting paradigmatic examples of the non-physical as physical. So we apparently have the tools for creating a negative necessary condition for physicality, and it will stipulatively avoid the most important counterexamples to its extensional adequacy.[17] So, on a basic version of this view a property would be physical if it is not a mental property. This is not adequate, of course, since it would presumably require that physicalism entail eliminativism. But we surely want to allow that the existence of mental properties is consistent with physicalism. So, we might alter the definition to say that a property is physical if it is not fundamentally mental. But now what does it mean to be fundamentally mental? Although one could hope for more precision at this point, because "fundamentally F" is here a technical term, the idea seems to be that something is fundamentally mental just in case its mental aspects cannot be fully grounded in the non-mental.[18]

To succeed, the *via negativa* must specify which properties count as "fundamentally mental," and we must have a firm grasp of those

as physical. If physicalism is true, the demonstrative definition would succeed. But the very fact that we have to talk about the propitious conditions for the demonstrative theory shows that we have something more fundamental in mind—the way the world would have to be for the conditions to be propitious.

[17] For a definition including this necessary condition on physicality, see Montero (2001), Wilson (2005 and 2006), and Howell (2009).

[18] "Fundamentally F" is in common parlance, but it means something different, at least to my American ears. To say Brian is not fundamentally racist is *not* to say that he is racist but that his racism can be explained by non-racist features of Brian!

properties—a better grasp than we have of what it is to be physical. Current defenders of the *via negativa* tend to point to two such mental features: intentionality and phenomenality.[19] So "physical" in the narrow sense might simply mean fundamental, concrete, and not intentional or phenomenal.[20]

Though these negative definitions are tailored to capture what is at stake in the current arguments for and against physicalism, they aren't satisfactory. Suppose it turns out that both physical and mental properties emerge from some Ur-property which is neither intuitively mental or physical?[21] Should this sort of neutral monism count as physicalism? It is not clear to me that it should. But even if negative definitions are extensionally adequate, there is something unsatisfying about this route. For one thing, it would be far preferable to have a definition that said what physical properties *are*, rather than what they are not—is there really a unified nature shared by all things not mental, unlike the nature shared by things that are not cucumbers? And while the negative definitions might satisfy participants in the debates about consciousness and intentionality, it would be better to have a definition that captures what is at stake in closely related philosophical discussions. There is, for example, some question as to whether the truth of vitalism would falsify physicalism. Many philosophers are inclined to believe it would, but the *via negativa* would consider a ghostly element which bestowed life on inorganic material to be physical.[22] Might we find that there are other peculiar properties of the mind, or of other "higher level" entities that seem to elude explanation in terms of the microphysical? Do we want to rule out that these things might in the end pose a challenge to physicalism? It would seem far preferable to have a definition that could guide us in future

[19] Montero (2001) and Wilson (2005).

[20] Papineau and Spurrett (1999); Papineau (2002). This could be seen as another way of framing the debate as Montero (2001) does. I have substituted "concrete" in this definitions where Papineau and Spurrett focus on the contingent. This is in part because I assume that a necessarily existent God would falsify physicalism in an intuitive sense. Thanks to a referee for pushing this point.

[21] It is not easy to find clear adherents to this view. Nagel (1986) seems to flirt with such a view, and philosophers who could be interpreted as having some sympathy with the view include Feigl (1958); Strawson (2003 and 2006); and McGinn (2004). A version of this view might be what Chalmers calls panprotopsychsim in Chalmers (2010).

[22] Stoljar (2010) seems to—the example is from him.

debates and that could apply to past debates as well.[23] Negative definitions then, to the extent that they are definitions at all, seem to be wanting.[24]

Despair

The difficulty of finding a satisfying definition of "the physical" and "physicalism" has led quite a few philosophers to claim that such a definition cannot be found. According to Crane and Mellor, for example, "there is no divide between the mental and the non-mental sufficient even to set physicalism up as a serious question, let alone a serious answer to it. Physicalism is the wrong answer to an essentially trivial question."[25] Earlier, the same point was made by Noam Chomsky: "In short, there is no definite concept of body. Rather, there is a material world, the properties of which are to be discovered, with no a priori demarcation of what will count as 'body.' The mind–body problem can therefore not even be formulated. The problem cannot be solved, because there is no clear way to state it."[26] Barbara Montero concludes that "it seems that a solution to the body problem, or at least one that helps us better understand the mind–body problem, is not forthcoming. And I take it that this indicates that, at least for the time being, we should focus on questions other than the question 'Is the mind physical?'"[27] Alyssa Ney follows Bas

---

[23] Ney (2008). There is admittedly a bit of tension between the desire for a definition of "physical" to apply to different debates and my earlier insistence that the notion could be interest relative, depending in effect on the debate. What I have in mind here, though, is a group of philosophical debates about the reduction of contingent phenomena to the physical—whether, for example, chemical interactions reduce or whether they are emergent. It seems desirable to have a consistent notion of "physical" for these debates, even if issues in the philosophy of physics might require a different definition.

[24] Wilson (2006, pp. 75–6) answers this criticism, by saying that it can be turned aside because as a matter of fact all of the possibilities that we would like to rule out (such as vitalism or moral agency) have either been accounted for in terms of more fundamental unobjectionable entities, or they presuppose mentality.

There are two problems with this response. First, as Wilson acknowledges in a footnote, this will not satisfy us if we are looking for a definition which would cover other possible worlds, such as worlds where life could not be explained by more fundamental phenomena. Second, I don't think she canvasses all the relevant options. It is not incoherent, for example, to believe there are fundamental, non-natural and objective features of the world that make certain actions right. The *actions* might presume mentality, but the *right-making* features might not. Don't we wish to say such things are not physical? The *via negativa* would allow that they are.

[25] Crane and Mellor (1990, p.206).

[26] Chomsky (1995, p.145); see also Chomsky (1968).

[27] Montero (1999, p.194).

van Fraasen in a move that similarly gives up on the traditional project of defining the physical by construing physicalism as an attitude.[28] On this view, physicalism is neither true nor false.

These authors differ about the consequences of this definitional failure for traditional problems in the philosophy of mind, but they all agree that pursuing the same old paths by trying to define physicalism is wrong-headed.

Physicalism, Old School

I disagree. Though it is admittedly futile to legislate what future philosophers or physicists will call "physical," we can define a positive notion of the base-physical that captures what is at issue in the mind–body debates and that captures the spirit of what many philosophers have intended. We can discern what philosophers have intended in part by looking at the definitions we have found unsatisfactory. We can get a sense of what sorts of views philosophers have intended to exclude, and to avoid changing the subject we should search for a definition that excludes those views as well. (Letting something in the door by a technicality will do little more than offer a chance to solve the mind–body problem by definition.) A view such as Russellian Monism, for example, which some have wanted to include under the umbrella of "physicalism," would blatantly violate the intuition behind the *via negativa*.[29] A view which allowed for properties that were undetectable in principle by any possible science, and offered no explanatory value should be suspected as well as it would clearly run afoul of the methodological conceptions.

We can develop a view that accommodates these general constraints without moving far from the view offered by Descartes. As we saw, Descartes thinks something is physical if and only if it is extended. Unfortunately, this view doesn't accommodate intuitively physical items such as

---

[28] Van Fraasen (2002); Ney (2006).

[29] Philosophers such as Stoljar (2001) and Pereboom (2011) have provided senses in which Russellian Monism can be considered physicalistic, and in a sense they are correct. My definition, on the other hand, excludes them because my main interest is whether the anti-materialist arguments work as they are intended to work by their proponents (who tend to consider themselves anti-physicalists). These arguments are not inconsistent with Russellian Monism, though, and are not meant to be. So my more restrictive definition makes it clear I am asking the question I intend to ask.

electrons, and physical properties such as charge. Nevertheless, Descartes had a crucial insight that tends to get left behind: being physical is closely tied to spatiality. Electrons are not extended, but they are in space. Charge might not require that its bearer be extended, but its instantiation does place requirements on other things that are in space. Put crudely, physical things and properties seem to have, by their very nature, spatial implications. They seem, in fact, to be defined by these implications. What it is for something to have charge (in the basic sense in which an electron is charged) is for it to repel or attract other things, and attraction and repulsion are clearly spatial notions. Consider, on the other hand, what the dualist says about qualia—say the sensation of pain. Something is painful in virtue of how it feels, not by how it causes the bearer of pain to act. How something feels doesn't have any immediate spatial implications—neither does having an intentional state, a state that is about something else.

Calling a property physical because it has spatial implications is in the ballpark, but it is still inadequate. For one thing, this might at best be a necessary condition for physicality. That is, one can imagine a property dualist who maintained, for example, that the instantiation of pain always requires that something spatial happen—that the bearer recoil, or even that an atom move a smidge. This would not make the quale physical. Why? Because according to the dualist even if qualia have physical implications, they are not *fully characterized* by those implications. I maintain that physical properties, on the other hand, are. In other words, it seems as though the addition of a physical property to a world does nothing more than place conditions on how things can be distributed in space and time in that world.

This suggests the following, neo-Cartesian definition of a physical property:

> *Neocart*: A property is physical iff it can be fully characterized in terms of the conditions it places on the distribution of things in space over time.

What does it mean to place conditions on the distribution of things in space over time? These "conditions" can be understood by thinking about what happens to the world when a property is instantiated in it. If you insert a property in the world, you have inserted a new condition on the way things are in that world. The conditions properties place on the world are closely associated with laws. The laws of a world place conditions on how things must be in that world. The instantiation of a property, then, simply places the conditions on the world that the laws of nature which mention that property entail.[30] So, for example, if a negative charge is instantiated in a location at a particular time, this might not nomologically require that any repulsion or attraction actually occur. But it does require that something else that is negatively charged, for example, will be repelled from that charge if it is within a certain distance of it. (Of course this condition, as stated, is *ceteris paribus*, and a full condition will mention many other factors which must or must not obtain, but if physicalism is true, these further factors will similarly mention only dispositions of things to be in spaces at times.) According to the neo-Cartesian definition, if you insert a physical property, you have inserted a condition on the way things in that world can occupy space over time and nothing else. Physical properties are exhausted by the spatio-temporal conditions they place on the world.

In simpler terms, once you have specified what a physical property necessitates about the orientation of things in space over time, you have fully described the property. For non-physical properties this is not the case. One must say something more—perhaps that the property generates or constitutes a phenomenal feel, or perhaps that the property makes its bearer aware of something. A world is physical, then, iff all the contingent properties of this world supervene upon all the properties in this world that are exhausted by the conditions they place on the distribution of things in space over time.[31]

As it stands, Neocart seems to catch the spirit of the Cartesian view while avoiding its difficulties. Nevertheless, a new problem arises.[32] According to some views, a property is something over and above the powers it contributes to its bearer: the dispositions conferred by a property must be grounded in some categorical basis.[33] Something is not simply

---

[30] I am attracted to the view according to which property instances simply are "particularized laws." Laws are typically thought of as general—they do not mention particular times, places, or things. A property instance can be viewed, on the other hand, as a *particularized law*: the instantiation of a property in a region of space–time is simply a matter of the laws governing that property going into effect in that particular region of space–time. On this view, Neocart would hold that physical properties are identical to "particularlized laws" which do nothing but specify how other things can be distributed in space and time in relation to the region of space–time at which the property is instantiated.

[31] I intend "distribution" to include "orientation" as well. E.g. the laws can determine not only where a sphere is, but which side is facing which way.

[32] Versions of this objection have been articulated (in conversation and correspondence) by Phillipe Chuard, David Chalmers, Brad Thompson, and James Blackmon.

[33] This is denied on "dispositionalist" views such as that of Shoemaker (2003).

fragile because it has the disposition to break—there is something that grounds that disposition: its base. The problem is that these categorical bases look to be something over and above the "conditions" the property places on the distribution of things in space and time, and according to Neocart this disqualifies any property with categorical bases (thus arguably any property at all) from being physical. That's not good.

It is tempting to think that this problem can be easily fixed, simply by limiting the scope of Neocart to the dispositional aspects of properties, thus giving the categorical bases a free pass. As long as the dispositional aspects are exhaustively characterized by their spatio-temporal implications, the property would count as physical on this view. But this will not do. The categorical aspects of some properties make them paradigmatically non-physical. On the most popular form of property dualism, for example, phenomenal properties are phenomenal and conscious not because of the dispositions they confer on a bearer but because of something categorical: their intrinsic feel. Within a world, given the psycho-physical laws of that world, these phenomenal properties might confer certain powers on their bearers, and these powers might be fully characterized by their "spatio-temporal" implications. We can imagine, for example, that there is a phenomenal property Q that, given the laws of nature, bestows all and only the powers bestowed by negative charge. On the reading of Neocart that gives categorical bases a free pass, a property like Q will count as physical. Thus, Neocart counts property dualism as a form of physicalism. Again, not good.[34]

The problem can be put in the form of a dilemma. Either Neocart will count paradigmatically physical properties as non-physical because they involve categorical bases in addition to the powers they confer, or Neocart will have to give categorical bases a free pass in which case paradigmatically non-physical properties get counted as physical.[35] To get out of this dilemma, we must find a way for Neocart to allow charge to count as physical while Q is non-physical.

[34] The problem is even more obvious for those forms of Russellian Monism which think that phenomenal, or protophenomenal, properties form the categorical basis for all properties. See, for example, Maxwell (1979) and Stoljar (2001).

[35] The problem is there even if categorical bases are not given a free pass but are counted as physical if their powers are all spatio-temporal.

I think there is a way out of the dilemma even accepting the view of properties that gives rise to it. But it is worth noting that the troublesome view of properties can be denied. This view of properties has two parts. The first is that every property divides up into a categorical base and the dispositions it grounds. The second is that the connection between these two things is contingent. The first part of the view can be resisted by denying that dispositions need categorical grounds.[36] Categorical bases are mysterious things, like classical substrata, undetectable outside of the dispositions they ground. If we do away with them, we lose little. Following this path stops the objection to Neocart at the first step. The problem with this is that to many of us, the idea of dispositions grounded in nothing at all sounds absurd.[37] We do, it seems, have a conception of a metaphysical ground for dispositions, and this is reflected by the fact that we often think that one and the same property could ground different dispositions depending on the laws of nature.

Another view would allow that there are categorical bases, which are distinct from the dispositions they ground, but would claim that we are wrong to think that the bases are only contingently linked to the dispositions they ground. Categorical bases necessitate their dispositions on this view, so that if one fixes the properties in a world, one fixes the dispositions—no further laws can alter those dispositions. One worry about this, though, is that it is not clear what would ground the necessities between the bases and the dispositions. This worry is based on a version of Hume's dictum: If they are really distinct, it is unclear what the necessary connection between them would be. One can deny Hume's dictum, but for many that will be implausible.

A closely related, but significantly more elegant view, is to deny that there are really two ontological pieces of properties—the base piece and the disposition piece. Instead, properties can be described in dispositional terms and categorical terms, but these descriptions don't pick out meta-physically distinct parts of properties.[38] Thus it is true that there are categorical bases, and it is also true that there are dispositional elements of properties, but since these truths do not reflect different parts of a property but are merely different ways of representing the same thing,

---

[36] This is the view often attributed to Holton (1999) and Shoemaker (2003).

[37] This intuition is well captured by Blackburn (1990).

[38] This is the view urged by Martin (1997) and Heil (2003).

there is no mysterious necessary connection in need of explanation. (Even if there is a sense in which identities such as "x = y" need explanations, as I think there is, the explanation will certainly not be to posit a relation between two things, x and y.)[39] This view not only avoids the need to posit ungrounded necessities, it also avoids the implications of the view that categorical bases are mysterious hubs of power which are contingently linked to dispositions. Among these implications is the fact that there can be two instances of a property (in two different worlds) that have something in common even if they bestow none of the same powers upon their bearers. It also seems that on the mysterious bases view there could also be instances of two different properties that confer precisely the same powers upon their bearers. (It might even be the case that there are two properties within a world that confer the same set of powers! This raises the possibility of an odd sort of skepticism.) It further seems consistent with this view that in some worlds certain properties bestow no dispositions at all. These sources of similarity and difference between properties will not be detectable using the methods of the physical sciences, or perhaps by any other methods. These bases don't actually seem to do anything that makes a difference to a world at all.[40] Theorists of any stripe, physicalist or no, should avoid positing things like this.[41]

On the view of properties which eschews the metaphysical distinction between categorical bases and dispositions, Neocart does not face the problem of qualitative bases, for it isn't remotely plausible that qualia—should they exist—are *identical* with dispositions or conditions on the spatio-temporal arrangement of things in the world.

While this "dual aspect" view of properties ducks the problem of categorical bases, it will not be acceptable to everyone. It does have the strange consequence, it seems, that the laws of nature are necessary. In any case, it would be preferable to have another solution. What is needed, recall, is a way to allow categorical bases of physical properties to count as

---

[39] See Block and Stalnaker (1999). Block and Stalnaker's correct point about identities does not show that we don't need explanations of some sort in the case of informative identities.

[40] Although Heil is not considering this issue in terms of physicalism, many of his arguments for an "identity theory" of dispositional and categorical properties provide reason to reject the view of properties presupposed by this objection. See Heil (2003, chs 8–11).

[41] Although Heil is not considering this issue in terms of physicalism, many of his arguments for an "identity theory" of dispositional and categorical properties provide reason to reject the view of properties presupposed by this objection. See Heil (2003, chs 8–11).

physical, but to exclude phenomenal categorical bases. We need, for example, a definition that distinguishes between phenomenal property Q, which bestows the powers of charge, and charge itself. There is, of course, an intuitive difference between the categorical bases of these properties. There is a sense in which the categorical base of Q is "juicy" or thick while the categorical base of charge is empty and thin. Even if the categorical base of charge bestows the powers it does only contingently, within a particular world it appears to contribute nothing more to its bearer than a set of powers. Meanwhile, Q contributes the powers plus a phenomenal feel.[42] But since we want to avoid making a property's properties in this world essential to the property—which would result in necessitarianism—we have to characterize that property more broadly. We can do so using the notion of Trans-World Disposition Sets (TDS). Each property confers a set of dispositions within a world. The TDS of a property is the set of dispositions the property gives rise to in each world. So, for example, charge gives rise to a certain group of dispositions D in world 1, but a different set of dispositions D2 in world 2, etc. The TDS for charge can be characterized as a set of pairs of worlds and dispositions $\{<w1, D1>, <w2, D2> \ldots <wn, Dn>\}$. Even if the powers of a property differ from world to world, its TDS does not—it is a necessary feature of the property.

Using this notion of TDSs, we can characterize the difference between properties that have thick categorical bases and those that have thin bases. Thin properties are individuated by their TDSs in a way that thick properties are not. In particular, thin properties obey the following individuation principle:

Th-individuation: If the TDS of P1 and P2 are the same, then P1 = P2.

Thus, among the set of thin properties, there can be no two properties with the same TDS.[43] This preserves the intuition that there are categorical

---

[42] A referee for OUP suggests that it is not clear that "the difference between the categorical bases for charge and Q are thickness rather than in our accessibility to them." I find this an interesting suggestion. I take it the suggestion is that just as Q gives more to the world than charge dispositions, so does the categorical base of charge—we are simply not privy to the "juice" in that base. If this is the case, though, such bases really do seem mysterious. They are inaccessible natures that can vary despite the fact that the dispositions they ground do not. I can't argue that such posits are impossible, but it does seem they are otiose.

[43] Thanks to Doug Ehring for his help formulating th-individuation.

bases (contra the dispositionalist) and that the categorical bases have their powers within a world only contingently (contra the necessitarian), without making the categorical bases mysterious things beyond description. The bases of thin properties are individuated by their dispositions, only across worlds instead of within worlds. Thick properties, if there are any, cannot be individuated solely by the powers they bestow, even across worlds. Further differences can be introduced between thick properties based upon the "juice" in their base. If the bases are phenomenal, for example, there could be two properties R and G which both have the same TDS but differ because R is a red quale and G is a green quale.

A physicalist should allow only thin properties in the base.[44] To embrace thick properties, one must believe that there is some feature of a property that is over and above that which is necessitated by the powers the property contributes. For my part, the only such feature I can think of that is suited for this job is an intrinsic feel or quale, but whatever it is it would of necessity be beyond the pale of any possible science and could have no explanatory value. Any physicalist worth her salt should steer clear of such things. But she should not countenance all thin properties. If a thin property P has as a disposition in the actual world to cause a subject to feel a certain way, and there is no physicalistically acceptable account of that disposition, P isn't purely physical either. Physical properties must not only be thin, they must also confer only spatio-temporal powers in the actual world. This provides a version of Neocart for the theorist who believes properties have their powers only contingently.

> *Neocart-con*: A property P is physical, iff (a) in the actual world P confers only spatio-temporal powers upon its bearer, and (b) P is a thin property.

Thus physical properties can have categorical bases, but that doesn't give the bases of properties a "free pass." By letting only thin categorical bases count as physical, Neocart-con escapes the contingency theorist's dilemma.[45]

---

[44] Remember, I am at present only talking about the properties in the narrow supervenience base. Whether or not all physical properties are thin is not my present concern.

[45] There is actually a further problem with Neocart-con that will not affect the debate, since it won't affect the definition of physicalism, but is a problem nonetheless. Suppose dualism is true of this world, and there is a psycho-physical law that C-fibres give rise to the non-physical quale pain. Clause (a) of Neocart-con would seem to imply that C-Fibres are thereby non-physical. This is odd enough, but the non-physicality of C-Fibres will

Objections to the Neo-Cartesian Account

The traditional counterexamples to spatial definitions of physicalism can be handled by the new account. Physics does posit some odd, seemingly ghostly things: fields, forces, quark-colors, etc. But all of these entities and properties have implications for how other properties or things are distributed in space over time, and there don't seem to be any other features that distinguish them from one another. There might still be some concerns about the neo-Cartesian account.

> *Objection 1*: Even if all current physical properties can be exhaustively described by their spatial implications, there is no guarantee that all future properties that will be discovered by physics will be this way.

Response: As Hempel's dilemma teaches us, there is no telling what the future science of physics will posit. Physics might go off the rails and embrace the paranormal for all we know. So the fact that physics might posit something that disagrees with our theory is not an objection. Nor is it an objection that we will in the future call properties "physical" that elude our definition. It is only a problem if a future physics discovers properties that do not satisfy our definition and *those properties should legitimately be called physical*. But unless the objector has a superior account of what determines whether properties should be so deigned this objection amounts to little.

> *Objection 2*: It is conceivable that there be a physical property that is epiphenomenal and that therefore has no implications for anything in space and time.[46]

Response: I'm not sure this is conceivable, in part because I don't know what it is I am supposed to be conceiving. I can, of course, conceive of

---

presubably spread to anything with a disposition to affect C-Fibres, and so on. The result might be that a dualistic world is really, by this definition, a strange sort of idealist world! The solution to this problem will again depend on particularities of the metaphysics of properties, in particular the trans-world identification conditions of properties. If properties have certain dispositions essentially, then the fix is easy: change (a) to say that P's essential dispositions are spatio-temporal. If properties do not have essential dispositions, the matter is harder, but perhaps the right thing to say is that physicality of properties comes in degrees on this view, and whether or not a property satisfies condition (a) is a contextual matter. These issues threaten to explode beyond what can be covered here, but since the issue of physicalism is not affected I leave the puzzle for a future occasion.

[46] Thanks to an anonymous referee from OUP for pressing this objection.

physicists talking about such particles and perhaps even stipulating their existence. But it is hard to see how they could play any theoretical role, or feature in any scientific predictions if they are completely epiphenomenal without any implications for spatio-temporal things.[47] In addition, such properties would only be counterexamples to my definitions if they are not only actually epiphenomenal, but have no relevant dispositions in other worlds as well otherwise the properties do have spatio-temporal natures, defined by their TDSs. It is hard to imagine a property that would necessarily lack any causal dispositions, unless it was something like a quale. Here again, it is important to remember that the purpose of our definition is to understand the mind–body problem. Suppose that the objection is right, and there is some sense of "physical" where this necessarily epiphenomenal particle would count as physical. Is this the sense that would be of use in these debates? Suppose it turns out that qualitative conscious experience did not supervene upon the things that are physical in my sense, but do supervene once these mysterious "physical" properties are added. Would this really vindicate the physicalist picture, given that conscious experience fails to supervene in the way biological or chemical properties do, but instead require something non-spatio-temporal to necessitate them? Far from vindicating physicalism, this just seems to be a version of non-physicalism! Given this, even if there is some reason to include such mysterious properties under some definition of physicalism, it would seem more in line with the debates about consciousness to rule them out.

Objection 3: What if our theory of space–time proves to be incorrect? Surely that won't imply dualism![48]

Response: The view here does not take a stance on a particular theory of space and time. All it requires is that there is space and time. As long as we don't become eliminativists about space–time, therefore, our definition will survive. People before Einstein were not wrong in saying things like "The hands of the clock overlap once an hour," though their conceptions of simultaneity and the nature of space and time were incorrect. Similarly,

---

[47] My emphasis on detectability and explanation here and in other responses does not compromise the metaphysical nature of the definition of physicalism. Even if we want a purely metaphysical definition of physicalism, it is appropriate to adduce epistemological considerations to evaluate the plausibility of counterexamples and objections to the definition.

[48] Montero (2001, p.31).

if it turns out that space–time is radically different than we take it to be, it doesn't follow that the spatio-temporal conditions associated with being an electron, for example, are not really necessary conditions for being an electron. It just means that those necessary conditions amount to something other than what we previously thought. (It is worth bearing in mind that the debate between substantivalists and relationalists about space and time is not a debate about the existence of space and time, despite their having quite different pictures of what space and time amount to.)

Suppose though, physics takes a surprising turn and our final science is eliminativist about space and time. Isn't this possible? In answering this, we should make a distinction between two different things we might mean by our final science being eliminativist about space and time. One construal might be that physicists find that talking in terms of space and time has no place in describing the fundamental level of reality, perhaps because they feel space–time emerges from something more fundamental. This would not necessarily falsify characterizations of things in terms of space and time any more than general relativity falsified statements about space. Another construal of the eliminativist hypothesis would be more dire. It might be meant that the implications of physics show that our statements about things in space and time are never true. It would be difficult to see how physics could show this, since whether or not this is the case is a matter that depends a great deal on the nature of semantics and it is seriously doubtful that the correct semantic theory would result in this sort of eliminativism. (A model might be the relative stability of "solidity" talk despite the discovery that there is "more space than stuff" in paradigmatically solid objects like tables.) Suppose, though, that physics points to an incoherence so deep in the notions of space and time that no consistent semantics could preserve the truth of our spatio-temporal claims. In such a case, I'm inclined to say that we will also find it difficult to preserve a meaningful semantics of "physical" and that physicalism is false, or at least an infelicitously formulated doctrine.[49] At the very least, it seems to me that such a development would have such a shattering implication for our metaphysics that our current debate about the mind–body problem would lose

---

[49] It might be responded that a simple semantics is in the offing—to be physical is to be whatever physicists say is at the fundamental level, or something of the sort. In fact, I don't think its obvious that even this definition will survive, since it is not at all clear that if such an extreme space–time eliminativism is true that there are in fact any physicists.

almost all of its grip. So my position could very well be conditional—to the extent that we want a definition that helps us with the current mind–body problem, mine is the most desirable.

Objection 4: What if Space and Time are emergent?

Response: Apparently some physicists claim it is a live hypothesis that classical space–time is emergent.[50] While this might not threaten the truth of our space–time talk, it does threaten the claim that physical properties can be exhaustively characterized by their spatio-temporal implications. After all, if space and time emerge from some lower domain, presumably that lower domain cannot itself be fully characterized in spatio-temporal terms, and yet surely the properties there deserve to be called physical if they are posited by our best physics. So, my definition is inadequate.

A full discussion of this issue would require more space and intelligence than is available here. I am therefore willing to offer a concessive plan B should brighter minds find this to be a genuine threat to my view. First, though, I want to offer a couple of reasons to think it shouldn't pose a real threat. First, the way many physicists seem to put the issue is in terms of the emergence of "classical" space–time. This leaves open the possibility that classical space–time emerges from another state space that is non-classical. For example, there is the suggestion that the Riemannian structure of classical space–time could be seen as emerging from a more fundamental, infinite dimensional Hilbert space.[51] If this is the case, the spatio-temporal definition is only threatened if it is wedded to characterizing things in terms of classical space–time. But there is no need to limit it in this way. The essence of the definition would remain intact, for example, if it turned out that physical properties were those that are exhaustively defined by their implications for the distribution of things and properties over a Hilbert space. The definition can be viewed as flexible, with no loss to my purposes, substituting the more fundamental space for the classical space–time.

---

[50] See Greene (1999) and Seiberg (2005). In fact most physicists, and scientists in general, are not particularly clear about what is involved in emergence. They usually don't seem to mean, for example, anything like what Broad and the British Emergentists meant. Their conception seems to me more epistemic. For the purposes of this objection, even a fairly weak sense of emergence will be adequate. Thanks to Alyssa Ney for bringing this issue to my attention.

[51] Kryukov (2003).

If, on the other hand, it is maintained that classical space–time emerges from something that is fundamentally non-spatio-temporal, such that the notions of "space" and "time" simply make no sense below a certain scale, and there is no single multi-dimensional state space which embraces the workings of the non-spatial but from which the spatio-temporal can be derived, there might be a problem. But I'm not sure the problem will be entirely with my view. Such a situation seems quite an unfortunate result for physics. Two related problems come to mind. On the one hand, it seems we would lose a desirable transparency about the relation between the different scales of physical explanation. It is an intuitive desideratum that we be able to see how the events at one scale derive from the events at a lower scale. It is not at all clear that this would be possible on the divided picture we have imagined. This explanatory failure would be paralleled by a methodological difficulty. A clear methodological desideratum of our basic science is that its claims be experimentally testable. String theory has already received many complaints that it does not yield to experimental tests, leading some physicists to despair of its tenability.[52] A theory that posits a brute emergence of the spatio-temporal from the non-spatio-temporal is bound to have worse difficulties. For surely the methods of empirical verification at our disposal are limited to the spatio-temporal. The instruments we use, including the scattering of particles, are clearly spatial, and our very conception of experimentation presupposes events unfolding over time.[53] It is hard to see what sort of confirmation this brute emergence view could enjoy.

It might be too much to say that a physics positing the brute emergence of space–time would be off the rails, but it is worth considering the similarities such a view would have to traditional philosophical views. There is no question that what we have here is a sort of dualism, even if it is not a mind–body dualism. And just as substance dualism faces the damning problem of explaining how a substance that is not spatio-temporal can interact with one that is, so the brute emergence view would have a difficulty explaining how the base domain, and the things in it, give rise to or interact with things in the spatio-temporal realm.[54] It also bears

[52] See Smolin (2006).

[53] Seiburg (2005) shows sensitivity to concerns like these despite suggesting this sort of emergence. Tim Maudlin (2007) seems to be arguing something like this.

[54] In perhaps the best explanation of why substance dualism has a problem with mental causation, Jaegwon Kim points to the fact that spatial relations are what allow us to distinguish "intrinsically indiscernable objects in causal situations" which is required to ground the

some striking similarities to Kant's transcendental idealism. Although the brute emergence view has no commitment to the spatio-temporal world being a construct of the mind (though the eliminativist view mentioned earlier might!) it similarly posits a spatio-temporal realm that looks a great deal like the phenomenal realm of Kant, and it claims that behind it lies a realm immune to empirical investigation that cannot be helpfully connected explanatorily to the spatio-temporal realm. Needless to say, this begins to look a great deal like the noumenal realm that post-Kantian thinkers found distasteful and subject to elimination by Occam's Razor. It would be ironic if modern science wound up reviving it and crowning it with physical respectability. If things wound up this way, I wouldn't feel too repelled from the further ironic claim that physicalism turns out—by the verdict of physics—to be false.[55]

This brings me to a more concessive response to this concern. If one is convinced that the brute emergence of space–time is a real possibility, and one is unhappy with the idea that this would falsify physicalism, I could still state the view that is relevant to the mind–body problem. This view talks about the physical★, which covers properties that satisfy Neocart definitions, and claims that physicalism★ is only true if the relevant mental properties (such as the phenomenal and intentional) supervene on the physical★ properties. This seems to capture what we care about—if the phenomenal doesn't supervene on the things in space and time, but is either (a) basic, or (b) supervenes not on the spatio-temporal but on some sub-quantum non-spatio-temporal realm, physicalism is false.[56] Why is physicalism false if (b) holds? If (b) is true, then essential features of the psychological—such as the phenomenal—are unlike the events and properties of chemistry, biology, or any other science on the books. The facts of

discriminating nature of causal relations (Kim 2005, p.85). The point is that the dualist has no answer to the question which of two souls, A or B, causes spatio-temporal event C, because there is no system of relations to secure the "pairing" of A to C versus B to C. It would seem that a similar pairing problem would face the brute emergent space–time view. Put another way, if there is a system of relations that could pair processes (or whatever) in the base, non-spatio-temporal domain, with processes or events in the emergent domain, then the emergence would no longer be brute.

[55] This is probably a good place to restate that I am not defining "physicsalism" or making statements about what is legitimate business for physics. I am defining physicalism. The former could be true while the latter is false.

[56] The second, b-possibility is interesting and is perhaps a version of neutral monism, but it is not physicalism in the sense that interests most participants in the debate.

these sciences are fixed by the physical★ properties, and while we would like to find a bottom in physics, we don't need to do so in order to see how these special sciences relate to the overall picture of the world. There might be multiple (logically) possible stories of how the 'physical' is fixed, but these will not essentially change our understanding of why, say, cell membranes form. It would be an uncomfortable anomaly, on par with panpsychism or neutral monism, if psychological facts could not be fixed by the quantum (or what are now the lowest known level) facts but instead require a particular realization in terms of the sub-quantum. This is something physicalists should shun, so even on this concessive response our neo-Cartesian definition of physicality serves its purpose.

> *Objection 5*: Being non-spatio-temporal is not even necessary for dualism, since if mentality were a fundamental spatio-temporal feature of the world, physicalism would still be false.[57]

Response: The case here is under described, but if it turned out to be the case that some fundamental property, which did nothing but determine the distribution of other properties in space over time, constituted a phenomenal (or intentional, or whatever) state, the physicalist would be surprised but not dismayed. It seems very unlikely that a property that only characterizes individuals of great complexity would be fundamental. But if it were, and it could be characterized fully in terms of spatial implications, the reductive physicalist would surely be vindicated beyond his wildest dreams!

The Base Problem: Conclusion

The development of physics since the days of Descartes has led us to acknowledge some entities and properties that Descartes would have found well beyond the pale of what he considered to be physical. To be physical, for Descartes, was to be extended. We are now willing to admit that this is probably false. The lesson that has been drawn from this definitional failure has often been that we should follow the lead of physics in defining what is physical, but this approach faces Hempel's famous dilemma: current physics is incomplete, and there is no telling what future physics might bring. The result has been a sort of despair over finding a

---

[57] Montero (1999).

definition of physicalism. I maintain that this despair is misguided, because the wrong lesson was drawn from Descartes' error. Descartes' was wrong to tie the physical to the extended, but right to recognize that spatiality is closely tied to physicality. The neo-Cartesian proposal is intended as a refinement of this insight.

This proposal is closely related to certain attempts to characterize the physical in terms of structure and dynamics.[58] It is an advance over those attempts for several reasons. One is that "structure and dynamics" is rather vague. At the very least, the neo-Cartesian proposal provides one of many possible ways of making it precise. Second, the idea of non-physical structure and non-physical dynamics doesn't seem contradictory, so "structure and dynamics" can only be sufficient for physicalism if it is *physical* structure and dynamics. This risks running in a pretty tight circle. Relatedly, it doesn't seem beyond question that certain sorts of structure and certain sorts of dynamics are sufficient to define things that are ultimately non-physical. Phenomenal experiences change over time, and they also have structure. Aqua is lighter than green, red and green cannot coexist at the same place at the same time, intense pains tend to leave haloes of pain after their departure, etc. Some philosophers believe that the structure of phenomenal space is sufficient to define phenomenal character.[59] It is coherent to hold this view as a dualist. So, a world determined by structure and dynamics cannot be guaranteed to be a physical world. There is a final worry, which is that it seems conceivable that there be a world with one unstructured, unchanging physical object in it. This world would lack structure, and would not be dynamic in any sense, but it seems intuitive that it could still be physical.[60]

What is suggested by definitions in terms of structural dynamics, and what is essentially Descartes' insight, is that physical properties only concern the location of things in space over time. What makes things such as thoughts or phenomenal states seem, at first blush, non-physical is that they do not seem to be fully describable by their spatial implications. Their natures, the feels and the "aboutnesses," seem to elude spatial description.

---

[58] Russell (1927); Alter (2009); Chalmers (2010).

[59] See Kirk (forthcoming).

[60] Imagining such things is difficult. Perhaps this is an incoherent supposition after all. The fact that it seems conceivable, however, points at the very least to the fact that the metaphor of "structure and dynamics" is not as clear as it needs to be.

Perhaps the anti-physicalist is wrong, and these features of the world are necessitated by the distribution of things in space over time, but that is, simply expressed, the question of whether or not physicalism is true.

If my arguments to this point are acceptable, there is a coherent neo-Cartesian conception of physicalism which insists that though physicality doesn't require extension, it is deeply intertwined with the way physical properties exist in space–time. While this does show that a sort of definitional despair is unwarranted, the mere coherence of a view is not much of a recommendation for it. Even though I began the chapter by offering some considerations against other views, I have hardly done away with the competition. In particular, there will remain those who are unimpressed by Hempel's dilemma and who will feel that a definition that sidesteps what physicists actually say is bound to be of limited interest. What is there to recommend our neo-Cartesian account as the right account of what it means for a property to be "physical?"

As I have noted earlier, it is doubtful that there is only one conception of the physical, and it would be silly to claim to have found Adam's definition. Nevertheless, I think there is a good deal to recommend the neo-Cartesian definition at least for the purposes of the mind–body problem. Perhaps most important is that the mind–body problem is first and foremost a metaphysical problem. It is about whether or not the stuff that makes up the world is of one fundamental type or not. Though it is a metaphysical problem, we will see that the challenges to physicalism involve epistemic premises and intuitions. As such, it behooves us to be particularly clear in this debate about what is epistemic and what is not, and to give metaphysical notions such as "physicalism" purely metaphysical definitions. To do otherwise might be to give the anti-physicalists an undeserved leg up. If, for example, a property was considered physical only if a description provided in the language of physics could convey a perfect and exhaustive understanding of that property, any argument which established an epistemic gap between the understanding of the physical and the phenomenal—as the knowledge argument attempts to do—would immediately have physicalism on the ropes. One of the most popular responses to such arguments is to accuse them of a form of epistemic fallacy, drawing a metaphysical conclusion from an epistemic premise. This objection cannot easily stick if the very definition of physicality is partly epistemic.

A definition in terms of physics risks being epistemic because it ties the nature of the physical to the results of a particular way of knowing the world. This way of knowing the world rightly places extreme emphasis on intersubjective testability and experimental verification. A strong defense of physicalism should not leave an opening for the dualist—or the neutral monist, panpsychist or anyone else—to insist that the physicalist is only dogmatically insisting on a particular way of knowing the world. Dualism is not, or should not be, merely a skeptical epistemological position about the limitations of physics. By focusing on the issue of whether or not the world is fully determined by properties that are exhausted by their spatio-temporal implications, attention is drawn to the metaphysical heart of the puzzle.

None of this is to say that one cannot defend a physics based physicalism from the threats posed by phenomenal qualities. In fact, I think few of the arguments in the rest of the book depend deeply on this particular definition of physicalism.[61] There are other definitions which, if defended appropriately, could work as well. Nevertheless, it is a good deal easier to enter these debates with a clear sense of what we are talking about, and it is not easy to do this by appealing to the findings, current or future, of our most developed physics.[62]

---

[61] A referee has suggested that the very fact that this definition allows for subjective physicalism must mean it is wrong. In fact, though, my definition allows for subjective physicalism, so would a physics based conception so long as the subjective part did not intrude at the base level. As will be seen, it is not a commitment of my view that it does.

[62] A final reason to prefer the neo-Cartesian definition is that it seems very close to the definitions offered by anti-materialists themselves. It is, as we have noted, close to the notion of "structure and dynamics" appealed to by Chalmers, Alter, and others. By sticking close to the anti-materialists definitions, we can focus on places where we disagree further down the road.

2

Supervenience and the Relation Problem

Though we have made headway on defining the physical base, or what we might call, for short, the physical*, we still face the relation problem. It seems unlikely that we want to say that all properties are physical*. For one thing, the metaphysics of properties that is presupposed in both forms of Neocart is only plausible for basic properties. (It seems much less plausible, and quite difficult to understand, how the property of being a car can be defined in terms of a Trans-World Disposition Set (TDS), and no one is inclined to be a necessitarian about such higher level properties.) Unless we wish to rule out that there are physical properties that are non-basic, we need an account of the relation non-basic properties must hold to physical* properties if they are to be physicalistically acceptable. My proposal, following many others but against recent trends to the contrary, is that the appropriate account is to be given in terms of supervenience.

The notion of supervenience was introduced into the contemporary discussion of the mind–body problem by Donald Davidson but there has since been a productive cottage industry spelling out different varieties of supervenience and examining their philosophical uses. Most important is the notion of strong supervenience (SSV). Jaegwon Kim formulates this as follows:

> SSV: For two domains of properties A and B, A strongly supervenes on B just in case: Necessarily, for any object x and any property F in A, if x has F then there is a property G in B such that x has G, and necessarily if any y has G, it has F (Kim 1993, p.181).

Less formally, the idea is that if you fix an object's B properties, its A properties will also be fixed, and this is true in all worlds as well as across worlds. The modality employed in SSV can vary, but, as I will argue, metaphysical necessity is what is desirable for defining the terms of this debate. This suggests the following basic supervenience definition of physicalism (SSVP):

> SSVP: Physicalism is true iff all properties strongly supervene with metaphysical necessity on the basic physical properties.[1]

SSVP looks promising as a definition of physicalism because it maintains that in some sense everything depends upon the physical: if God, when constructing the world, fixed all of the physical properties, he would not have to do anything else; the rest would come "for free." Although SSVP captures the spirit of the physicalist doctrine, two issues suggest that it is not perfectly adequate. On one hand, SSVP as formulated—in terms of SSV— might seem to make physicalism inconsistent with externalism about the content of mental states. I have thoughts about water, my twin has thoughts about twater, yet we are physical twins—the difference between us depends upon our histories or upon the substance with which we actually interact. This type of consideration has led many to prefer global supervenience theses which formulate physicalism in terms of the necessary similarity of worlds taken as a whole. In the end, I am convinced that GSVP claims aren't ontologically superior, but they might in the end be clearer.[2] So consider the following:

> GSVP: Physicalism is true iff a world that is a physical duplicate of our world is a duplicate *simpliciter* of our world.

The problem with GSVP is that it seems to make physicalism false if ghosts and non-physical minds are even *possible* in worlds that have the same physical furniture as our world. Such worlds would, after all, duplicate our world but contain spirits. Most think that this shouldn't lead us to claim that physicalism is false about our world. In fact, I am not convinced that the metaphysical possibility of ghosts should be countenanced, but perhaps

---

[1] As Schaffer (2003) has noted, there are issues surrounding the assumption of a "fundamental level" of reality in these sorts of supervenience definitions. I don't think this threatens the SVP thesis I advance shortly. Montero (2006) discusses other ways of defining physicalism without the assumption of a "fundamental level" of reality.

[2] See Bennett (2004). This is given a few assumptions about how the GSVP is formulated as well as a closure condition on properties. Stalnaker makes a similar point about the equivalence in ontological power in Stalnaker (2003b).

one should be agnostic about such things.[3] Given this, it seems best to say that physicalism is a thesis about our world, where other worlds are part of the thesis only insofar as they demonstrate the modal robustness of the relations that obtain in our world. One must be careful about how "our world" figures into the supervenience thesis, however. Jackson's well-known formulation (JGSVP), for example, fixes the problem of possible ghosts but runs into other problems. He proposes the following thesis:

JGSVP: Physicalism is true iff any world which is a *minimal* physical duplicate of our world is a duplicate *simpliciter* of our world. (Jackson 1998, p.12)

A "minimal physical duplicate of our world is a world that (a) is exactly like our world in every physical respect . . . , and (b) contains nothing else in the sense of nothing more by way of kinds or particulars than it *must* to satisfy (a)" (Jackson 1998, p.13). In other words, a minimal physical duplicate of our world contains the physical properties, with no gratuitous additions.

This thesis fails, however, because of the possibility of what John Hawthorne calls "blockers" (Hawthorne 2002). Suppose that in our world the connection between physical configuration P and mental property M is such that P necessitates M only if there is no B in the world. Bs are not in our world—they are alien, non-physical entities which only sever the connection between Ps and Ms. The intuition is that physicalism should not tolerate this looseness of connection between mental and physical properties, and yet JGSVP would be insensitive to this because we are only looking at minimal duplicate worlds, not worlds with new things like Bs in them.[4]

To solve this problem, I suggest the following, which is indebted to a suggestion by Chalmers (1996, pp.39–40 and 364):

SVP: Physicalism is true of our world iff any world that is a physical duplicate of our world is either a duplicate of our world simpliciter or it contains a duplicate of our world as a proper part.

To say that a world contains a duplicate of our world as a proper part is just to say that it is our world with some additions. So the idea is that if physicalism is true, God can make a duplicate of our world *simpliciter*

---

[3] I am sympathetic with the arguments offered by Levine and Trogden (2009) that we should not even view ghosts and such as possible.

[4] This problem confronts David Lewis's supervenience thesis tailored to avoid the problem of ghosts; see Lewis (1999b, p.37). For the problem with his thesis, see Hawthorne (2002).

simply by duplicating the physical properties in our world. What's more, supposing God then decided to add things to that duplicate world, his additions would not change the intrinsic properties of what he had already created. So suppose our world had immaterial souls in it. SVP would deem physicalism false about our world, because replicating the physical features of our world would not produce a duplicate of our world—the souls would be missing.[5] Nevertheless, ghosts in *other* worlds would not falsify physicalism, according to SVP, since they would include our world as proper parts, and the possibility of blockers would falsify physicalism since blocker worlds would not contain a duplicate of our world. This is the result we want.[6]

Perhaps counterintuitively, SVP does allow that physicalism is true even if there could be a physical duplicate of our world where one of the individuals in that world had one further mental state, or where things thoughtless in our world had active mental lives. Since worlds where these scenarios obtained would have our world as a proper part, SVP would be satisfied. But such scenarios—allowing mental discernability despite physical indiscernability—sound like just the sort of thing supervenience was meant to rule out.

This problem can seem worse than it is. Physicalism, according to SVP, does allow that my physical duplicate has, say, a pain I don't have. It doesn't allow, though, that this new pain be of the same ontological type as the pains I actually have. My pains are physical, and my physical duplicate will have just those physical pains and no other physical pains. If he has further pains it will be because in his world there are pains made of different stuff. So though SVP doesn't provide the classic guarantee of

---

[5] SVP does not say, for example, that once we duplicate the physical base properties of our world then we've duplicated everything physical. It says that when we duplicate the physical base properties then we've duplicated *everything* and no further additions to the world can change that.

[6] Leuenberger (2008) argues that blockers are not inconsistent with a reasonable construal of physicalism. His claim, I take it, is that even if the physical explains the mental only given that there are no alien properties (or *ceteris absentibus*, as he puts it) the physical still explains the mental, which is what physicalism requires. We often accept *ceteris paribus* explanations without those implicit conditions being part of the explanation, so we can similarly accept *ceteris absentibus* explanations without the alien blockers being part of the explanation. But even if we accept *ceteris paribus* explanations sometimes, would we really be happy with *ceteris paribus* physicalism? He says, "Intuitively, physicalism is not a claim about such merely possible facts" (p.155). I do not share this intuition. To say that one event explains another is to take on commitments about what would happen under other circumstances.

mental indiscernibility across worlds given physical indiscernibility across worlds, exceptions to this thesis only come with worlds that have some fundamentally alien stuff. These exceptions seem to come with the territory of allowing for the possibility of ghosts. If we are to allow for the possibility of non-physical minds, it would seem hard to rule out the possibility of "free-range" mental properties that can latch onto brains or rocks, adding sensations and thoughts that are not present in the actual world. It has to be remembered, however, that this definition of physicalism is meant to capture the sense in which *this* world is physical. If physicalism as defined by SVP is true, the dynamics of things in this world do, in fact, follow the intuitive physicalist behavior: mental changes require things to change physically. It is only when alien things are inserted into our world that the mental comes unmoored from the physical. In other words, physicalism should just say that nothing in our world is weird. If some physical duplicates of our world have thinking rocks, that is a sign that those worlds are weird, not that our world is weird. Nevertheless, if one is still bothered, I think one will be forced to go beyond a contingent physicalist thesis, accepting GSVP as the definition of physicalism.[7]

A final worry about SVP is that it looks as though it is consistent with the actual existence of necessary ghosts—or a necessary God. For if there is a necessary ghost, then any physical duplicate of our world will contain our world's ghost as a proper part, because any physical duplicate of our world—indeed any world at all—contains our ghost. Since we want to allow for possible ghosts but not actual ghosts, this is a problem for SVP.

This objection only works if necessary ghosts are really metaphysically possible, but there is little reason to think this is the case. As we shall see later, we must be careful in these debates to remember that there is no such thing as an accidental necessary truth. If there could be a necessary being there is one. A physicalist should not allow this. The space of worlds is necessary, and it is also very large. Unless we have a strong argument that there is a ghost in every world, we should deny it.[8]

---

[7] Even if a physicalist should think ghosts and qualia are possible, it might well be she should not think that ghost worlds are too close. It seems likely that the holding of physical laws in our world should guarantee that no close world has ghosts in it.

[8] Giving this objection a full airing would involve rehearsing the ontological argument and its responses. The interested reader is directed to the voluminous Oppy (2007) for discussion.

The Challenge to Supervenience Definitions

Many recent philosophers, including early supervenience champion Jaeg-won Kim, no longer feel supervenience can be much more than a necessary condition of physicalism.[9] Because it leaves the reason for mind–body co-variation unspecified, it is compatible with numerous non-physicalist doctrines.

> . . . both emergentism and the view that the mental must be physically realized (we can call this "physical realizationism") imply mind–body supervenience. But emergentism is a form of dualism that takes mental properties to be nonphysical intrinsic causal powers, whereas physical realizationism is monistic physicalism. (Kim 1998, p.12)

I think Kim might be overly pessimistic about the possibilities of supervenience. If emergentism is the reason why a supervenience formulation of physicalism is extensionally inadequate, perhaps we can fix the problem by strengthening supervenience.

Supervenience is a modal notion, and as such it involves the typical ambiguities generated by the possibility of different domains for the modal operators. It is particularly important in this context to distinguish between nomological and metaphysical supervenience, where in the former the necessity operator has only nomologically possible worlds in its domain and in the latter all metaphysically possible worlds are considered. So if the mental supervenes nomologically on the physical, physical indiscernibility entails mental indiscernibility in all worlds with the same laws as ours.[10] If the mental supervenes metaphysically on the physical, physical indiscernibility entails mental indiscernibility in any metaphysically possible world whatsoever.[11]

---

[9] Though in his (2011) Kim argues that supervenience is sufficient for physicalism after all. His argument is quite a bit different than the one here.

[10] The relevant notion of indiscernibility needs clarification, but for my purposes it can remain intuitive. For clear and adequate senses, see Paull and Sider (1992); McLaughlin (1995); Stalnaker (2003b); Bennett (2004).

[11] In enumerating the relevant types of supervenience, I do not consider the third option of logical supervenience which would have the necessity operator ranging over all logically possible worlds. This only differs from the metaphysical thesis on the assumption that there are logically possible worlds that are not metaphysically possible. Most people support this assumption, but it is not obvious to me that they should, at least when doing metaphysics. Nevertheless, physicalists who do adhere to such a distinction are probably unlikely to think physicalism requires anything as strong as a logical supervenience thesis, and emergentists certainly don't wish to claim anything as strong as logical necessity for emergence laws.

Emergentism about minds threatens supervenience theses of physicalism because it maintains that everything is determined by the physical★ properties, but that not all properties are physical. Some new properties "emerge" in a law-like fashion at certain levels of organizational complexity, endowing the new structure with features that could not have been predicted from the lower level properties alone.[12] But the emergence that threatens physicalism is not of this *epistemic* variety, which merely claims that new patterns emerge that we cannot discern by looking at the lower level properties. It is *metaphysical* emergentism that is the threat. These properties are "new" in that they bear significantly novel powers or characteristics that are not *metaphysically grounded* in the powers or characteristics of the elements from which they emerge but appear given particular configurations of those more basic elements. (One can have epistemic emergence without metaphysical emergence if one's knowledge of the base properties is limited—for example one didn't know the base had these properties until one observed the higher level phenomenon.) In the metaphysical case, properties that are irreducibly mental—in virtue of endowing their bearer with phenomenal feelings or intentional thoughts—emerge on purely physical configurations. In at least some sense, they supervene upon those basic characteristics: given the way things work in this world, if you fix the basic configurations, the emergent properties come for free. If they supervene in the same sense of supervenience meant by SVP, then SVP fails because basic mental properties supervene upon the basic physical properties despite the fact that they are not physical★.

An intuitive response to this argument is that given the radical "newness" of the emergent properties SVP can be saved by strengthening the type of supervenience it involves. Since properties emerge only given the existence of emergence laws, this line of response continues, they emerge nomologically but not metaphysically. The emergence laws may hold in this world, but there are surely worlds without such laws, and if that is the case SVP stands. Following a suggestion by James Van Cleve, we might define emergence as follows:

---

[12] For excellent discussions which, among other things, lay out the basic tenets of British Emergentism, see McLaughlin (1992); Kim (2000).

A property P emerges given a configuration of properties C iff P supervenes with nomological necessity, but not with metaphysical necessity, on C. (Van Cleve 1990, p.222)

If this definition of emergence is adequate, then SVP would seem to remain extensionally sound, excluding emergentism by definition. However, as we will see, some think Van Cleve's definition is not adequate because emergence laws could be metaphysically necessary. I maintain, however, that if emergence laws are necessary (and Van Cleve's definition fails) SVP is still sound because the properties upon which mental properties emerge will no longer be purely physical.

Supervenience and Emergence

Some emergentists claim that properties emerge with metaphysical necessity, making the emergence laws examples of the necessary a posteriori. Of course it falls to a defender of such a position to explain what is so special about emergence laws. There is no obvious reason to maintain that emergence laws are necessary while the basic laws of physics are contingent. If anything, emergence laws seem particularly inapt to be considered necessary because of the strange "newness" of the emergent properties with respect to their bases.

If an emergentist is going to claim metaphysical necessity for emergence laws, her best strategy is to claim that it is because laws of nature in general are necessary.[13] In a recent paper, Jessica Wilson has argued just that (Wilson 2005). She maintains that there are persuasive reasons to accept the thesis that the laws of nature are not just well-confirmed generalizations, but are necessary truths. The natural laws exemplified in our world might not be exemplified in every world—a world with different stuff entirely will exemplify different laws appropriate to that stuff. Nevertheless, natural laws are necessary if they are laws at all. Wilson then points out that if this is the case the distinction between nomological and metaphysical supervenience is vacuous. Emergent but non-physical properties do supervene metaphysically on the physical, so SVP and similar supervenience definitions of physicalism fail.

---

[13] My argument also would work against someone who thinks that only emergence laws are necessary.

Necessitarianism about natural laws is a contentious thesis and most philosophers who are inclined towards supervenience definitions of physicalism will be apt to elude Wilson's argument by rejecting necessitarianism outright. In fact, this would leave another, similar problem: physicalism cannot be defined in terms of supervenience since it is conceivable that dualism be true, but that God set things up so that in every world with a certain set of physical properties there is a certain set of dualistic properties.[14] Thus, say these critics, supervenience is consistent with dualism. Even if necessitarianism about laws were rejected, this objection would remain, so a defense would do better to focus on whether or not necessary emergence is a threat to supervenience definitions.

Defending Supervenience Definitions

Even given necessitarianism about laws, emergentism is not a counter-example to SVP. The basic argument is that if emergence laws are necessary, and the emergent properties are "new" enough to count as non-physical, then the supervenience base will be polluted and will no longer be purely physical.[15] If this is the case, then SVP will judge an emergence dualist world to be non-physical, because duplicating the purely physical properties will not duplicate the world *simpliciter*.

Let's suppose with the emergentist that there is a genuinely new emergent property E which emerges necessarily from C. We can suppose, for example, that E is the property of having a phenomenal pain. It seems that any plausible version of necessitarianism will entail that properties are (at least) in part individuated by the properties they necessitate, be those properties emergent or otherwise. This might be because necessitarianism follows from one's view of properties or it might be because one is forced to this view of properties by one's necessitarianism.[16] Either way, the result is that C is individuated in part by the disposition to give rise to E.[17] Is this

---

[14] Melnyk (2003, p.58).

[15] If the "emergent" properties are not substantially new, it doesn't seem physicalism should have a problem with them, so even if they supervene on the physical they would not provide a counterexample to SVP.

[16] Since Shoemaker's necessitarianism is driven by this sort of view of property individuation, my point is clear in his case.

[17] This is to say that what makes C *that* property, and not another very similar type, is that disposition.

disposition a physical disposition? It is hard to see how it is, given our solution to the base problem. By hypothesis, E is a fundamental, mental property, which means that C is essentially characterized by the disposition to produce a fundamental mental property. On the assumption that qualia are as the dualist describes them, this means that E cannot be exhaustively described in terms of its spatio-temporal implications. C is not purely physical, and any supervenience base that includes C must include the dispositional property of C to produce E (call this second order property $C_{1.1}$). Otherwise there would be nothing to distinguish C from $C^\star$ which is just like C only lacking that disposition. Intuitively, and by Neocart, $C_{1.1}$ is not physical. (How could the dispositional property to give rise to a new, non-physical property itself be physical? Even if one wanted, *pace* Neocart, to call C itself physical, the property that is nothing but the disposition to give rise to something non-physical surely is not.) Thus, if necessitarianism is true and emergentism is true, there must be non-physical properties in the supervenience base to necessitate the emergence. If this is the case, however, there is no counterexample to SVP: a purely physical duplicate of our world would not have our world as a proper part, because some of the fundamental stuff of our world necessarily involves non-physical properties like $C_{1.1}$.

Though I have presented the previous argument in an *ad hominem* fashion, as if it depends upon necessitarianism about laws, it is really based on intuitive considerations about property individuation. Properties are at least in part individuated by their necessary connections. If P necessitates $P^\star$, but G doesn't, then P is not the same property type as G. The necessitation of $P^\star$ is part of what makes P the type of property it is. If it turns out that part of what makes electrons what they are is that they give rise to "unpredictable" qualitative experiences when in a certain setting, then it seems that electrons are somewhat magical and are at least partly constituted by non-physical dispositions. To make a crude comparison, suppose we found out that our world had schmairs in it. Schmairs are just like chairs, except that when zombies sit in them they are suddenly conscious. This is just a brute disposition of schmairs. Assuming zombies can purely be described physically, the existence of schmairs in our world clearly suggests that some of the fundamental furniture of our world is not exhaustively describable as physical. Schmairs might not themselves be conscious, but a fundamental, irreducible part of what makes them what they are is the disposition to confer consciousness. This is not purely a physical disposition, and that's why schmairs are magic chairs. If electrons, or the basic constituents of our world, have a similarly brute non-physical disposition, then the basic stuff of our world is infused with mentality in a way that is quite surprising. It contains properties that are not in the natural purview of physics, and as such do not belong in a purely physical super-venience base. In such a world, a sort of quasi-panpsychism is true: at least some of the basic stuff in our world is not conscious, but it is infused with mentality in that it is individuated by the brute tendency to produce it.

My argument depends upon the claim that properties are in part individuated by their necessary features, so if C gives rise to E in all possible worlds, that fact is part of what makes C the property it is. One might object to that claim, claiming that C can give rise to E necessarily, even though C is not individuated by the disposition to do so. Perhaps, one might say, it is just a basic fact that the mental properties emerge on their physical bases in all possible worlds, but not because it is part of the individuation conditions of the base properties. Thus, the argument continues, basic mental properties supervene with metaphysical necessity on a purely physical base, and we finally have a counterexample to SVP (Melnyk 2003).

This response doesn't really outline a coherent possibility. Given configuration base C and emergent property E, if C gives rise to E in every possible world, part of what individuates C is that it does so. This can be seen by considering how C differs from C⋆, which has all the same propensities except that of giving rise to E. If C⋆ is possible, which there is no argument that it is not, then it must differ from C, and this difference must ultimately be grounded in something about C. If this is the case, my argument remains intact. Compare the case of mass. One might say that though mass is not defined by the causal propensities it bestows, things having it necessarily obey the inverse square law. But then what distinguishes mass from schmass, which attracts other schmassy things in a way that could be described by an inverse cube law? There must be something about the properties in virtue of which one falls under one law and one falls under the other. One could, perhaps, deny that schmass is a possible property, but that seems speculative and unfounded. What could possibly ground such a necessity? Denying the possibility of schmass or similar properties seems a desperate way out, and if there are such possible properties then the necessitarian must individuate properties in part by the necessary laws that govern them.[18]

There is a lesson to be learned here.[19] Some philosophers dismiss supervenience formulations of physicalism because it seems a coherent possibility that the space of possible worlds could be such that all possible worlds with physical bases like ours have dualistic mental properties. There could, according to them, be a sort of modal accident that every world with a certain purely physical base has certain purely mental properties. There are two, related problems here. First, there simply are no modal accidents: the space of possible worlds is necessarily what it is. It makes no sense to say it could possibly be otherwise, since talk of possibilities itself is grounded in the space of possible worlds. One cannot simply posit a total distribution of worlds as a possibility—that distribution either necessarily is, or it necessarily is not. One can, perhaps, locate a possible subset of such worlds where there is an accidental match between the physical properties and the mental properties, but if the match is indeed accidental, there will be other worlds that exist where it does not occur, and there will not, therefore, be metaphysical supervenience. If there is metaphysical supervenience, on the other hand, then it is no accident—the worlds where supervenience fails are ruled out by necessity.[20] If this is the case, my previous arguments apply. What is it that guarantees that these possible worlds are ruled out? It seems there is no other explanation than that it is part of the individuation conditions of the properties in the supervenience base to give rise to the supervening properties.

This can be put even more intuitively in terms of the objection that God could make it such that every world with a physical base came paired with a certain set of non-physical properties. We can ask the following question about this situation: did God have to make things this way or not?

---

[18] For the record, Wilson, Shoemaker, and most other necessitarians in this debate do not deny the possibility of properties such as schmass or $C^\star$.

[19] What I have to say here bears important similarities to arguments provided in (Paull and Sider (1992).

[20] I have Melnyk (2003) in mind here. In fact, Melnyk probably doesn't really believe necessary brute dualism is possible, since he is a physicalist. One cannot be a physicalist and believe in the possibility of necessary emergence since if it is possible that physical properties necessarily give rise to dualistic properties, then there is a world such that it is true of that world that emergentist dualism is necessary (i.e. it is true in that world that it is true of every world that dualistic emergentism is true). But if that is the case, it is true of every world, including this one, that dualistic emergentism is true, and physicalism is false.

If he didn't have to, then there are other possibilities and thus other possible worlds where there isn't the pairing, and supervenience fails. If God did have to make things this way, why? Presumably for the same reason he cannot make squares without corners—just as corners are part of the nature of squares, certain dualistic states would have to be part of the nature of "physical" states.

From what I have argued, it looks as if a necessitarian with emergentist sympathies will be forced either into a type of quasi-panpsychism, where our basic physical properties contain the illicit seeds of mentality at their core, or she will be forced to admit that emergence laws are not necessary after all. In neither case is there a counterexample to SVP. In the first case, a purely physical duplicate of our world would not look anything like our world, since the basic properties that give rise to mentality will not be duplicated, because they are not purely physical. In the second case, emergence laws would be well-confirmed generalizations that hold in our world, and perhaps in all neighboring worlds, but not in all metaphysically possible worlds. If the necessitarian takes this course, however, there is obviously no counterexample to SVP since the mental properties will not emerge with metaphysical necessity but only given the contingent emergence laws.

Conclusion

The definition of physicalism can be put as follows:

> Physicalism: Physicalism is true iff the concrete properties and things in this world supervene upon the properties in this world that are exhausted by their implications for the distribution of things over space and time.

Given our particular interpretation of supervenience, provided by SVP, this means that if physicalism is true, then any world which contained all of the "spatio-temporally exhausted" properties in our world would contain our world as a proper part.

This definition not only fairly parcels out the terrain in the mind–body debate—putting panpsychists and dualists on one side and functionalist and identity theorists on the other—it doesn't stack the deck unfairly against either side. Physicalists should be happy that the resulting definition is clearly metaphysical, and dualists should be happy with the fact that the base notion doesn't endorse an overly permissive notion of "physical" according to which anything real counts as physical. In my view both physicalists and dualists should feel comfortable basing physicalism in the notion of supervenience, for even though we will no doubt want a more specific explanation of the mental/physical relationship, we can remain agnostic about those specifics while the relevant sciences are still building and testing theories.

PART II

The Threat of the Subjective

With a clear notion of physicalism before us, we can begin to consider physicalism's primary threat: conscious phenomenal states. Although there are several anti-physicalist arguments that stem from the recalcitrance of phenomenal states to physicalistic analysis, I will focus upon Frank Jackson's Knowledge Argument. Other arguments will be addressed later, in Part III. But the Knowledge Argument is the best place to start for at least three reasons. It is extremely simple to comprehend, it serves to highlight precisely the sort of "consciousness" which poses a problem for physicalism, and it is rather up front about the fact that it is getting at intuitions about metaphysics from intuitions about epistemology. Since most physicalists see this as the downfall of the anti-physicalist arguments, it will be instructive to see what is and what is not true in their criticisms.

I maintain that the Knowledge Argument is much more difficult to resist than it has appeared. In particular, I will argue that what many have taken to be the most attractive sort of response to the knowledge argument is in fact unstable. I have in mind those responses defending what Chalmers calls Type-B physicalism according to which Mary learns something new when she leaves the room, but that this does not threaten physicalism. In other words, these philosophers deny the metaphysical step of the argument while embracing its epistemic step. Although I think a position like this can be maintained—indeed I myself maintain such a position—it comes with more cost than many physicalists would be willing to bear. I believe, actually, that when pushed most of these epistemicists will turn out to be hardliners in epistemicist's clothing. The alternative, I argue, will threaten the view that an objective picture of the world can be complete, which could be seen as a threat to physicalism itself.

In Chapter 3, I will present what I find to be the best version of the Knowledge Argument. I will argue that on this version at least, it does not commit the "epistemic fallacy" that it is sometimes accused of committing. I will then argue that all of the epistemicist responses to the argument, which grant that Mary enjoys an epistemic achievement when she leaves the room, ultimately collapse to subtle variations of the "acquaintance theory." I will not, however, do much to motivate the epistemic step of the argument. In other words, I leave it open for the physicalist to retreat to the hard line Type-A position which denies that Mary learns anything upon leaving the room. While I myself think she must learn something, there is little one can do to argue against someone who lacks that intuition or who is willing to abandon it once its consequences are clear. On this issue my own intuitions will not lie down, so I find myself stuck with an acquaintance theory.

In Chapter 4, I will argue that commitment to an acquaintance theory involves denying Objectivism, the view that an objective picture of a world with consciousness can be complete. This will involve, among other things, becoming clear about what it means to call a theory object-ive, and what it means to call a theory complete. As we found in Part I, such definitional projects are not always entirely straightforward, and just as there is nothing to force someone to use "physical" in the way I understand it, so there is no forcing anyone to embrace my picture of what a complete objective theory would involve. I will argue, however, that the picture I present captures a natural sense of the term as it is used in these debates.

3

Phenomenal Knowledge and Acquaintance

A brilliant scientist, Mary, has spent her life within a black and white room. According to the original story, from within that room, she learned all the facts about color and color vision: how light reflects off of the surfaces of objects, how that light affects the eye and the optic nerves, and how that information is eventually processed in the brain.[1] Furthermore, Mary is able to draw all the logical consequences from this knowledge: she's not only well informed, she's logically infallible. Thus, from within her room, Mary knows all of the physical information about color vision and its logical consequences. After a while, her captors relent: she is released from the room, and as a token of apology she is presented with a red rose. The question is, when she sees the rose, will she learn something new?

Most people who hear this story, though not all, have the strong intuition that she will. When she sees red for the first time, she learns something that no amount of study and reasoning from within the walls could provide: she learns what it is like to have a red experience. What she gains, in other words, is phenomenal knowledge, and in doing so, she learns something that she did not know before: that an experience of red is like *this*. But, since she knew all of the relevant physical information before she left the room, and she learned this new information upon leaving the room, the physical information is not all there is. Physicalism is therefore disproved by the existence of phenomenal knowledge.[2]

There are a couple of tweaks, which are often implicitly made, that make this argument a bit clearer and a bit more powerful. First, we ought to assume that Mary has all the physical facts about the world, not just

---

[1] Jackson (1982).   [2] Jackson (1982).

those in neural and optical science. If we are to have a valid argument against physicalism, we can't limit Mary's information to a subset of the physical information. So, this involves a big expansion of Mary's inferential base. On the other hand, we have to be careful that if we include psychology and neuroscience in the base, that phenomenal information is not somehow snuck in there. When we talk of neuroscience, we often talk of things like the neural correlate of the pain sensation. So, if we allow Mary to know neuroscience, what do we give her? Can we give her the pain sensation? If not, how is she to understand the neural correlate talk so popular in neuroscience?

It is not important that Mary have in her inferential base everything said by psychologists and neuroscientists, even with their completed theories. For just as physicists might include intuitively non-physical things in physical theory sometime in the future, so too psychologists and neuroscientists might absorb phenomenal talk into their theories. (In fact, one suspects they already do so.) The knowledge argument is about whether or not Mary can get from complete knowledge of the physical to knowledge of the phenomenal, and this is supposed to bear on whether or not physicalism is true. According to the work in Chapter 1, this means that we are supposed to use the knowledge argument to determine whether the phenomenal properties supervene on the physical★ properties, or the properties which can be exhaustively characterized by their spatiotemporal implications. Given this, it is appropriate to think of Mary as having complete knowledge of the physical★ properties in the world, and to the degree that this knowledge can provide her with a complete knowledge of neuroscience as well, she has that. But if a complete knowledge of neuroscience is supposed to include understanding of what I mean when I talk about a neural correlate of pain (which assumes an understanding of the phenomenology of pain) we cannot assume that she has that.

The refined argument thus maintains that Mary knew all the physical★ information in her room, as well as anything she could reason to from that knowledge. When she left the room to encounter the rose, she learned something new: what it was like to see red. So the physical information is incomplete.

Of course this argument does not simply apply to what it's like to see red.[3] It applies to all states for which there is something it is like to have them. The

---

[3] The "what it's like" terminology comes from Thomas Nagel (1979a). I will use "what it's like to see red" and "what it's like to have a red experience" and other such locutions

delicious state we find ourselves in when smelling bacon in the frying pan, the feeling we get when standing in a cold shower, and the feeling of pain all have this associated "phenomenal feel." Mary, it would seem, cannot have full knowledge of such states without undergoing them. The states of having high blood sugar or of having a heart murmur do not, usually, come associated with such a feel, and as such Mary can come to know all about them through studying them from within her room. The "problem of phenomenal consciousness" is largely the problem of figuring out how to reconcile the existence of such phenomenal "feel" states, which do not seem to be fully understandable on the basis of physical descriptions, with the fact that this appears to be a physical world.

The Importance of Deducibility

It is worth guarding against at least a couple of confusions. First, according to the argument, before seeing the rose Mary was not merely ignorant of what it was like for *her* to see red. She was ignorant of what it was like when *other people* had red experiences. She knew that when they looked at roses their brains entered into certain states, and perhaps she knew that these people associated the color with love and warmth and that they said it made them feel good, but she didn't know everything about what it was like to be in that state[4] (Churchland 1985; Jackson 1986).[5] Second, despite initial appearances the knowledge argument does not claim that there is no way for Mary to come to know what it's like to see red from within her room. Daniel Dennett among others has pointed out that she could almost certainly do so. She could press on her eyelids, stimulate her brain appropriately, or simply use her great powers to imagine accurately. She might be able to invent x-ray vision and see through the wall to the roses outside! But none of these points undermine the knowledge argument. The point of keeping Mary locked in her room isn't to show that knowledge of

interchangeably, meaning in all such cases to refer to the phenomenal quality of a red experience.

[4] For an example of the first confusion, see Churchland (1985). Jackson clears things up in his (1986).

[5] It's not unusual that students object: "We don't really know whether other people feel red like we do anyway, so she still doesn't know what other people feel when they see red." This objection, though, grants the very premise it challenges since it claims that all the physical information doesn't give us knowledge of what it's like for others to see red.

physical information cannot help Mary get herself into a red-seeing state, thereby knowing what it is like to see red. The point is that she cannot *deductively reason* from her physical knowledge to knowledge about what it's like. This is in stark contrast to knowledge about, say, whether an elephant would crush a bird—even if her physics lectures didn't mention that fact explicitly, she could figure it out. This is the asymmetry the knowledge argument is getting at.[6]

To guard against these confusions, I suggest the following bare-boned version of the knowledge argument:

1. There are truths that are not deducible from the physical truth, namely, those Mary learns when she leaves the black and white room.

2. If there are truths that are not deducible from the physical truth there are truths that are not necessitated by, and so do not supervene on, the physical truths.

Therefore, physicalism is false.[7]

I would prefer to be able to give as precise a characterization of deduction as I have for the physical, since deducibility carries a lot of weight in these arguments. Alas, this is not very easy to do. Some things can be said, however. First, the notion of deducibility here is not necessarily tied to that of provability within a particular logical system. In my view it is more basic than that. For no matter what system of axioms one has, there must be some further fact about what it is legitimate to deduce using those axioms. On can add these to the system as inference rules, but some rules are good additions for a deductive system and others are not. We decide which are which based on a prior notion of what follows deductively from what, and with any luck our notions about this correspond to what really does follow from what.

Ultimately the notion of deducibility at play here is strongly tied to the notion of a priori reasoning.[8] When we imagine Mary with all the physical facts, we shouldn't really imagine her with just the physical facts and nothing else. The physical facts, I take it, don't include *modus ponens*.

---

[6] A thorough response to Dennett and a development of these arguments can be found in Torin Alter (2008).

[7] This is a modified version of the argument presented in Alter and Howell (2009).

[8] This is emphasized by Chalmers and Jackson (2001).

When we imagine her to be a perfect reasoner we imagine that she follows the appropriate reasoning rules, such as *modus ponens*. Which rules are appropriate? It is difficult to say more than that they are the rules which are knowable a priori. This ultimately means, I think, that serious skepticism about the a priori should generate some skepticism about the knowledge argument. How such skepticism affects the knowledge argument and the consciousness debate is an under-discussed question. Not just any skepticism will be important. If, however, one is skeptical that there is any difference between "traditional" a priori inferences ("if something is scarlet it is colored") and inferences about the identity of phenomenal states and brain states, the knowledge argument will lose a lot of power. This is no easy out, however, for we must be aware of selective and convenient skepticisms. Many physicalists want to claim that arguments for the existence of God are not good, for example. By some inference rules, however, they are splendid. (Modus Aquinas: "If anything exists, there must be an intelligent creator of that thing.") These inference rules are, in fact, pretty intuitive to a lot of people. Those who are skeptical about the a priori to the extent that they want to include physical/phenomenal inferences in the same class as traditional a priori judgments will need to explain why those inferences are acceptable while the theist's arguments simply "don't follow" from his premises.[9]

Even if we feel like we have a grasp of deduction and are willing to admit that deductive inferences have important epistemic properties, we might wonder why it is so important that Mary be able to *deduce* the phenomenal facts from the physical facts. The reason is that no other way of reasoning from the physical facts to the phenomenal facts guarantees that the physical necessitates the phenomenal, which is what is required by physicalism. Consider, for example, inductive reasoning. Suppose I am pulling marbles from an opaque jar. I have removed 999 marbles and they have all been black. There is only one marble left. I have very good inductive evidence that the last marble will be black. But the fact that the first 999 marbles have been black does not *necessitate* that the last marble is black—it could be that the one white marble just happened to rest on the bottom of the pile. I can only find a fact necessitated by my data—say, that there are more

[9] More should be said on this score, I think, and I thank Philippe Chuard and Clayton Littlejohn for pressing me on this.

than three black marbles—by deducing that fact from my data.[10] The same worry holds for abduction, or reasoning to the best explanation, since even if p is the best explanation for a (potentially conjunctive) fact q, this doesn't rule out the possibility of some r such that p is not the best explanation for q&r.[11]

None of this is to say, of course, that one cannot be justified to conclude that a necessary relation holds based on induction or abduction. It might be, for example, that my justification for the belief in Fermat's Theorem is based on its truth being the best explanation of the agreement by mathematicians that Wile proved it. And perhaps that is sufficient for knowledge of the necessary truth that Fermat's Theorem is true. Nevertheless, my inductive evidence does not entail the necessary truth. And if that evidence was all the evidence there was (which of course it is not, because Wile proved the theorem deductively) then all the evidence—both empirical and otherwise—would not entail the truth of the necessity. If this is the case, it appears we have a wholly ungrounded necessity. This appears untenable. Since Mary is supposed to be a perfect reasoner in possession of all the physical information (which is all the information, according to the physicalist) such ungrounded necessities would have to hold if Mary's justification were merely inductive or abductive. So we must insist on deducibility.

The Three Camps

The knowledge argument tends to divide philosophers into three camps. First are the hardline physicalists, who deny premise one. These hardliners, whom Chalmers calls "Type-A materialists," maintain that there is nothing Mary cannot deduce about the world from the physical facts. She has everything within the room, and when she leaves it there is no

---

[10] The phrasing of this might invite an easy, but misleading, counterexample. Necessary truths are necessitated by the data and in some sense they can't be deduced from the data alone since the data are irrelevant to their truth. It's more accurate, perhaps, to say that necessitated truths must be deducible given the data. This deduction/necessitation principle will discussed later at length.

[11] Note, I am not arguing here for the claim that there is no necessitation without deducibility. Here I am not blocking the move that denies premise 2 of the knowledge argument, but am answering an objection to the epistemic step (premise 1) which claims that Mary can know what she needs to know, but by something other than deduction.

epistemic accomplishment. Second are the epistemicists, who roughly correspond to Chalmers' Type-B materialists. These philosophers grant premise one of the above argument but deny premise two. There is something Mary cannot deduce from within the room, but this is not a sign that physicalism is false. To think otherwise, according to these philosophers, is to draw an illicit metaphysical conclusion (physicalism is false) from an epistemic premise (there are truths Mary cannot deduce from within her room). Mary would have an epistemic accomplishment of sorts when she leaves the room, but this indicates nothing metaphysical. Finally, there are the non-materialists, who buy the argument lock, stock, and barrel. Some of these non-materialists are property dualists, others are pan-psychists, and others are neutral monists, but they do not, in the end, believe in physicalism, at least as it has been defined in Part I.

Unsurprisingly, most philosophers find themselves attracted to the epistemicist position. It is, in a way, the have-your-cake-and-eat-it position. No one really wants to reject physicalism. It's just bad business. Rejecting physicalism not only flies against the naturalistic tide that has ripped ever faster through the intellectual waters, it also risks losing conscious experience in the epiphenomenal doldrums. On the other hand, how can we deny that Mary would learn something upon leaving her room? There is, to be sure, not much she will learn. She knows about how patterns in the world are encoded and transmitted to be stored in the brain, and she knows how the brain takes that information and transforms it into other information or other behavior, but how could she deduce from the fact that there is an organism with such states that there is a particular way it is feeling? If physical properties are ultimately exhausted by their implications for how other properties and objects are distributed in space–time, Mary must somehow get from this sort of description of the world to an understanding of how it is to see red, feel pain, and taste chocolate. To think she can reason from the former sort of information to the latter seems akin to a category mistake—it is like insisting that $2 + 2 = 4$, $2 + 2 + 2 = 6$, but if you add two enough times it equals red! So, at risk of sounding absurd, many philosophers naturally want to grant that Mary learns something but that this is no threat to the *metaphysical* view of physicalism. There appear to be numerous ways to grant this. One could claim that she comes to know old facts in new ways, or one could appeal to the idiosyncrasies of phenomenal concepts, or one could claim that Mary merely has new indexical knowledge. All of these options and more have been tried, and most philosophers find comfortable haven in some part of the epistemicist camp.

Hardliners and Faith

I ultimately wish to focus upon this epistemicist view, arguing that the path it maps is neither as wide nor as easy as it first appears. First, however, it is worth solidifying the intuition that Mary will learn something upon leaving the room. We have seen that it is a mistake to object that Mary could gain enough knowledge to put herself in a state corresponding to perceiving red, by stimulating her brain or otherwise. But another version of that mistake should also be avoided. It is tempting to argue that we think Mary would learn something only because we underestimate what would be involved in knowing all the physical information, and we have no way to estimate what a logically infallible being could infer from that information. There is obviously something to this, but that alone can't prevent us from following the argument to its conclusion. We also have no idea what would be involved in knowing the proof of Goldbach's conjecture or what a logically infallible being could infer from such a proof, but we know that whatever such a being infers, it's not going to be able to infer, on the basis of mathematical knowledge alone, that abortion is wrong. To make the hardline response stick, it helps to have some story to tell, speculative or not, about how Mary is going to come to know what it's like to see red.

Perhaps there are satisfying stories to tell that will be told by future philosophers. But there are stories one might be inclined to tell that don't do the trick. For example, it is tempting to imagine that at some point Mary can, based on her current experience and her knowledge of neuroscience, infer what it would be like to have experiences other than those available in her boring room. It's not so difficult to think, for example, that she can figure out the neural difference between seeing a lit wall and seeing a wall with a shadow across it, and based on that difference (and her knowledge of neuroscience, and her knowledge of what state people's brains are in when they say "this is blue") she can infer what it would be like to see blue. Perhaps Mary can then work from there and come to know what it is like to see red. Even if this is the case, it doesn't vindicate the hardline position, and for two reasons. First, it is almost certain that this is not deduction. Perhaps abduction or induction is involved, but it is difficult to see how this could imply deducibility. Second, in such a case Mary would not be deducing phenomenal facts from physical facts alone. She is also using as premises her knowledge of what it is like to see a lit wall and a wall cast in shadow. These are phenomenal facts, not the sort of facts that could figure in a physical base.

It is worth recalling the results of Part I at this point. Physicalism maintains that everything in this world supervenes upon the physical, construed (according to Neocart) roughly as those properties which are exhausted by their spatio-temporal implications. Although it is typical—and indeed much easier—to speak of higher level sciences when talking about Mary, there is a danger in doing so. The danger is that some of the concepts of higher level sciences are penetrated by the phenomenal and are not completely physical themselves. To keep this from happening, it is worth keeping in mind that Mary needs to deduce from physical facts of the sort in the supervenience base—that is, of the sort described by Neocart—to the supervening facts, which must include phenomenal facts if physicalism is true. Thus phenomenal facts cannot be included in the base, and if one insists they can be included one should give some sense of how they can be the sort of property described in purely spatio-temporal terms, as required by Neocart. I'm very skeptical that this can be done.

So, at least one tempting sketch of a story about how Mary might come to know what it is like to see red proves unavailable. Perhaps, though, we can back off some of the details and just insist that given a certain amount of physical knowledge—who knows how—it will gradually dawn on Mary that there is something it is like to see red and it is like *this*. Like the computer wizards in *The Matrix* who can look at the numbers cascading down their computer screens and "see" the tables and chairs of the phenomenal world, perhaps Mary will become so fluent in the language of physics that she will be able to "see" the phenomenal world it manifests. Perhaps, but once again this doesn't sound like deduction. It doesn't sound, in fact, like reasoning at all. One can imagine that God made it so that particularly bright humans would come to know the truth about the morality of abortion when they proved (or disproved) Goldbach's conjecture—it could just dawn on them, so that they saw the impermissibility of abortion peering through the numbers—but that would not show that abortion facts were necessitated by facts about numbers. This is again why we must keep deduction squarely in mind.[12]

Another tack for the hardliner might be to insist we've been coming at things the wrong way. We've been making the object of Mary's knowledge too mysterious. Let's instead look at what she will say and do. She will, it might be said, be able to do all the things that constitute knowledge of what it's like to see red. Dennett suggests something like this in Consciousness Explained.[13] If Mary didn't know what it was like to see yellow or blue, one would expect us to be able to fool her by, say, handing her a blue banana, leading her to come to believe that that is what yellow is like. But Mary will not be easily fooled. If Mary's captors handed her a blue banana, she would immediately recognize that it was blue, and would say "You're trying to trick me! Bananas are yellow, not blue!" This seems to indicate, he thinks, that she already knew about what it is like to see yellow and blue and would receive no surprises whatsoever. There are various ways she could manage this, perhaps by knowing the physical fact that yellow things cause brains like hers to enter physical state x, that this banana is causing her to enter physical state y, which is what blue things would cause her to enter.[14] Dennett is right about this, and defenders of the knowledge argument should agree with him. But they will say that Dennett is looking for the wrong surprise: being able to discriminate between blue and yellow things is not the same as knowing what it's like to see blue and yellow. The intuition isn't that she couldn't sort all the things in the world into appropriate bins. The intuition is, in fact, that she could do all this without knowing what it's like to perceive such things.[15] The lesson from this case generalizes: showing that Mary would be behaviorally indistinguishable from someone who knew what it was like to see red or blue doesn't show that she knows what it's like to see red or blue.[16]

---

[12] Of course it might be that this "seeing" of consciousness could reflect a subconscious deduction or something like that, but in that case a conscious deduction should be possible and it is that which we should imagine.

[13] Dennett (1992).

[14] Dennett's point requires that Mary retains her physical omniscience—including her knowledge of what states her brain is in—after leaving the room. This is a legitimate requirement, and it makes things clearer in my view, since it emphasizes that the real issue is not what Mary can know from within her room, but what can be deduced from what.

[15] This criticism of Dennett is in Robinson (1993).

[16] Many of the recent arguments regarding "Zombie Mary" fail for this very reason. See, for example, Vierkant (2002) and McGeer (2003).

None of this, of course, shows that the hardliner is wrong. It would be no more than dogmatism at this stage to insist that he is. But these sorts of blind alleys make it so that many of us just can't see a way for him to be right.[17] Perhaps that's our shortcoming, but it leads us to look for another way. One is reminded of the debate between theists and atheists about the problem of evil. Atheists find enough evidence in the existence of apparently needless suffering to believe that an all powerful loving God doesn't exist. Theists insist that we simply can't comprehend what is available to an all knowing, perfectly reasoning God. When theists point out possible reasons for suffering, atheists show they are inadequate. But theists are right to insist that we mere mortals can't prove that there is no possible reason for suffering and that we would be dogmatic to insist otherwise. Acknowledging this certainly doesn't lead us to be theists, and it doesn't lead most of us to be agnostics. The fact that we simply cannot imagine how it could be so is reason enough for us to look elsewhere. Those of us who find the hardliner response unattractive find ourselves in a similar position to the atheist. Perhaps there is a solution to our worries, but without a more convincing positive story we must look elsewhere.

From Deduction to Necessitation

Since epistemicism offers a way between the hardliner's leap of faith and the dualist's anti-naturalism, it's no wonder the path has proven so popular. The past twenty years have seen a proliferation of ways to be an epistemicist. The general intuition behind most of these views has been in play since the early days of the knowledge argument debates: the argument commits a fallacy involved in moving from epistemic premises to metaphysical conclusions.[18] Of course the argument as we've stated it

---

[17] Pereboom (2011, chs 3 and 4), advances a new possibility that might seem to help the hardliner. He raises the possibility that when we introspect qualitative states, we represent them inaccurately and that they do not in fact have the properties which are recalcitrant to physical explanation. I largely agree with the points made by Alter (forthcoming, b) but would add that even granting the representational account of introspection, Mary still seems to have some ignorance from within her room, but this ignorance is about the misrepresentations. In particular, she is ignorant of the particular way in which people misrepresent their qualia—as phenomenal yellow vs. phenomenal green, etc. Even if nothing has those properties, the instrospective error is substantive and that leaves open the question of which misrepresentation people are guilty of. The argument seems to reapply at this level.

[18] As in Horgan (1984).

doesn't really commit a fallacy—it owns up to the move in the second premise: If there are truths that are not deducible from the physical truth, physicalism is false. The argument is committed to a principle that can be put more generally:

DN: P necessitates Q only if Q can be can be deduced from P.

The epistemicist must ultimately disagree with DN, and few of them are reluctant to do so. To some, its falsity might appear obvious. "Deduction is an epistemological matter about what an individual can do with a representation," they might say, "while necessitation is a metaphysical matter that holds between facts. Why think the ability of a reasoner to move among representations should map onto the metaphysical structure of the world?" Though this objection might seem initially compelling, in fact it risks misconstruing the claim of DN and the arguments based on it. The notion of deducibilty employed by DN does not tie necessitation to the contingent abilities of humans. One thing can be deducible from another in this sense even if there are no beings capable of performing competent deductions. (A is deducible from (A and B), even if no one can understand the deduction.) This is often explained in terms of "deducible by ideal reasoners" though the appeal to ideal reasoners is only a heuristic. What is really at issue is not the existence or possibility of ideal reasoners, but the question of whether one thing follows logically from another. Once the operative notion of "deducible" is made clear, the epistemic premise in these arguments doesn't look as epistemic as it did on first blush, and the complaint that the argument moves from a premise about knowledge or reasoning to a metaphysical conclusion loses some of its force.[19]

Setting aside this sort of objection, it might still seem that there are cases where DN fails.[20] One obvious circumstance jumps to mind: when the

---

[19]   The premise is still epistemic in some sense, however. In this context "x follows logically from y" does not simply mean "y entails x." If it did, these arguments would beg the question. "Logically follows from" in this context is in a circle of notions including "is a priori derivable from" and "is deducible from" and it isn't obvious that these notions can be given non-epistemic analyses.

[20]   It has been suggested to me by Chris Hill and Katherine Dunlop that there might be problems of a Godelian variety with some implications of DN, and that DN might run into problems when it comes to domains with a non-denumerable infinity of objects. This might be right, and but these points don't seem directly relevant to the argument here. Chalmers does address these issues, however, in Chalmers (2012).

connections between facts reflect a posteriori necessities.[21] In fact, it might seem that DN is simply committed to the denial of a posteriori necessities. It says, after all, that if f necessitates g then a proposition describing g must be deducible from a proposition describing f, and since knowledge generated by deduction is typically a priori, it looks as though if DN is true there can be no a posteriori necessities. This argument is fallacious, however. Acknowledging a posteriori necessities only requires us to acknowledge that some necessary truths can only be discovered upon empirical investigation. It doesn't follow from this that there is no way to deduce the relevant necessary truth. It only follows that performing this deduction— perhaps coming to know one of the premises—requires some empirical knowledge.

Take the example "Where there's water, there's hydrogen." This is a paradigmatic a posteriori necessity, but it's being so does not contradict DN. For given a complete description of water, which would involve its molecular composition you could deduce the presence of hydrogen. It's just that to know the complete description of water you have to do some empirical work—merely having the concept "water" doesn't get you there.

Tye (2009) strongly rejects the sort of picture I have painted about deducibility, and considering his objection will help clarify the dialectic. He claims there are plenty of cases where there is necessitation without deducibility (or as he puts it, a priori reducibility). In fact, he claims that any truth which involves a concept from the "manifest image," such as truths involving tables, water, trees, etc., is unlikely to be deducible from the microphysical truths alone. He claims:

But why should we accept that we can move a priori from the microphysical and (allowed) indexical facts to watery stuff facts? After all, something is watery stuff just in case it is a clear, colorless, tasteless liquid that comes out of taps, falls from the skies as rain, and fills rivers and lakes . . . . But the terms here are as much a part of the manifest image as the term water. They are not a part of the scientific image (to put the point in Sellarsian language). Why think that the link these terms bear to the microphysical is any more secure, *at an a priori level*, than the link the term water bears? Why suppose that there are *a priori* sufficient conditions for the

---

[21] Chalmers has responded to these counterexamples and more in several places, such as Chalmers (2004b), and making the case for something like DN is the central purpose of Chalmers and Jackson (2001). My coverage here will be quick, but the reader should look to these sources for more in-depth arguments.

application of such concepts as *river, sky, tap,* and *colorless* that do not themselves involve concepts from the manifest image?[22]

Note that Tye's criticism is not that one cannot deduce chemical facts expressed in the language of chemistry from the micro-physical facts. He expresses no qualms with this. Tye's criticism is that non-scientific concepts like water—which are associated with concepts like "colorless" or "wet"—are not a priori derivable from microphysical facts, at least not without the aid of other concepts from the "manifest image."

In fact, the defenders of the knowledge argument should grant Tye that water facts, etc., cannot be a priori derived from microphysical facts without the aid of other "manifest image" concepts.[23] This is because the "manifest image" is suffused with phenomenality, and the manifest image concepts are intertwined with phenomenal concepts. (After all, "manifest image" concepts have to do with how things manifest themselves, or appear to us.) Anyone who denied that phenomenal facts were deducible from physical facts must deny that manifest image facts are as well, so it is no objection to defenders of the knowledge argument that manifest image facts are non-deducible. Tye might reply that given the mass of cases that falsify DN, we have little reason to believe it. But if we can ascertain that DN failure always stems from phenomenal non-deducibility—and non-phenomenal cases don't suffer from it—this is telling. Removing the bite of DN in this context requires showing that it fails for non-phenomenal reasons, and we can use the manifest image facts to see whether it does. Simply add the phenomenal concepts to the deductive base, along with the microphysical facts (and indexical facts).[24] It is much more plausible that someone who knows the behavior of microphysical facts and these facts—that this stuff feels wet, etc.—will be able to conclude that water is present using deductive reasoning.[25]

---

[22] Tye (2009, p.62).

[23] Chalmers and Jackson (2001) are actually explicit that qualitative facts are necessary for the deduction. Alter (2011) points this out as well.

[24] Why include the indexical facts? It is generally accepted that these cannot be derived from the physical facts, yet does anyone think that indexical facts aren't necessitated by the physical facts? Why isn't this a counterexample to DN? I think it is a counterexample, but that is because indexical knowledge is dependent on phenomenal knowledge. See Howell (2006).

[25] Of course the conclusion will not be a priori, since the premises are empirical, but the reasoning is deductive.

It would, in fact, be somewhat disastrous for DN to fail in cases like this. To believe that it does is to believe there is a sort of opacity in the explanatory order of the world. Granted, it sounds a bit strange to say that the chemical facts are deducible from the physical facts. But if they weren't—and for a while the British Emergentists thought they weren't—we would be unable to see why a certain physical situation required that a certain chemical be present. We would have to accept "with naturalistic piety" that one fact required another. It is a major achievement of science that this is not the situation we find ourselves in.[26]

In the end, there are only two circumstances in which it would turn out that there was necessitation without deducibility. One way does involve a type of a posteriori necessity that is stronger than the typical examples. In the case of these *strong necessities*, as David Chalmers calls them, one could not deduce them even given a full description of the necessarily related facts.[27] What would make these necessities unusual would not be that they are a posteriori necessities, but that they are necessarily a posteriori! Think about what these necessities really involve. In these cases, two facts are necessarily related but those relations could not be deduced from a full description of the properties and relations that constitute the facts. Strong necessities are brute necessities, ungrounded in the non-modal features of the facts. Such necessities seem counterintuitive. For the instantiation of a property F to necessitate the instantiation of a property G, it looks like there had better be something about Fness or Gness that makes this the case, and a description of Fness or Gness that left this out would be an incomplete description. (If there were not some property of Fness that made that the case, what would distinguish an instance of Fness from an instance of Eness which is just like Fness but without the modal implications?) Electrons might (according to a necessitarian) necessarily repel things of negative charge, but that is because part of what it is to be an electron is to be negatively charged and part of what it is to be negatively charged is to repel other negatively charged things. If you didn't know this feature of electrons, you would clearly be missing something about the nature of electrons. This necessity is, in other words, deducible from a full description of the facts involved.

---

[26] "Naturalistic Piety" is from Alexander (1920). An excellent discussion of what is involved with such emergentism, and why most now reject it, is McLaughlin (1992).

[27] Chalmers (1996).

There is another way that the DN might fail, however, without appealing to strong necessities. DN might fail if there is a feature of some facts that can stand in necessitation relations but that cannot be represented and so cannot be the premise or the conclusion of a deduction. On the face of it, though, this doesn't seem like an attractive option either. For one thing, it would seem that unrepresentable parts of reality are nothing to us—they don't make a cognitive impact upon us. So, though there might be necessitation relations galore among such things, we would never know it and should not care. Furthermore, this option won't look good in the context of this debate, at least to the traditional physicalist who wants to say that the physical description of reality can be complete. According to this response, the physicalist description, like any description, will leave something out—the unrepresentables.

Given this, the non-deducibility argument against physicalism seems to have a lot going for it. One might in the end reject DN, but it is difficult to deny that DN captures a sense in which necessary connections should be "epistemically transparent" once all the information is in. This transparency doesn't seem to exist in the case of consciousness and the physical, and one way to explain this explanatory gap is in terms of a metaphysical gap.[28]

Epistemicism and the Collapse to Acquaintance

Most versions of epistemicism maintain that there is another way out, gained by positing a very particular sort of difference between our ways of thinking about phenomenal states and our way of thinking about physical states. This is a promising strategy, and there are many different ways philosophers have tried to fill in the details. I will argue, however, that there are not as many options as it first appears and that in fact the epistemicist approach is ultimately unstable. Many of those who consider

---

[28] The "epistemic transparency" terminology comes from Chalmers and Jackson (2001) in their response to Block and Stalnaker's (1999) challenge to deducibility conditions on reduction. The arguments of Block and Stalnaker are subtle, as are the responses by Chalmers and Jackson. With very few exceptions I think Chalmers and Jackson's responses are adequate, but even if one doesn't agree it is hard to see how the points of Block and Stalnaker address the apparent asymmetry between typical reductions (such as that of heat or water) and those proposed in the case of consciousness. The solution offered in the final chapters addresses this, and in a way that gives Chalmers and Jackson their key premise.

themselves epistemicists will, under pressure, have to become hardliners. The others will ultimately have to adopt an acquaintance theory to get out of the knowledge argument. This comes with its own costs, and is likely to make epistemicism less attractive than it first appears.

I argue that there is a dilemma for epistemicists—they must either become hardliners or they must become acquaintance theorists. We have seen what the hardliner arm of the dilemma involves—it involves claiming that Mary will in fact learn nothing upon leaving the room because she can know everything pre-release. What is involved in the other arm? What is an "acquaintance theory?"

The notion of acquaintance I have in mind goes back to Bertrand Russell's distinction between knowledge by description and knowledge by acquaintance.[29] The notion has had various explications and uses, and many of those commitments will depend on one's other epistemic and metaphysical views.[30] In an attempt to argue in as theory-neutral a way as possible, I will consider an *acquaintance theory* to be *a theory which holds that there is a way of knowing one's own experiences that provides a grasp of those experiences that no other way of knowing can provide.*

It is worth mentioning just how peculiar such a relation must be. There are, to be sure, unique relations which happen to provide unique avenues for knowledge. I am the only one who can be the eldest brother to my brother. And, it might be the case that this has given me a unique perspective on his character. But that it does so is not because of the relation itself—I could easily have been his eldest brother without ever knowing him. Further, that it is a unique perspective is only a contingent fact—someone else could have the same perspective, they just don't as a matter of fact. Acquaintance is not like that—the mere presence of that relation is enough to generate a necessarily unique perspective on its object. This is unlike any other relation in nature, so one might think twice about embracing it. It might not be much less outlandish than the metaphysical view one is fleeing from.

It might seem that things are not so dire. One commonsense response to the Mary argument is to claim that this mysterious "acquaintance" is simply a matter of Mary becoming "hooked up" appropriately to a system she knew everything about. In the room, she knew everything about

[29] Russell (1912, 1914/1971).
[30] For a nice discussion of the varieties and discussions of them, see Gertler (2011).

brains, and knew what it was for brains to be in red states. But upon exiting the room, she herself gets into that state and becomes "hooked up" to phenomenal redness. But this alone will not do. Being "hooked up" is not sufficient explanation for Mary's epistemic gain. To see this, consider the following corollary to the Mary case:

> Meet Mary's lesser known, but still impressive twin brother Mark. Mark, brilliant as genetics would have it, has decided to become a doctor who specializes in complications with that elusive organ, the pancreas. Mark knows all information remotely relevant to the pancreas. He has discovered that a particular chemical, xtose, when digested causes interesting changes in the lining of the pancreatic duct (changes that might, say, make the pancreas less affected by alcohol abuse). He has witnessed this process in many of his patients and knows precisely the physical effects of the ingestion of xtose, but he has never ingested xtose himself. One day, as a practical joke, one of his colleagues slipped a little xtose into Mark's grape-nuts. When his friend told him, Mark was surprised, but after a couple of chuckles and I'll-get-you-for-that-ones, Mark goes on about his work.

Mark knew everything about his own pancreas before the dose was taken. Is there anything Mark doesn't know about what will happen to his pancreas? Is there anything special about its being *his* pancreas? No. The fact that his pancreas is now hooked up to the relevant causal network is irrelevant. Being hooked up does not necessarily provide new knowledge, and thus it is not sufficient to explain Mary's epistemic advancement. There needs to be some explanation of what is unique in the case of phenomenal knowledge that makes being hooked up so enlightening.

The answer, according to the acquaintance theory, is that being hooked up in the appropriate way generates acquaintance with the object. It must be admitted that at this point the answer is not very informative. It can be made more informative, perhaps, by saying more about what cognitively enables acquaintance. On the physicalist side the two options which have attracted the most adherents are the indexical strategy and the phenomenal concept strategy. These views must ultimately succumb to the dilemma, forcing adherents to either become hardliners or acquaintance theorists.

The phenomenal concept strategy

According to the phenomenal concept strategy, there is a certain sort of concept that we employ when introspectively considering phenomenal states that we cannot have without having been in that state.[31] Most

---

[31] This description of the phenomenal concepts strategy owes much to Chalmers (2004c).

dualists will agree with this much. It is arguable, in fact, that everyone should believe in phenomenal concepts, since there seems to be a way of thinking about phenomenal states that Mary gains upon leaving the room, and this way of thinking can enter into inferences, can satisfy generality constraints, and bears most of the other earmarks of conceptualization. The proponent of the phenomenal concept strategy, however, argues that this knowledge using phenomenal concepts is knowledge of the same facts that Mary knew from within her room. She cannot deduce the phenomenal knowledge from the scientific knowledge because the phenomenal knowledge essentially employs concepts she cannot possess while she is sequestered in her room. While this response has force, it doesn't go far enough. For suppose we give Mary the relevant concepts, perhaps by giving her the experience. Of course she no longer would learn anything when she left the room, but the important part of the argument still remains. She still cannot deduce the phenomenal knowledge from the physical knowledge. The deduction version of the knowledge argument, in other words, still goes through.[32] For this reason it is important that phenomenal concepts not only (a) cannot be had by a subject who has not had the relevant phenomenal experience, but also (b) are cognitively isolated from other concepts that are not experience-dependent. Most advocates of the phenomenal concept strategy hold this stronger view.

So, what are phenomenal concepts? Why are they so special? There are many different stories. According to some, they are recognitional concepts, closely related to perception and our use of demonstratives. To others they are associated with different faculties and cognitive roles, and for still others they are peculiar because they act in a quotational manner to refer to the experiences. There are many interesting strengths and weaknesses of the various accounts, but for our purposes we can focus on what they have in common: that phenomenal concepts are experience-dependent and cognitively isolated.

The appeal of the phenomenal concept strategy is fairly obvious: it argues that *metaphysical dualism* can be avoided by acknowledging *conceptual dualism*. A good scientific and fully physicalistic picture of the mind must recognize that there are phenomenal concepts because of their unique cognitive roles (or what have you). But that means that far from being

---

[32] The conceivability argument against physicalism can basically be seen as making this point. Chalmers (2004c) and Alter (2005) both make this point.

inconsistent with Mary's predicament, the correct scientific picture of the mind actually predicts it!

One question that should be asked about phenomenal concepts, but that is often overlooked, is whether or not the unique features of phenomenal concepts are contingent or necessary.[33] Must any creature that has phenomenal knowledge have concepts with these unique features? If the cognitive isolation of phenomenal concepts is a contingent feature of them, then the phenomenal concept strategy only explains the fact that *humans* cannot deduce phenomenal facts from physical facts. But the non-deducibility intuition is not so limited. That intuition is grounded in the fact that physical properties seem to be exhaustively described by how they are, or how they dispose things to be, in space over time. If there are "what it's like" features of the world at all, they seem to be over and above such features of the world. It's not clear that the phenomenal concepts strategy addresses this source of the non-deducibility intuition. The result is that the phenomenal concepts strategy becomes a version of the hardline response (or, perhaps, as a particularly pessimistic version of the ignorance hypothesis, which is ultimately a sort of hardline response.) A suitably impressive Mary, who might not be human, would not have this brute conceptual block between concepts. She could perform the required deduction from physical to phenomenal facts. How she would do so is beyond us, but she would ultimately know "what it's like" from within her room.

There are those, however, who seem to understand that this cannot be a merely contingent matter.[34] The strongest challenge to this phenomenal concepts theory comes from recent work by David Chalmers.[35] Chalmers argues that any phenomenal concepts strategy must accept some thesis C that attributes certain psychological features to humans (that we have cognitively isolated concepts of a certain sort, etc.). It must claim that C both explains the existence of the epistemic gap, and can itself be explained in physical terms. Chalmers argues that this cannot be done: either C is not physically explicable or it does not explain the epistemic gap.[36] We can recast his argument as follows:[37]

[33]   Alter and Howell (2009, pp.64–7).

[34]   Papineau (2002) would seem to be an example.

[35]   Chalmers (2006a).

[36]   Chalmers (2006a, pp.172–3).

[37]   Chalmers casts the argument in terms of conceivability, which would add unnecessary complications to our discussion. Here I try to translate his argument into the terms of the

Take P to be the complete micro-physical truth about the world:

1. Either C is deducible from P or it isn't.
2. If C is not deducible from P, then C is not physically explicable.
3. If C is deducible from P, then C cannot explain our epistemic situation.

Therefore,

4. Either C is not physically explicable or it cannot explain our epistemic situation.

Let's consider the first horn of the dilemma. To say that C is not deducible from P is essentially to say that knowing everything about P would leave it open whether or not C was present. The phenomenal concept theorist should not accept this if she wants to claim that the explanatory gap is predictable by the physical story of the world, or that it is physically explicable. If C can't be deduced from the physical description of the world, we have only replaced one mystery with another.[38]

The second horn of the dilemma holds that if C is deducible from P, then C cannot explain our epistemic situation—or in other words, it couldn't explain Mary's enlightenment when she leaves the room. Why? The phenomenal concept theorist grants that the phenomenal truths, call them Q, are not deducible from P. Chalmers seems to think there is some problem with granting this, while still claiming that C, which explains Mary's enlightenment, is deducible from P. Why?

Chalmers' argument is complicated, but perhaps it can be put this way.[39] There is nothing, strictly speaking, wrong with saying that C is deducible from P but Q is not. Many dualists would want to say such a thing. But unlike the dualist, the phenomenal concept theorist cannot appeal to features of Q to explain the unique epistemic gain that Mary experiences when she leaves her room. For them, phenomenal concepts provide the explanation, and so it must be C that explains Mary's illumination. But if C is fully physically explicable (i.e. deducible from P) then Mary can know all about C from within her room. Given this, it is not clear where the phenomenal concept theorist thinks the illumination comes from.

knowledge argument as I have presented it. His argument is can be found at Chalmers (2006, p.174).

[38] Chalmers (2006a, pp.174–5).

[39] Chalmers's discussion involves the conceivability of zombies, and the comparative epistemic status of zombies and others. This is tough going, and perhaps a bit far out. I again, hopefully without violence to his points, try to translate his argument into our terms.

An example will perhaps make it clearer. Suppose there is an indexical expression "apant" which, just as "here" delivers a subject's location, delivers the state of the pancreas. And, suppose that Mark is wired such that this concept is cognitively isolated from his scientific pancreatic knowledge. All of this can be easily understood—we can "build" a model of this. Now suppose Mark thinks "My pancreas is apant!" Will that deliver any sort of illumination? There is no reason to believe that it would. This is because the features specified (C, in Chalmers' argument) while easily deducible from the physical description do not explain any illumination.

There is a way out of his argument. I will say more about this in Chapter 6, but for now we can note that this way out requires that the PC theorist embrace acquaintance. The phenomenal concept theorist should say that Mary's enlightenment (and our epistemic situation) is explained by C which is deducible from P. But this doesn't mean that understanding that explanation actually provides that enlightenment, since understanding C does not make it the case that one has the features described by C. It doesn't make it the case, in other words, that one occupies the state which provides Mary's enlightenment (and that ultimately provides the phenomenal part of our epistemic situation). The phenomenal concept theorist believes that knowing Q in the right way requires *being* in C, and no other way of knowing (including descriptive or theoretical knowledge of C and Q) can provide the same illumination. But this, then, makes the phenomenal concept theorist an acquaintance theorist, since she believes that there is a way of knowing one's experiences (Q) which no other way of knowing can provide.

So even though there is a way out of Chalmers' argument, that way out reinforces our initial dilemma. The phenomenal concept theorist, in an attempt to avoid being a hardliner, admits Mary can come to new knowledge, or have a sort of revelation when she leaves the room. The only way it can do so, consistent with its own commitments, is to collapse into an acquaintance theory.[40]

---

[40] Papineau (2007, pp.111–44) makes part of this argument. He seems to concede that it is being in C, not knowing about it, that provides Mary's illumination. This amounts to a concession that he is not explaining why Mary cannot deduce all the facts about P and C from within the room. He is instead explaining why Mary cannot possess a certain sort of first-personal knowledge of phenomenal states, and this is to be explained by the fact that in her room, she is unable to instantiate the properties described in C. It's not clear that he realizes that

Indexicals and phenomenal knowledge

The indexical account of phenomenal knowledge gains much of its plausibility from parallels between the knowledge argument and the puzzles surrounding first-person indexicals.[41] To see some of these similarities, consider the famous case of Rudolf Lingens:

An amnesiac, Rudolf Lingens, is lost in the Stanford library. He reads a number of things in the library, including a biography of himself, and a detailed account of the library in which he is lost. He believes any Fregean thought you think might help him. He still won't know who he is, and where he is, no matter how much knowledge he piles up, until that moment when he is ready to say,

This place is aisle five, floor six, of Main Library, Stanford. I am Rudolf Lingens.[42]

Lingens seems very Mary-like: one can even imagine him gaining her physical omniscience while still being lost in the Stanford library (assuming, of course, that there are physically identical libraries elsewhere in the world).[43] But does anyone draw the conclusion that physicalism is false from the fact that indexical knowledge seems to be something over and above knowledge of non-indexical matters of fact? No. Nor should we jump to such conclusions in Mary's case, says the indexical theorist, because her case is essentially the same. Consider how she expresses her new knowledge when released from her room: "*That* is what it looks like to see red." She uses a demonstrative—a type of indexical—to articulate her new knowledge, because any non-demonstrative description seems simply to restate things she already knows.

---

this substantial difference essentially commits him to an acquaintance theory. It can, at times, appear as though the phenomenal concept theorist is not trying to explain Mary's epistemic gain at all but is only meant to explain why we think there will be an epistemic gain. (Papineau at times appears to argue this way, for example.) If this is what is really being argued, then the phenomenal concept response is really either a hardline response, thus succumbing to our dilemma, or it is a form of the ignorance response, which will be dealt with later in the chapter. In the end, I don't think this is a good interpretation of the phenomenal concepts response. If it were, phenomenal concepts wouldn't enable a new epistemic perspective on their objects (for otherwise Mary would learn something) but if phenomenal concepts don't do this there seems to be little reason to insist we are dealing with concepts instead of some brute mental block.

[41] The indexical response has recently been championed by Perry (2001a) and Stalnaker (2008). It was defended somewhat earlier, though, by Tye (1995).

[42] Perry (1979).

[43] For this reason, Lewis's case of the two gods might be preferable; see Lewis (1979).

I think it is highly doubtful that these parallels bear fruit, but to the degree that the indexical theory does seem to have plausibility, it presupposes something like acquaintance.

To evaluate the indexical response, we need to determine what role is being played by indexicals, and what role is being played by factors that usually accompany the use of indexicals. In normal circumstances, when I am suddenly in a position to say "That is John Perry!" I learn a great deal of new information that is over and above the indexical information. I learn, for example, much about his height, the state of his beard, his manner of dress, etc. All of this is perceptual knowledge, not the indexical knowledge Perry has in mind.[44] So, in evaluating the epistemic achievements we get when using indexicals, we need to strip all of that away.

Once we strip that away, what is left? For this, we can follow John Perry himself, since he has both developed a sophisticated account of indexical knowledge and is one of the main proponents of the indexical solution to the knowledge argument. According to Perry, indexical knowledge of this sort is essentially a matter of connecting folders of "detached" information to each other, or folders of information to perceptual buffers.[45] So, what is happening when I say "That is John Perry" is that I connect my current perceptual buffer with a "folder" containing my detached (objective?) knowledge of Perry—that he was a professor at Stanford, that he runs a radio show, etc. What is important to notice here is that the indexical knowledge is not the perceptual knowledge, but the knowledge that results from the connection between the perceptual knowledge and the pre-existing detached knowledge. It is what Israel and Perry call "architectural" knowledge.[46]

All of this remains somewhat abstract, and the true view can only come out once we see what "files" are being connected and how.[47] But we

---

[44] It is not implausible that perceptual knowledge is indexical in some sense. (See, for example, Brewer (1999).) The contents of perception might perhaps involve, "That ball is red," or "that is thus" or something. While this confuses matters, it doesn't vitiate the main point for two reasons. First, we can still distinguish between the indexical element of this content and the sensual element (or between the "that" and the "thus") which allows us to ask the main question—where does the real enlightenment come from, the sensual part or the indexical part? More importantly though, this is not the indexical knowledge that Perry is talking about since, among other things, this indexical knowledge delivers information about particular objects in the world, not experiences.

[45] See Perry (2001a, pp.120–1, and 2001b, p.94).

[46] Israel and Perry (1991).

[47] This criticism has a close relative in Stalnaker (2008, ch. 2).

might wonder whether this seems like the right approach in general. When Mary leaves the room, is her phenomenal knowledge simply the learning of a connection between two known pieces of information, or is it a matter of her gaining new information which then might be connected to previous information? Is it the connection that is new for Mary, or is it one of the things connected (perhaps in addition to a connection)? While it is question begging to insist that it is the latter, it is worth seeing if the indexical theory retains its initial intuitive attractiveness when it is forced to admit that it must be the former. Imagine for a moment that Mary's brother Max is, like Mary, physically omniscient but he is phenomenally omniscient as well. So, he knows exactly what it is like to see, hear, taste, etc., everything, and he knows how these phenomenal properties are tied to the physical things. He has never seen red, but he knows what it's like to see red. He is clearly not thereby omniscient with respect to indexical knowledge. He does not know, for example, that "That is John Perry" because he has never met him or been in a position to gesture at him. Now, suppose he enters the APA smoker and sees Perry. He now can know "That is John Perry." What has he learned? Well, he ties his previous knowledge of Perry to his current perceptual buffer, but since he is phenomenally omniscient that buffer contains no significant new information. Max's new knowledge is very thin indeed. Suppose Max looks away and then looks back and thinks, "That is John Perry" yet again. What is the difference between what Max learns in this second instance and the first? In both cases, Max already could conjure a perfect picture of what Perry would look like in that particular circumstance. And in the second case, no less than the first, Max connects all of his previous Perry knowledge (including the "what it's like" to see Perry knowledge) to his perceptual buffer. The second case is new knowledge no less than the first, because the perceptual buffer is numerically different from one moment to the next.[48] So Max does gain new indexical knowledge when he meets Perry, but he gets the same sort of new knowledge when he glances at Perry again. This emphasizes just how little indexical knowledge really

---

[48] Numerical difference is all that is required for new indexical knowledge. If it were not, Perry could not solve several puzzles including Austin's (1990) two tubes or any case where there is the possibility that "That is that" comes out false despite the fact that the subject's experiences are qualitatively identical; see Perry (2001b, ch. 5).

gets us when it does not come with new perceptual or phenomenal knowledge. Is Mary's knowledge this thin?

Anyone who thinks Mary's knowledge is this thin is basically a hardliner. At least apparently, Mary gains new things to make connections with, not just new connections. This point can be made in terms of a Lewisian picture of *de se* knowledge. Lewis ingeniously argues that while most knowledge consists in determining which worlds are candidates for the actual world, indexical knowledge locates us within a world.[49] Non-indexical omniscience would thus allow one to know which of all infinite worlds the actual one is. But it would not necessarily tell you which being you are in that world. Let's think of Mary's knowledge using this framework. Because Mary knows all the physical facts, and this is all the facts for the physicalist, she must know precisely which world is actual. But does she? Take the brain state R, which humans occupy when they see red. Now consider a phenomenal color spectrum—r is what it's like to see Red, y is what it's like to see Yellow, b is what it's like to see Blue, etc. Now, when Mary exits the room she learns that when humans are in R they have r. This is not merely location within a world. Mary is ruling out the world where R is associated with y, with b, with g, etc. She is, in fact, discovering that this is a world where r is instantiated! It is thus not indexical knowledge.

I have not shown that this is how the indexical theorist must think about indexicals, but there is at least a serious challenge here. Lewis's model appears to account for all other cases of indexical knowledge, so for the indexical response to retain plausibility we need an account of how Mary's knowledge is not, as it appears, a matter of ruling out possible worlds but is instead a way of locating Mary within the actual world. I, for one, do not see a plausible way this can be done.

Perhaps, though, I have moved too quickly. Perhaps the defenders of the indexical account can respond by making clear just what is being connected to what in phenomenal knowledge. Perry offers an account according to which what is learned involves "reflexive content." What is the reflexive content of "This is what it's like to see red?" Perry gives it in terms of the following truth conditions: "This is what it's like to see red" is true "iff the act of inner attention to which it is attached is of the subjective character of the experience of seeing red."[50] So what Mary learns is that a

---

[49] Lewis (1979).   [50] Perry (2001a, p.148).

particular act of inner attention has the subjective character of the experience of seeing red. She already knows everything about the subjective character of seeing red. That is not what she learns on this model. She simply learns that this act of attention has that subjective character. But is this what the intuitions behind the Mary experiment has her learning, or do they suggest that she is learning what the subjective character of seeing red is in the first place? If it is the former, then she continues to learn things of the same exact significance every time she looks at red, since each time she looks at a future rose she learns of that act of attention that it has the subjective character of seeing red. But clearly the epistemic gain Mary enjoys from the first look at a rose to the second look at a rose is not the same. (If it were, there would be no point in isolating her in the room.) It is Mary's first look that gets her the epistemic gain, not the second look, so anything in common between the two cannot be what she learns. Thus, the indexical knowledge cannot be what she learns. There must be something about the indexical knowledge involved in her first release from the room that is special. But now it seems that the indexical alone is not doing the work; it is the peculiar sort of state Mary enters upon leaving the room. Perhaps this involves an indexical, but what is unique about it is the epistemic access that it enables.

The fact that the indexical knowledge is not what she gains can be reinforced by the fact that Mary's new knowledge is not threatened by forgetting which particular act of perception (or attention) provided it. If upon leaving the room, Mary encounters a whole garden of flowers, she will very quickly learn many new things: what it is like to see yellow, what it's like to see orange, green, etc. On the indexical model, she is learning something about the particular acts of attention she is engaged in. But with only a slight weakening of her mental prowess, one can imagine that she loses track of the individual acts of attention. She might wonder, which act of attention was the one of seeing red? Which one was of seeing orange? Despite being hopelessly confused about which particular acts of attention were which, she would not thereby lose the knowledge of what it's like to see red. So, the reflexive indexical knowledge, tying subjective characters to acts of attention, cannot be the knowledge of what it's like.[51]

---

[51] Can Perry respond by saying that Mary does retain her knowledge, but not under the description "the subjective character of act of attention x?" I don't think so. The point of this view is to say that Mary already knew "what it's like" under many modes of presentation

In fact, I am inclined to believe the indexical model makes a mistake when moving from the linguistic domain—which is the domain for which the Kaplaninan view was developed—to the domain of thought.[52] Mary's is no normal use of indexicals. It is not linguistic in nature. Her knowledge of her qualitative state employs an internal sort of demonstrative—one associated with an act of attention or introspection—and it is doubtful that it can yield a Kaplanesque treatment. The problem is that the typical candidates for the character of the indexical are inadequate. The Kaplan-like demonstrative gets its cognitive significance by a character which can be formulated like a description—"The object which is related by R to subject S" (e.g. I = <the utterer of the sentence>, you = <the person addressed by S>, etc.).[53] Now for this to provide cognitive significance for the subject, she must have an independent grasp on R and S. In the normal case, this seems to be no problem, because R and S are independently identified. Now take the internal indexical, "this," when a phenomenal property is ostended. What is the character here? The most promising candidate is "The property that is the object of ostension F." But this will not do, for how is ostension F grasped? If it is not independently grasped, then this cannot provide the cognitive significance for the internal "this."[54] Perhaps the character of the internal "this" should be "the property that is the object of this ostension." But then, of course, we have an embedded demonstrative within the description. What is the character of this "this"? (i.e. How does the subject know which ostension?) It seems an infinite regress ensues unless we allow that there is a more fundamental internal "this" which is not subject to Kaplan-like analysis. Since there is intro-spective demonstration there must be a more basic "this," and it seems that

(or descriptions) but that this indexical one is what she learned. If there is another, more fundamental mode of presentation which can survive Mary's loss of the knowledge by the indexical mode of presentation, the indexical theory is at best incomplete leaving us in need of a story of this more fundamental mode.

[52] Adapting the Kaplanian picture to the domain of thought can be seen as one of the projects of two-dimensional semantics. Something like this adaptation must be possible if the indexical model is to be used in response to the Mary case. I provide an account of indexicals of this sort in Howell (2006).

[53] The "cognitive significance" of an expression, as I am using it, refers to the role that the expression plays in the understanding. So, for example, part of the puzzle of indexicals is to explain the difference in cognitive significance between "I" and "Robert J, Howell" since they refer to, and ultimately have the same content.

[54] F cannot simply be a name, because this just pushes the problem back: how is the cognitive significance of the name secured?

phenomenal properties are the most obvious objects of these basic internal demonstratives.[55]

If the indexical model is modified so as to provide for an internal "this," however, it has basically preserved its explanatory power at the cost of collapsing into just another response from acquaintance. The new knowledge comes from the employment of a basic internal "this" that is unlike other indexicals, and it generates a substantively new perspective on its object. If this indexical is to play a role in a solution to the knowledge argument, it is presumably because there is a way of knowing associated with inner demonstration that can only be fully understood when one is performing the inner demonstration and when the state is one's own mental state. Remember the case of Mark and his pancreas. When he ingests xtose, he can now say "I am undergoing this state," (or he could use our made up indexical "I am apant") but his indexical reference to the state clearly doesn't count as the sort of knowledge that generates Mary's epistemic gain. Mary's internal demonstrative generates a substantially new perspective on her object, and it is a perspective which she can have only by undergoing the phenomena in question. This is again an example of the answer from acquaintance. The indexical response ends up in the same camp, really, as the PC response: they are both best construed as stories about the nature of acquaintance. The only difference is in the detail of those stories, but in the end, the relationship of acquaintance provides the epistemic gain.

It might be objected that though in a sense these views are acquaintance theories, they are ultimately more informative because they explain what acquaintance merely names. It's not hard to see that this is not in fact the case. Where precisely is the explanation? The functional isolation of phenomenal concepts is not, as we have seen, really doing the work. There could be functionally isolated concepts which were not phenomenal concepts. What is doing the work is that they enable a unique perspective on their object, one not available to anyone else. That is, they enable the subject to enter a relation of acquaintance. This is not much of an explanatory advance—any mystery about the relationship of acquaintance becomes a mystery about what makes a concept a phenomenal concept versus some other functionally isolated concept. The same

---

[55] Perry (2001a, p.148) seems to admit the equivalent of the "inner this" by focusing upon acts of attention.

problem holds, as we saw, for indexical concepts. Indexicals in general do not yield unique and informative epistemic perspectives. Some indexicals do, of course, but these are precisely those indexicals that are in need of explaining. They are those indexicals that put the subject in a relation of acquaintance with the object they refer to. Again, any mysteries about acquaintance translate completely into mysteries about these sorts of indexicals.

Abilities and Ignorance

So far, I have overlooked two popular, or at least well known, approaches to the knowledge argument: the abilities hypothesis and the ignorance hypothesis. It is true that they do not fit nicely into the dialectic as I have cast it. Nevertheless, I think there is still reason to think they succumb to the dilemma.

The ability theorists agree that Mary learns something new when she leaves the room, but they deny that what is learned is propositional knowledge.[56] What she learns is know-how, not knowledge-that. In other words, she gains an ability. Much as you could study all the manuals in the world on bike riding, and know all the physical facts about riding a bike, you might still not know how to ride a bike. For that you usually actually have to practice and ride a bike. You knew all the facts and you learned something new, but that type of learning doesn't consist in knowing new facts but in gaining new abilities.

What new abilities does Mary gain when she leaves the room that accounts for her revelation? Accounts differ, but proposals include the ability to imagine having a red experience,[57] the ability to recognize and remember red experiences[58] and the ability to distinguish red experiences from others.[59] Actually, these abilities are pretty clearly not what Mary gains. If physicalism is true, Mary could have already had these abilities within her room. Suppose a red experience is just the activation of brain state B. She could easily detect the activation of such brain states and

---

[56]   The ability theory was first advocated in Laurence Nemirow (1980), but received more thorough defense in David Lewis (1999c).

[57]   Nemirow (1980).

[58]   Lewis (1999c).

[59]   Bence Nenay (2009).

distinguish them from other brain states before leaving the room, and if she saw brain scans where B was activated she could imagine seeing them again. What is true, of course, is that she was not able to recognize a red experience in the way that we typically do—by introspection. This looks like a fine fix to the problem, but only until we ask what it is about introspection that makes it crucial that *this* is the cognitive ability that is gained. It is precisely the fact that introspection is a faculty that presents a unique perspective on its objects, one that is only available to the subject who introspects. In other words, it looks like the ability Mary gains is to come to recognize, etc., red experiences by being acquainted with them. If the ability hypothesis is forced to this, the ability hypothesis presupposes no less than the others that there is a relation of acquaintance.[60]

The ignorance hypothesis comes in various guises, but they all respond to the knowledge argument by claiming that drawing the anti-materialist conclusion ignores the possibility that we are misled by our ignorance and cognitive limitations. We can divide the ignorance posited by hypothesis into two types. There is base ignorance, which is ignorance about important facts about the physical base. These facts will either become available with a scientific breakthrough, or they won't because it is simply beyond human understanding. There is also inference ignorance, which is ignorance about how those base facts determine the nature of phenomenal consciousness.[61] The defender of the ignorance hypothesis can commit himself to one or the other view, but he will probably advocate the disjunction—that the knowledge argument seems plausible either because we have base ignorance, inference ignorance, or both.

The ignorance hypothesis is different from the other responses to the knowledge argument we have canvassed because it doesn't commit to a view of what is going on in phenomenal knowledge. It is a sort of meta-philosophical position encouraging us to be cautious and skeptical in the face of this problem, and it defuses the argument essentially by maintaining that such skepticism must keep us from inferring anything metaphysical from the argument.

Despite its noncommittal nature, there are still reasons, I think, to feel that our dilemma applies to the ignorance hypothesis. Or rather, what

---

[60] A version of this argument is in Gertler (1999), as well as Howell (2007).

[61] For the best statement of this position, see Stoljar (2006), though its first influential formulation is from McGinn (1989).

remains is a related trilemma: the knowledge argument will force philosophers into either non-physicalism, hardline physicalism, or the acquaintance theory. What seems most likely is that the ignorance theorist will
either be a sort of non-physicalist or is just a hardliner in disguise. Which it
is depends, I think, on whether the ignorance theorist thinks our current
ignorance is about the base properties or about the way Mary deduces
phenomenality from them. The inference ignorance theorist who maintains the latter just seems to be a slightly more cautious version of the
hardliner we met before, insisting there is a way to do it but we can't see
how yet. Though there is really no *refuting* this position, we can answer it
in the same way we did the hardliner. Given our intuitions to the contrary,
and no particular hypothesis about why those intuitions are wrong or how
the difficulties can be overcome, we must look elsewhere. The base
ignorance theorist, on the other hand, is no hardliner, bur nor is he likely
to be a true physicalist.

The suspicion about the physicalist credentials of the base ignorance
theorist stems from the intuitions behind the knowledge argument paired
with the notion of physicalism outlined in Chapter 1.[62] The intuition
behind the knowledge argument is not simply that there isn't the right
sort of particle or field in the physical base to explain consciousness. If, as
currently seems likely, the Higgs-bosun is found, advocates of the knowledge argument won't be phased. They don't think that anything of that
sort is going to help because the problem is with the general type of thing
physics will posit in the base. Given our discussion in Chapter 1, we can
make the worry clear: physical properties are exhausted by their implications for the locations of other properties in space and time. The problem
of consciousness, as highlighted by the knowledge argument, is that we
cannot see how something like this could ever give rise to a phenomenal
feel. Or, put in explicitly epistemic terms, it seems terribly unlikely that a
full understanding of phenomenal states can be deduced from knowledge
about things like this. Perhaps we are wrong and that somehow it is
deducible—this is the modesty recommended by the hardliners and the
inference version of the ignorance hypothesis. But the base ignorance
theorist places hope for new discoveries in the base, and as long as those
new discoveries are discoveries of physical properties in our sense, the

---

[62] The argument in this paragraph owes greatly to Alter (forthcoming, b).

problem will not go away. Perhaps, however, the hoped for discovery reveals a hidden nature of phenomenal properties from which we can deduce the existence of phenomenal facts. The problem is that such hidden natures are incompatible with physicalism, as we argued in Chapter 2. The result, it seems, is that the ignorance theorist succumbs to one of the arms of our dilemma—if this is in fact a physicalist response to the knowledge argument, it must ultimately be a form of the hardline response, though perhaps a more modest one that places emphasis upon our current or permanent cognitive limitations.

Conclusion

If I am right, the promising epistemicist response to the knowledge argument either collapses into the somewhat mysterious acquaintance response, or it adopts hardline physicalism with its commitment to a mysterious inference that we may or may not one day understand. From this point on, we'll set the hardliners to one side and focus upon the acquaintance theory. Though I ultimately find this theory the most attractive, it is a bit mysterious. The mystery might be dissolved by further scientific work and so might not in the end be problematic. In fact, though, there is reason to believe that subscribing to an acquaintance theory involves the rejection of a doctrine that is plausibly intertwined with a naturalistic approach to the world: Objectivism, or the view that an objective theory of the world can be complete.

4

Acquaintance and Objectivity

The intuitions behind the knowledge argument make, in the end, commitment to an acquaintance theory extremely attractive. An acquaintance theory, recall, is a theory which holds that the knowledge argument can be answered by an appeal to acquaintance, where acquaintance is a way of knowing one's own experiences that provides a grasp of those experiences no other way of knowing can provide. Appeal to such a relation is, however, in conflict with a thesis that seems to be an implicit part of the naturalistic worldview. The thesis, which we can call *objectivism*, holds that a complete objective description of our world is possible.

The most important thing to notice about objectivism in this sense is that it is about theories, or the ways of knowing and representing the world, not about the world itself. As such, embracing objectivism—or its denial, subjectivism—is not yet to draw a metaphysical conclusion about the world. To this extent it is to be contrasted with physicalism as we defined it in Part I. Denying physicalism denies things about the nature of properties—perhaps that they are not exhausted by their spatio-temporal implications—and the things they necessitate—perhaps it is denied that the physical properties necessitate qualia. To deny objectivism, on the other hand, is to deny something about the nature of theories and our ability to understand them in a certain manner.

Objectivity

There are many different notions of objectivity, and by insisting on one of them I am in no way denying that other notions are legitimate or have important application. I am simply clarifying what I am meaning by the term. I am not alone, however. What I have in mind is what Thomas Nagel, arguably the progenitor of the problem of consciousness, means by "objectivity" and "subjectivity." In many ways, therefore, I take myself to be explicating the notions he is employing.[1] Here's Nagel:

> It is beliefs and attitudes that are objective in the primary sense. Only derivatively do we call objective the truths that can be arrived at in this way. To acquire a more objective understanding of some aspect of life or the world, we step back from our initial view of it and form a new conception which has that view and its relation to the world as its object. In other words, we place ourselves in the world that is to be understood. The old view then comes to be regarded as an appearance, more subjective than the new view, and correctible or confirmable by reference to it. The process can be repeated, yielding a still more objective conception.[2]

Though I don't wish to tie myself completely to what Nagel says, his words provide guidance. And so here are more of them:

> A view or form of thought is more objective than another if it relies less on the specifics of the individual's makeup and position in the world, or on the character of the particular type of creature he is.[3]

Objectivity thus comes in degrees, with its ultimate goal the elimination of essential reference to a subject's point of view.

> It's essential character ... is externality or detachment. The attempt is made to view the world not from a place within it, of from the vantage point of a special type of life or awareness, but from nowhere in particular and no form of life in particular at all.[4]

The goal of objective theorizing, in other words, is a "view from nowhere."

Following Nagel, the notion of objectivity I am employing is thus to be contrasted with several other notions. One notion is objective as true, or real. Although philosophers rarely speak this way on the job, it's not uncommon to hear people talking as though being anything other than objective is to be in error. Such a notion would be no help here, since we only want to be talking about true theories. Closer to what we want is the notion which is more pervasive in, for example, the literature about perception and secondary qualities. According to this notion, to be objective is to be mind-independent.[5] This still falls short of what we are looking for, in part because we are talking about theories and our question

---

[1] I have in mind Nagel (1979b as well as 1986).
[2] Nagel (1986, p.4).   [3] Nagel (1986, p.5).
[4] Nagel (1979b, p.208).   [5] See, for example, Cohen (2009, p.144).

is not the somewhat arcane one of whether a theory can be mind independent. (If theories are propositions, it seems all of them are mind independent, but if theories are sets of beliefs, none of them are.) Nor does it help to modify this notion and talk about a theory's being objective if it is about mind independent things, since this would make it trivially true that theories of minds could not be objective. Another, related conception of objectivity, finds expression in meta-ethical writings and certain debates about the nature of truth. According to this notion, roughly, a theory (or judgment) is objective if its truth does not depend upon what anyone thinks about it. (It could be true, for example, even if no one believed it.)[6] The issues surrounding that notion, however, are far more general than the ones that concern us here.

What we are looking for is something much more *epistemic* than any of these notions of objectivity. It has to do with what it takes to understand the world, or to fully grasp a theory of it. Understanding an objective theory does not require that one occupy a particular point of view in order to grasp it. Of course in some sense, any theory requires that one occupy a particular point of view to grasp it: it requires the point of view of a subject grasping that theory! What requires emphasizing is that in some sense that point of view is *subjective*. Again, though, in some sense every point of view is subjective since every point of view is the point of view of some subject. We can perhaps gain a little guidance by considering cases that do not appear to be cases of objective knowledge. Before having children, I saw little value to the project of parenthood. I was told by friends and family, however, that it is only by having children of my own that I can understand this value. This is quite different from the way I understand electrons. I must have electrons in order to understand them, of course, since without electrons I wouldn't exist. But I don't need to know something about *my* electrons in order to know something about electrons in general. Objective knowledge is, among other things, impartial knowledge. We can use this idea to develop the following *necessary condition for theory objectivity*:

> Understanding an objective theory of Ts cannot require that it is only by coming to know a fact about one's own T's that one comes to understand that fact about T's in general.

---

[6] See, for example, Shafer-Landau (2003, p.8) and Wright (2003, p.16). It actually seems to me that both of these philosophers sometimes talk about even other, slightly different notions—such as the investigation independence of truth, etc.

If a theory fails this condition, that theory cannot embody a view from nowhere. Understanding the theory requires that one have particular states and that only by understanding one's own states can one come to understand a general theory of such states. Such a theory is, in a sense, epistemically partial and not fully objective.[7]

The Search for Completeness

Given this condition for theory objectivity, it remains to explain what it means for a theory to be complete. Again, completeness comes in varieties—there is the notion of completeness operative in metalogic, the notion involved in talking about completed actions, etc.—but these are not very helpful in this context. One way, of course, that a theory could be incomplete is if it left something out: if there is a fact that the theory fails to depict, the theory is incomplete. In this sense a theory is incomplete iff the theory could be true of more than one possible world.[8] A theory can pass this standard for completeness rather easily, however. Wittgenstein's Tractarian statement "the world is all that is the case" passes that standard. So does "the world is thus" when accompanied by a sufficiently expansive demonstration, or "Bob is Phi" where "Bob" is the name of the world and "Phi" is the conjunctive property that characterizes the world. But this is not what we are looking for in theory completeness. It would be small reward if physics, or any other objective theory, were only complete in this sense. The problem these theories have is not simply with the grain of the description, although providing finer grain would help. The problem is that these theories do not convey a full grasp or understanding of what they are depicting, even to a perfect reasoner.

---

[7] In Howell (2007, p.149), I formulated the necessary condition for theory objectivity as follows: "An objective theory cannot require that one enter any token state of fully determinate type T in order to fully understand states of type T." This condition has its advantages—among others, it places the emphasis on the fact that in a non-objective theory one must enter a determinate state as opposed to entering a privileged relation to a state. This raises questions about what constitutes a determinate state, as well as the question of whether a determinate state of understanding must be entered into in order to understand anything at all. I still tend to think these questions can be answered (and do some work to that end in Howell (2007)), but the new statement simplifies things considerably.

[8] This requires that a complete theory include a "that's all" clause, so that it not only indicates what is in a world, but rules out worlds with further stuff as well.

What must a theory do to give complete understanding? I think it is not too much to require that a complete theory in this sense must not only suffice to locate the world among actual possibilities, but it must also be able to make it such that an ideal reasoner who believed the theory would also be able to eliminate any *epistemic* possibilities. That is, an ideal reasoner in possession of a complete (and true) theory in this sense would not be able to imagine any world (possible or impossible) that she could not rule out as being the actual world—except for the actual world. In other words, a complete theory cannot be such that an ideal reasoner believes the theory and yet does not know which of two conceivable worlds the theory is about. Anything less will leave questions unanswered for someone who knows the complete theory, and through no fault of her own. There is a clear sense in which such a theory leaves something out—even if it serves to cull a single world out of all possible worlds. So I propose:

> A theory is *complete* iff an ideal reasoner who fully grasped the theory could not conceive of more than one world (possible or impossible) that the theory could be about.[9]

This provides us with a better understanding of the necessary condition for theory objectivity, and it also provides us with an understanding of how an objective theory could fail to be complete even if it were true and specified all of the facts about the world. It also clarifies the commitments of objectivism. Objectivism claims that our world is such that an objective theory of the world would leave no doubt for an ideal reasoner about which of many conceivable worlds was ours.[10] Objectivism is false, on the other hand, if the ideal reasoner could only locate which world was hers by entering into a privileged position with respect to her own states.[11]

---

[9] It is an interesting question whether quantum indeterminacy would result in a theory's being incomplete in this sense. This depends, I take it, on whether the theory itself requires the indeterminacy or if it allows for the existence of "hidden variables." If the latter it is incomplete, but as far as I know there is no conclusive argument showing that it must allow for those hidden variables and not embrace real indeterminacy.

[10] Can any non-indexical theory be complete? According to my definition, Lewis's (1979) case of the two gods shows that it cannot. In fact, though, I think such a theory fails to be complete precisely because of its exclusion of phenomenal knowledge; see Howell (2006).

[11] Given that the condition for theory objectivity didn't mention privilege, it might seem odd to see it mentioned here. In fact, the existence of first-person privilege of some sort is entailed by the failure of theory objectivity since if objectivity fails it is only by knowing one's own states that one can come to a certain sort of understanding. Assuming others can occupy the same type of state, this implies privilege.

Acquaintance vs. Objectivity

Given these notions of objectivity and completeness it should be relatively clear how the acquaintance theory is inconsistent with objectivism. Objectivism requires that there can be a complete objective description of our world. The acquaintance theory acknowledges that Mary makes an epistemic gain when she leaves the room because she becomes acquainted with something that she previously knew about only by theoretical description. Upon leaving her room she knows more about the way the world would have to be in order for it to be true that people are having red experiences. She can now rule out conceivable worlds (though perhaps not possible worlds) in which people occupying brain states while seeing red things have the experiences we associate with seeing yellow things. The theory she had while in the room was thus incomplete, according to our definition of theory completeness. According to the acquaintance theory, she can only complete her picture of the world by entering into a privileged way of knowing her own experiences. Objectivism is therefore incompatible with the acquaintance theory. Furthermore, if the arguments of the previous chapter are sound, any non-hardline response to the knowledge argument requires embracing acquaintance. The vast majority of philosophers working on this problem will therefore have to deny objectivism, and to the degree that physics is an objective science, they will consequently have to deny that physics can be a complete picture of the world.

From one angle this is a surprising result, and it will not be appealing to those philosophers who saw epistemicism, or Type-B physicalism, as a way to remain robust about their commitments to physics. I suspect the first place of attack will be on the notion of theory completeness. My notion of theory completeness is admittedly a bit idiosyncratic. Unlike other notions, it seems to have a significant epistemic element. Thus, it could easily be complained that this is where I have gone wrong. Epistemology should not play a role in the completeness of a theory. It should, perhaps, play a role in what it takes to have a complete grasp of the theory, but that one cannot have a complete grasp of a theory without entering into a privileged perspective on objects in the domain of the theory does not indicate that the theory is incomplete or that it is anything but objective.

This is a very sensible complaint. I suspect it depends upon a conception of theories, though, that is rather abstract, formal, and well removed from what we really want theories to do. We want theories of the world to explain the world. We want them to inform us about the way the world is and ideally to generate an understanding of the world. If a theory can be complete while still leaving an ideal reasoner somewhat in the dark about the world, completeness has lost a good deal of interest. There is, though, no need to fight over words. Perhaps there is a good reason to retain a non-epistemic notion of theory completeness, and perhaps there is a way to do so.[12] This would be a merely verbal win for the objectivist, however. It is not the point of the knowledge argument, as I am making it, to establish a metaphysical conclusion. I will argue, in fact, that it does not show the falsity of physicalism. It does, however, show a limitation on theories and pictures of the world formed in a certain way, and it is a limitation we care about. Even if it is not a limit on some formal notion of theory completeness, it is still a limitation on the theory's ability to provide a complete understanding of the world. If the arguments so far are correct, objective theories will inevitably leave an ideal reasoner in the dark, and if physics is an objective theory it will still at its best leave ideal reasoners with serious questions about the way the world is. Perhaps this is a conclusion physicalists will accept in stride, but it is a conclusion that reflects more modesty than physicalists often demonstrate.

Another way out of this argument is to deny the necessary condition for theory objectivity. If however the notion of objectivity we have in mind is that of a "view from nowhere" it seems clear that any theory that requires not only that one be a particular sort of creature, but that what one studies must be one's own state, fails to be objective.

From another angle it might seem that the argument I have made is rather trivial. If you grant my conceptions of objectivity and understanding, the acquaintance theory commits one to the denial of objectivism by definition. This is true, of course, but it's only worrisome if objectivity and understanding are given meanings that don't reflect real theoretical desiderata. But as Nagel and others have pointed out, gaining a view from nowhere has seemed to be a driving force in scientific theorizing about the

---

[12] An intuitive, somewhat formal notion of theory completeness seemed to be embraced by no less a luminary than Einstein. "In a complete theory there is an element corresponding to each element of reality." See Einstein, Podolsky, and Rosen (1935, pp.777).

world, and if a view from nowhere will necessarily leave questions unanswered (even if those questions reflect merely epistemic possibilities) then that project must fail. If the argument in the past two chapters is correct, the only way to avoid that conclusion is to be a hardliner, and it has seemed that few have wanted to take that plunge. And there is good reason for it: to do so involves having a certain amount of faith in a proposition one's current evidence does not support, and that one simply cannot see being true.

Of course the real significance of the argument hinges on how worrisome it is that objectivism is false. I will argue in the final chapter that there are in fact reasons to be unhappy about this result. But a more pressing threat looms. Is denying objectivism consistent with physicalism as we have defined it in Part I? Several arguments have maintained, in effect, that it is not. This, I take it, would be a concern, so to those arguments we now turn.

PART III

Saving Physicalism

We have now seen what it takes for physicalism to be true. We have also seen that it is doubtful that objective science like physics can provide an understanding of phenomenal experience. I've argued that setting aside hardline responses, all responses to the knowledge argument depend on there being a state of acquaintance that generates a special sort of phenomenal knowledge that cannot be attained from "the outside." This results, I argue, in the inevitable conclusion that objective pictures of reality are incomplete.

None of this is yet to take any stand on physicalism or anti-materialism. The notions of objectivity and completeness employed are at least in part epistemic, and the notion of physicalism is robustly metaphysical. We cannot immediately get from the falsity of objectivism to the falsity of physicalism. But that we cannot get there immediately does not imply that we cannot get there eventually. Most of what I have said so far would be perfectly acceptable to the anti-physicalist, and for good reason. If there is an incompleteness in my sense, then one can still conceive of all the physical facts being true without there being any phenomenal states at all. There are well known arguments from this premise to the falsity of physicalism. It is also not easy to see just how there could be an incompleteness in my sense without there being some property that is left out by physics. How can Mary learn something new if there is nothing new out there to learn?

In the following two chapters, I address these explicitly anti-physicalism moves directly. In Chapter 5, I consider two anti-materialist arguments—the conceivability argument and the presentation argument—which would deliver metaphysical conclusions from what has already been admitted. I will argue that we can in fact resist those conclusions if we are again careful to keep epistemology out of our metaphysics. In particular, I will maintain that these arguments get their bite by individuating properties and possible worlds in ways that a physicalist should resist. If those basic metaphysical moves, apparently upstream of the current debate, are resisted, the move to physicalism can be blocked. This still leaves us, however, with a need to explain precisely how it could be that physicalism can be true despite the fact that Mary learns something new and despite the fact that the phenomenal facts are not deducible from the physical facts. A positive story of this epistemic gain is needed. Unsurprisingly, given what has been said, this story will be a sort of acquaintance story. It will be one, though, that is at least somewhat more informative than other such theories on the table, and it will be one that is consistent with physicalism.

5

The Ontology of Subjective Physicalism

If the previous chapters are correct, and phenomenal knowledge shows that there cannot be a complete objective picture of the world, then a certain sort of "objective physicalism" is not tenable. Before we fret overmuch, however, we should consider that the considerations of Part II threaten an "objective dualism" just as much. To see how this might be, consider an objection to the knowledge argument offered by Paul Churchland.

... if Jackson's argument were sound, it would prove far too much. Suppose Jackson were arguing not against materialism, but against dualism: against the view that there exists a nonmaterial substance—call it "ectoplasm"—whose hidden constitution and nomic intricacies ground all mental phenomena. Let our cloistered Mary be an "ectoplasmologist" this time, and let her know everything there is to know about the ectoplasmic processes underlying vision. There would still be something she did not know: what it is like to see red. Dualism is therefore inadequate to account for all mental phenomena![1]

Churchland is rightly pointing out that merely substituting some sort of psychic goo for the more conventional physical stuff will do nothing to satisfy the intuitions behind the knowledge argument. This does not, however, show that dualism is false. It only shows that a sort of "objective dualism" is false. Churchland's objection is ultimately ineffective against the knowledge argument since no dualist worth his salt is such an objective dualist. The dualist admits that these special mental properties can only be known in a certain way, and most dualists would probably be happy to say that they know them by acquaintance. Though Churchland's target is off,

[1] Churchland (1985, pp.24–5). While Jackson replies to this *tu quoque* argument in Jackson (1986), John Perry revives the criticism in Perry (2001a, sect. 7.5).

it would be a mistake to ignore his point. If dualism escapes the adapted knowledge argument because it is "subjective dualism," why can't there be a "subjective physicalism" that escapes it just as well?[2]

According to such a subjective physicalism, the world is completely metaphysically grounded in the physical★, in that all things, properties and states supervene upon contingent properties which are exhausted by their spatio-temporal implications. Nevertheless, some of those supervenient states and properties are "subjective" in the sense that they cannot be fully grasped except by an agent that is undergoing them. Thus there is a sense in which physicalism is true, despite the fact that physics—or any other objective science, for that matter—cannot provide a complete understanding of the world.[3]

Though there appears to be space for subjective physicalism, it can be difficult to keep the view from slipping towards dualism. The worry is that if physicalism is true there is little substantive sense to be given to Mary's learning anything upon exiting her room. If she does learn something new, on the other hand, she is surely coming to know *about* something and that looks like it must be a property.

This simple objection to subjective physicalism will linger, and it is best to get it out in the open early. In many ways, it crystalizes the point made by two anti-physicalist arguments: the presentation argument and the conceivability argument. The subjective dualist is not on the ropes, however, because this simple argument, as well as its more complex cousins, makes metaphysical assumptions that the subjective physicalist should deny. For one thing, even if Mary does come to grasp new properties, it is an open question whether those properties are physical or not.[4] For another, the persuasiveness of these arguments depends upon certain presuppositions about the individuation of properties and possibilities. These assumptions are quite natural, so they often slip by without notice. The lesson is that the physicalist must take a stand on metaphysical issues that are often left out of these debates. In particular, the subjective physicalist should adopt a fully extensionalist metaphysics that repudiates

[2] Interesting discussions of Churchland's argument, with a similar slant, can be found in Robinson (1993b) and Nagasawa (2008).

[3] For the sense of physicalism in which the resulting understanding is incomplete, see Chapter 3.

[4] Exclusive subjective physicalism, for example, would maintain that they are. The different incarnations of subjective physicalism will be discussed in Chapter 6.

methods of individuating properties and possible worlds in terms of concepts or cognitive capacities.

The Presentation Argument and the Metaphysics of Properties

Any view admitting that Mary actually learns something when she leaves her room runs the risk of slipping down the slope to dualism. If subjective physicalism is to resist this slide it had better have a clear response to the arguments that have traditionally pushed philosophers down that onto-logical slope. The first argument, which I call The Presentation Argument, is often attributed to Max Black, but has in recent years been revived by Stephen White.[5]

The presentation argument for property dualism

The simplest argument that pushes subjective physicalism towards dualism is articulated in J. J. C. Smart's early defense of the identity theory. After disposing of two less serious challenges to the identity theory, Smart considers the following challenge:

it may be possible to get out of asserting the existence of irreducibly psychic processes, but not out of asserting the existence of irreducibly psychic properties. For suppose we identify the Morning Star with the Evening Star. Then there must be some properties which logically imply that of being the Morning Star, and quite distinct properties which entail that of being the Evening Star. Again, there must be some properties (for example, that of being a yellow flash) which are logically distinct from those in the physicalist story.

Indeed, it might be thought that the objection succeeds at one jump. For consider the property of "being a yellow flash." It might seem that this property lies inevitably outside the physicalist framework . . .[6]

Smart's objector does a good job of expressing just how unavoidable property dualism can seem. The winnowing of one's ontological commit-ments by empirical discovery usually involves the recognition that what one previously thought to be two things is in fact one. When it comes to

---

[5] White (2010).
[6] Smart (1959/1971, p.63). The objection is apparently due to Max Black. See also Jerome Schaffer's (1961 and 1963), though in the end Schaffer seems more sympathetic to the type of view I propose than to simple property dualism.

things, this strategy is effective and uncontroversial: one's mistaken impression that there were two things can be explained by the fact that one came to know about a single thing by two distinct *properties* yet failed to realize that they were both properties of that thing. This ontological pruning does not seem to work in the case of properties themselves, however, for the simple reason that the explanation of the *appearance* of multiple properties will have to be explained by the *existence* of multiple properties (even if they are only properties of the original properties) that are responsible for those appearances. Ironically, therefore, when one makes an informative identity between properties one's ontological commitments actually increase!

This version of *the presentation problem* does not stem from anything particular to conscious states; it is a general problem for property reduction. In the case of mental properties, one initially thinks there are two properties, one well-groomed physical property, and one "touchy-feely" mental property known only "from the inside." After a little empirical work, one concludes that there really is only one property—the well-groomed neural property—previously known by two of its properties: its property of being a certain neural state, and the property of constituting a certain feeling for the subject that instantiates the property. It seems one has gotten nowhere when it comes to decreasing the number of properties to which one is committed or when it comes to eliminating touchy-feely properties. At best the touchy-feely property is now a second-order property, but it is no less troublesome for all that.

When presented in this way, the property dualist argument seems inescapable. It is telling, however, that the famous idiosyncrasies of qualitative consciousness are not playing much of a role. The problem doesn't stem from the peculiarity of consciousness per se, but from the fact that ontological "pruning" seems to be unachievable on the property level, at least given the model we apply to objects.[7] What we ought to question, it seems, is whether the "appearance properties," which provide the mode of

---

[7] Since the presentation problem does arise because of the existence of multiple epistemically individuated modes of presentation of one property, the role of mentality is not completely innocuous. It is not, of course, merely accidental that mental properties—such as qualia—wind up being the ones most resistant to reduction. My point here is just that we should be suspicious when the model of reduction increases ontological commitments when mental properties are *not* the targets of reduction. There is a sign of a problem, in other words, before we ever attempt to reduce the appearance properties themselves.

presentation of the property to be reduced, always deserve the same ontological status as the target property. We are, in fact, only forced to that view on a questionable assumption about property individuation. Once one drops this assumption, the dualistic argument can be blocked.[8]

The presentation argument and property intensionalism

It is crucial that we be clear about whether properties are to be individuated intensionally or extensionally. According to the intensional view, properties are individuated in part by the ways we can think about them. Extreme intensionalism about properties would hold that there is a property answering to every coherent concept, and if two concepts are distinct, so then are the properties they express. Extreme intensionalism can be regimented by specifying individuation conditions for concepts, or by appealing to possible concepts. For example, one might not want to say that the concept of being an unmarried male is distinct from that of being a bachelor. So, one might say that concepts are distinct iff a priori reflection could not establish that they necessarily have the same extension.[9] Connecting this condition to property intensionalism, one gets:

(PI) If it's not a priori that <F> and <G> are coextensive, $F \neq G$.

Where <F> is a concept and F is the property that satisfies the concept.[10]

---

[8] One of the only thorough critical discussions of the presentation problem I am aware of is Block (2007). Though Howell (2009), which was the ancestor of this chapter, was all but complete when I became aware of that piece, there are some similarities in our conclusions. Just how similar it is difficult to say, as our terminology and approach are different. Block does not focus on the individuation of properties, though it seems he is taking implicit stances on their individuation that are similar to those I support. Block thus does not criticize intentionalism as a metaphysics. Instead, he tries to dismantle arguments for some of the inferences intentionalism would sanction.

[9] Actually, this won't do, because an intensionalist might want to say that "equiangular-triangularity" and "equilateral-triangularity" are different concepts, yet they necessarily have the same extension. To get this result, one can distinguish between basic concepts and complex concepts, where the latter are concepts that are composed of other concepts and the former are not. Then one can say that concepts are distinct iff (a) they are basic and a priori reflection cannot establish their necessary coextension, or (b) they are complex and are composed of different basic concepts. Since equiangularity and equilaterality are not necessarily coextensive, and they are quite plausibly parts of "equiangular-triangularity" and "equilateral-triangularity," the latter can still be distinguished according to condition (b).

[10] I realize that there are complex issues surrounding concepts and properties, and this is merely a way to finesse the issue. Two-dimensionalism might complicate things here, but I think only in a way that would make the proof more complex, not unsound.

Intensionalism is attractive, in part because it makes the epistemology of properties straightforward. We can know about property identities and differences because they are metaphysically individuated by conceptual abilities. The extensionalist, on the other hand, insists upon mind-independent individuation conditions for properties. This leaves it an open question whether property identities are tracked by conceptual relations. One appealing view is to individuate properties by the causal powers they bestow on their bearers.[11] While attractive, this is only one possible extensionalist view. The general position is that properties are not tied to concepts in the way suggested by PI.

The presentation argument ultimately depends upon an intensionalist conception of properties. Recall the general problem: one cannot achieve ontological parsimony by property identification, because explaining the *appearance* of multiple properties itself requires that there *be* multiple properties. The extensionalist denies the necessity of this connection. It should, of course, be granted that a fully rational individual thinks there are two properties when there is really one only when that individual has two perspectives on that property that he cannot reason between a priori. But it is only by using PI that we get from this to the conclusion that there must be two properties in virtue of which the object is known. Otherwise, there being two perspectives on one property entails nothing at all about how many properties there are, second-order or otherwise.

Tensions within property intensionalism

Simply by examining the general structure of the presentation argument, we find reason to believe that intensionalism is bound to generate a profligate ontology. Ontological profligacy is not the only reason to be suspicious of intentionalism, however. Intensionalism makes knowing property identities a rather simple matter—depending on how idealized the relevant notions are—because it inserts the epistemic into something that is properly metaphysical. Concepts are individuated psychologically and have to do with the way that we think about things. It is therefore counterintuitive that properties, features of the world, should be hostage to concepts. To the extent that we wish to remain realists, maintaining that the world is not of our making and has the features it does independently

---

[11] See Shoemaker (2003), for example.

of our minds, we should keep concepts and properties clearly distinct and we should avoid tying them too closely to one other. This is not to say that we do not often have epistemic license to infer facts about properties based upon a priori conceptual reflection, but this should not be confused with a metaphysical principle of individuation.[12] Accepting property intensionalism is potentially a step towards anti-realism, and if it is optional, we should avoid it.[13]

At this point my argument must answer an obvious complaint. Defenders of the anti-materialist arguments, the presentation argument included, not only do not explicitly endorse the intensional individuation of properties, they would likely reject it. My interpretation of them, they would object, accuses them of a sort of anti-realism which they would deny. If they embrace PI, they do so in a realist manner, such that concepts pick out independently existing properties that are not metaphysically individuated by those concepts.[14]

This is undoubtedly the move the dualist will and should make, and we will see that the move will arise again when discussing the conceivability argument. The move depends on what one might call a rosy view of our cognitive capacities. According to the rosy view, PI is true not because properties are shaped by our concepts, but because our cognitive capacities, and the concepts they employ, track independently existing properties. So, the objection maintains that PI does not imply property intensionalism, but implies either property intensionalism or the rosy view. My complaints are about the former, but the anti-materialist accepts the latter.[15]

---

[12] The epistemic licenses would be defeasible and probably externalist principles, I suspect. It is my suspicion, actually, that the attraction to intensionalism is tied to an illicit attraction to a strong sort of internalist epistemology that would require, for example, knowledge of property identities to fall out of our concepts of those properties. I believe this epistemic internalism is implausible, but a defense of both that and my suspicion will have to wait.

[13] Stephen White in his (2010) presents an argument for intensionalism that appeals to its ability to get us out of Fregean puzzles. I both doubt its ability to get us out of those puzzles (see Howell (2006)) and doubt that it is required to get us out of them (see Salmon (1986) for example). In addition, his argument to the contrary depends upon PW below, a premise the subjective physicalist will not let him have.

[14] Thanks to the referee for pushing this objection. Thanks also to Torin Alter who raised a similar issue.

[15] Thanks to Brad Thompson and Torin Alter for forcing me to deal with this objection more explicitly, and to Brad for the designation "rosy view."

I think this objection is correct. We cannot infer property intensionalism directly from PI. But we have gained ground, locating an opening for
the physicalist. Most importantly, the presentation argument looks to
hinge on PI, PI is optional, so to have a good argument the anti-materialist
needs to defend either property intensionalism or the rosy view. At least in
discussions of the presentation argument, neither is typically defended.
I think we can push for something stronger, however. There are two
considerations that suggest that PI—at least when it is being used in the
presentation argument—is committed to property intensionalism. First,
there is evidence that properties really are being individuated intensionally
in these arguments. Second, there is reason to doubt the rosy view. Here,
I will focus on the first, and in the discussion we will find support for the
second. I will save further reasons to doubt the rosy view for the discussion
of the conceivability argument.

If the rosy interpretation of PI is true, we should expect the properties
that are picked out to have individuation conditions that are non-epistemic—that is they must have extensional individuation conditions.[16] It is
doubtful, however, that purely extensional individuation conditions can
be provided, at least for the properties that make trouble in the presentation problem. These are appearance properties, and as such will have to be
individuated epistemically, based on the way they appear.[17] Thus, it seems
implausible to say that these properties are simply "picked out" and not
shaped, in part, by our ways of picking them out.

The dualist will, of course, deny that this is the case. For her, the
appearances are real further features of the world, not defined by how

---

[16] Philippe Chuard has raised the following objection: if all concepts must have extensional
individuation conditions, where this means that they are not individuated in terms of our
concepts, then response dependent properties seem to be ruled out. But, the objection goes,
this is unreasonable so something must be wrong. Two points. In fact, I'm fine with the
consequences of this. I maintain that response dependent properties are often not really
properties at all but are instead concepts that locate properties. In general, though, the fact
that a property can be picked out intensionally doesn't mean that there are not in fact
extensional individuation conditions. The idea that there are real properties that can only
be understood in a response-dependent manner is implausible. More importantly, though, PI
specifies a very particular connection between concepts and properties and it's not clear that
denying PI requires eschewing response dependent properties.

[17] This is especially clear when it is argued that phenomenal properties ground the modes
of presentation of informative identity statements about them. White (2007) is explicit about
this, for example.

we access them.[18] There are, she will say, real resemblances between, say, two people instantiating a red quale, and these real resemblances can only be in virtue of real properties. Call them extensional, call them intensional, either way they are real features of the world.

There are three responses to this objection. First, of course it is true that the dualist will insist that these are real properties with real extensional individuation conditions. But this is precisely what the dualist needs to establish and intends to establish by the presentation argument. If the presentation argument itself assumes, without independent argument, that these are real further features of the world, we shouldn't be convinced. The dualist response I am considering does have an argument as well, however. There are resemblances between agents with certain qualitative properties, and these resemblances are objective features of the world. These resemblances thus demand real properties to ground them: the appearance properties. This leads to our second response to the objection. There is nothing strictly speaking wrong with grounding properties in resemblances, as long as those resemblances are not themselves subjectively determined. Relying on the rule that "there is a property for every resemblance" can be misleading if how things resemble one another is arbitrated merely by judgments of similarity. This is ultimately a way to let property intensionalism in the back door. Nevertheless, if he believes in phenomenal properties at all, the physicalist should grant (unless he wishes to be a hardliner) that there are resemblances between agents who are having "red appearings." And, he should also grant that these resemblances must be grounded in properties. What he should deny, however, and what is not argued for, is that these properties are different from the physical properties and that the resemblance is not a physical resemblance. For the dualist to show that this resemblance in appearings gives rise to properties other than the physical properties, the dualist must appeal to something like the presentation argument, and now the argument is circular. (The presentation argument works only given a dualist result from the resemblance argument, but the resemblance argument only generates a dualist result given something like the presentation argument.)

In fact, it should be clear that the appearance properties doing the work in the presentation argument are intensionally individuated. They are

[18] My thanks to Alyssa Ney for pressing this point. Similar points have been keenly expressed by Cory Juhl and David Sosa.

inevitably described quite generically as the properties that explain a particular mode of access to the target property. Of course at times a novel way of accessing a property requires that there be some other novel property which explains that access, but why think this is always the case? What is more likely is that our concepts often, perhaps even usually, latch onto independently existing properties in the way suggested by PI, but not necessarily. If this is so, we should be on the lookout for signs that our concepts have not succeeded in picking out such properties.

There are signs that when it comes to qualia and appearance properties we are not latching onto independent, properly individuated properties. This becomes clear when we consider another reason to prefer the extensionalist model of property individuation. We should expect properties with intensional individuation conditions to have trouble integrating into the causal and explanatory order of things. The intensionalist and the extensionalist should be committed to many of the same properties. After all, even the intensionalist must admit that in many cases our concepts are of properties that have completely objective individuation conditions—our concept of an electron, for example, or of mass. We should expect the intensionalist to have more properties in her ontology than the extensionalist, however, because in addition to those extensionally defined properties, there are some that can only be individuated partly in terms of the minds that know them. Thus the extensionalist's ontological commitments are a subset of the intensionalist's.[19]

The result is that in contrast to the extensionalist, the intensionalist has what might be considered a mixed domain of properties. The problem arises with the intensional properties—the properties to which the intensionalist is uniquely committed. Assuming realism about causation, the complete causal story about the world should be able to be told in terms of properties that have objective individuation conditions.[20] Thus the

---

[19] An intensionalist might respond that it is inaccurate to view the extensionalist's domain as a subset of the intensionalist's. This might be so, but even so, an analogue version of this mental causation argument goes through—the general version stated later in the paragraph seems indifferent to the many ways one might count properties.

[20] It should be noted that I am here talking about the causal relevance of properties, not the appropriateness of making causal explanations employing reference to such properties. Causal explanation might appropriately invoke properties that are not themselves causally relevant. This sort of thing is suggested by Yablo (1992)'s proportionality constraint and others. I am not inclined to think this mitigates the problem of causal relevance, but this debate deserves another locale.

extensionally individuated properties in the intensionalist's domain would seem to be responsible for all of the causal action, leaving no causal role for the intensional properties.

Put another way, the intensionalist would seem destined to recognize properties that are not identical to the extensionalist's properties, and the latter are sufficient to explain the causal order of the world. If this is the case, then the intensionalist's properties are not causally necessary. Unless there is overdetermination in the case of intensional properties, which seems a slender reed for such an ontology, they are bound to be epiphenomenal.[21] This is of course what tends to happen to qualia, but if my argument is right this has as much to do with the intensionalist method of property individuation as it does with any particular idiosyncrasies of conscious states.

If the foregoing is correct, we not only have a reason to prefer an extensionalist metaphysics to an intensional or mixed metaphysics, we also have our sign that in the case of appearance properties we are not latching onto extensionally individuated properties as the "rosy" interpretation of PI would suggest. Recall that one could hold that PI was true not because properties are individuated by concepts, but because concepts pick out independently individuated properties. We can grant that such a coincidence between concepts and properties could obtain, but we should also be alert to indications that it does not. We have found one sign: if properties lack extensional individuation conditions they will have difficulty integrating into the causal picture of the world. Since this is the case with the properties proffered by the dualist, we have reason to believe that at least in this case our concepts have not picked out independent properties but have led us to posit intensional properties with all of the problems that come with them.

This leaves us with the following situation. The presentation argument depends upon PI, which suggests an intensional picture of the individuation of at least some properties. These properties are apt to be causally inert and, indeed, the properties found by the presentation argument also threaten to be epiphenomenal. This means that dualism gains plausibility

---

[21] This is, of course, just a version of the argument from Kim, most easily presented in his (1998 and 2005). If what I have said is right, the problem of mental causation might be a species of a more general problem which doesn't stem from mentality so much as from the ways in which the relevant properties are individuated.

because of a metaphysics that eventually drives it towards incoherence. On an extensionalist picture we can resist the presentation argument for dualism, adopting instead a monistic ontology. This is the picture the subjective physicalist adopts, and it seems by far the preferable path.

The Conceivability Argument and the Metaphysics of Possible Worlds

In recent years, the presentation argument for property dualism has not been as popular as arguments from the conceivability of physical properties existing without mental properties.[22] According to these arguments, the conceivability of physical properties without mental properties indicates that it is possible that the two come apart. If it is possible that they come apart, they cannot be identical. David Chalmers has offered the most subtle defense of the conceivability argument in recent years, so I will focus on his presentation. Other versions of the argument can be handled in basically the same way.

In truth, the conceivability argument is a close sibling of the presentation argument, and it fails to undermine subjective physicalism for similar reasons. In particular, where the presentation argument presupposes a questionable metaphysics of properties, the conceivability argument presupposes a dubious metaphysics of possible worlds.

The conceivability argument

Chalmers summarizes the conceivability argument as follows:

According to this argument, it is conceivable that there be a system that is physically identical to a conscious being, but that lacks at least some of that being's conscious states. Such a system might be *a zombie:* a system that is physically identical to a conscious being but that lacks consciousness entirely .... From the conceivability of zombies, proponents of the argument infer their *metaphysical possibility* .... From here, it is inferred that consciousness must be nonphysical. If there is a metaphysically possible universe that is physically identical to ours but that lacks consciousness, then consciousness must be a further, nonphysical component of our universe.[23]

---

[22] Though Stephen White in his (2010) does a good job of resurrecting the argument. He does so, though, in part by making it closer to the conceivability argument than it first appeared.

[23] Chalmers (2003, pp.5–6).

Subjective physicalism would seem to be particularly vulnerable to the conceivability argument. The subjective physicalist admits, after all, that there is an epistemic gap between physical descriptions and conscious states. Thus, it is conceivable that there be zombies with no "subjective properties," and this will be conceivable even given a completed objective science of the mind. Zombies therefore seem possible, which means—according to our own supervenience definition SVP—that physicalism seems false.

The traditional response to conceivability arguments is to deny that conceivability entails possibility. This response is usually couched in terms of Kripkean a posteriori necessities: the fact that something is conceivable is ultimately an epistemic fact that does not inevitably reveal a metaphysical fact. We can conceive of the falsity of some necessities because they can only be discovered upon empirical investigation, but they are metaphysical necessities nonetheless. The conceivability argument has a response, however, as Chalmers—following in Kripke's own footsteps—has pointed out.[24] When we are thinking of the falsity of an a posteriori necessity, we are envisioning a real possibility. Our mistake is to describe that possibility in such a way that it conflicts with the a posteriori necessity. This can be explained using what Chalmers calls "two-dimensional semantics."

According to two-dimensional semantics, the necessary a posteriori is best described as a phenomenon at the level of statements. "Water is H_2O" is an example of the necessary a posteriori, and this is because our language associates it with two different propositions or "intensions." The primary intension is the meaning of the statement achieved by considering a range of worlds as candidates for the actual one. It is that in virtue of which the statement picks out what it does in any world in which it is employed. The primary intension of "Water is H_2O," for example, might be captured by something like "the colorless, odorless stuff in lakes, rivers and oceans is H_2O." The secondary intension is the meaning of the statement taking the semantic facts of the actual world as fixed, and considering the statement counterfactually. In other words, it is what the Kripkean would consider the content of the statement, and the sense in which the statement is true

---

[24] I have essentially given this response in Chapter 3, without employing two-dimensional semantics. Since we are dealing directly with Chalmers here, however, it will help to have his particular system before us.

in all worlds, whether the stuff in lakes is XYZ or otherwise. The primary intension is what determines whether a statement is a priori or a posteriori, and the secondary intension is what determines whether a statement is necessary or contingent. Statements that are necessary a posteriori, like "water is H2O," thus have a contingent primary intension but a necessary secondary intension.

Two-dimensionalism gains metaphysical bite when it is added that corresponding to the two intensions there are two senses of conceivability and possibility. To say that a statement is conceivable$_1$ is to say that one can conceive of a possible world where the primary intension is true, and to say that a statement is conceivable$_2$ is to say that one can conceive of a world where the secondary intension is true.[25] To say that a statement is possible$_1$ is to say that there is a possible world where the primary intension is true, and to say that it is possible$_2$ is to say that there is a possible world where the secondary intension is true. ("Possible" and "conceivable" are used in the *definientia* without subscripts because at the level of *propositions* conceivability and possibility are univocal. The subscripts just indicate which intensions are in the scope of the conceivability/possibility operators when they are applied to statements with two dimensions of meaning.) Given this, there no longer seems to be a problem with inferring possibility from conceivability, as long as one only infers possibility$_2$ from conceivability$_2$ and possibility$_1$ from conceivability$_1$. (Though one can, of course, infer possibility$_2$ from conceivability$_1$ when the primary and secondary intensions are the same, as Chalmers claims is the case with thoughts about consciousness.[26]) Concluding from the conceivability$_1$ of S that it is possible$_2$ is what the Kripkean thought experiments warn against: from the fact that we can conceive of its having turned out that watery stuff is not H$_2$O we cannot conclude that there are worlds where water is not H$_2$O. We can, however, conclude—by conceiving of the falsity of the primary intension—that there are worlds where watery stuff is not H$_2$O.

If two-dimensionalism provides the real story underlying a posteriori identities—and it has a distinct air of plausibility when applied to the traditional Kripkean examples—then it should also apply in the case of mind–body identities. If pain is identical to a physical state f, then it is not possible$_2$ that there be a zombie world. But we are conceiving of

---

[25] See Chalmers (2002) for this way of putting things.
[26] Chalmers (2009).

something when we are conceiving of zombie worlds: we are conceiving$_1$ of a possible world—namely, a world where the primary intension of "pains are identical with physical state f" is false. To find this proposition we must locate the primary intension of "pain" and it seems that here the primary intension is something like "the unpleasant feeling that comes when I am wounded" and—assuming the a posteriori identity holds—the secondary intension is the basic physical description of "f." So, according to two-dimensionalism, we are licensed to infer that there is a world where "that unpleasant feeling" does not pick out anything despite the fact that there is brain state f. But this is a zombie world, since it involves the supposed physical part of pain without the feeling part. Thus, since two-dimensionalism vindicates the inference from conceivability$_1$ to possibility$_1$, the conceivability of zombie worlds shows their possibility, and by the supervenience definition we proposed in Part I (SVP) physicalism is false.[27]

The conceivability argument and metaphysical two-dimensionalism

Two-dimensionalism is impressive because it seems intuitive while generating significant metaphysical results. One reason to be wary of two-dimensionalist arguments for dualism, however, is that what is intuitive about two-dimensionalism is distinct from what yields the metaphysical conclusions. For many of us, it seems obvious that there must be an element of thought content (if not of linguistic content) that captures the cognitive significance of our thoughts, and that this role cannot be satisfied by Millian or Russellian content. Thus, many of us are at least pre-theoretically committed to something like Chalmers' primary intensions, and Kripkean arguments usually persuade us that there are also secondary, Millian intensions. So far, however, this only commits us to a sort of minimal "cognitive" two-dimensionalism. This should not be confused with Chalmers' more "metaphysical" two-dimensionalism, however, and part of the persuasiveness of his arguments trades on our slipping from the former to the latter. Metaphysical two-dimensionalism requires that our primary intensions have possible worlds as their extensions. Since primary

---

[27] In much of what follows, including the proof that PI iff PW, I do not use the possibility$_1$ and possiblity$_2$ notions (and the conceivability counterparts) because they do not really indicate two different modal notions (or types of conception). Even on Chalmers' view there is only one sense of possibility and one sense of conception, it's just sometimes ambiguous what is being conceived and what is said to be possible.

intensions are epistemically individuated—designed, as they are, to capture cognitive significance—this implies that worlds are individuated, at least in part, epistemically.[28] This is in contrast to what is perhaps a more natural view, that primary intensions are simply conceptual in nature, and they may or may not deliver possible worlds, which are individuated extensionally. It is the implicit ontology of metaphysical two-dimensionalism that provides the dualist results, and that is what we should question.

The intensionalist about possible worlds roughly maintains that there is a possible world corresponding to every set of circumstances that can be consistently thought. In practice the anti-materialist arguments don't employ (though they likely depend on) this strong claim. Instead they rely on something like the following:

(PW) If it is conceivable that Fx & ~Gx, it is possible that Fx & ~Gx, and for possible worlds W and V, if it cannot be established a priori that V = W, then V ≠ W.

Where <F> is a concept and F is the property that satisfies the concept.

In other words, if it is conceivable that two properties are not coinstantiated, it is possible, and it is sufficient for difference between two possible worlds that their identity is not knowable a priori. This ties possible worlds rather strongly to their conceivability.

An extensionalist, on the other hand, maintains that possibilities are what they are independently of what we can think about them, and a priori it is an open question whether our ability to conceive possibilities tracks the relevant modal facts. It's not necessarily the case that all worlds of which we can have a consistent conception are really possible, and not all possible worlds need be conceivable.[29] Again, this is not to say that there are not inferential rules that connect conceivability to possibility, but such rules are merely defeasible epistemic licenses.

Against metaphysical two-dimensionalism and world intensionalism

For many, realizing that metaphysical two-dimensionalism is optional will be enough to lead them to reject the dualist argument. Dualism is, after all,

---

[28] Thus metaphysical two-dimensionalism is cognitive two dimensionalism plus a realist possible world semantics of thought. Both additions are optional.

[29] This makes it sound as though one must be committed to impossible worlds, but it needn't. It will simply turn out that one is not really conceiving of a world at all in such cases.

an attractive haven only for those who are forced to occupy it. There are independent reasons to reject the world-intensionalism that is part of the dualist argument, however.

First, world intensionalism and property intensionalism are mutually entailing, so any skepticism about one should cast doubt upon the other. I offer a more "formal" proof below, but the idea is actually pretty simple. When we conceive of worlds we do so by conceiving of the properties that make up the worlds, and when we conceive of properties being distinct, we do so by conceiving of worlds where they are not coinstantiated. It thus stands to reason that a commitment to a conceivability/possibility principle with respect to properties will be reflected in a similar principle with respect to worlds and vice versa.

We can start by considering the entailment from PW to PI. This is especially obvious if one thinks of worlds as properties—"worlds" are really just ways the world could be.[30] The recognition of a world distinct from the class of extensionally defined worlds would simply amount to the recognition of at least one intensionally defined property—the new world itself. One needn't view worlds in this way, however, for the entailment to hold. As long as for every world there is a corresponding property of being that world (or being identical with that world) the argument can go through. This commitment is optional as well, however. A contradiction can be derived by supposing PW is true and PI is false.

1. If PI is false, there is a pair of concepts <F> and <G> such that F = G even though it's not a priori that <F> and <G> are coextensive. (PI)
2. For any concepts <M> and <N>, if it's not a priori that they are coextensive, there is a conceivable world W with an object x such that Mx & ~Nx. (Premise)
3. For any properties J and K, if J = K then necessarily J = K. (Premise)
4. It is necessarily false that there is some x such that Fx & ~Gx. (from 3 and 1)
5. So if PI is false, it's conceivable but not possible that Fx & ~Gx. (from 1, 2 and 4)
6. So the falsity of PI entails the falsity of PW. (from 5 and PW) Therefore, PW entails PI. (from 6, contraposition)

---

[30] Stalnaker (2003a). The entailment does not hold without supplementary assumptions even here—something like the assumption mentioned next is probably needed.

PI also entails PW. We can see this in the same way, by deriving a contradiction from the supposition that PI is true and PW is false.

1. If PW is false, either (a) there are possible worlds V and W such that V = W even though the identity of V and W cannot be established a priori, or (b) it is conceivable that Fx and not Gx despite the fact that F = G. (PW)
2. For any properties J and K, if J = K then necessarily J = K. (Premise)
3. If (a), then there are concepts <F> and <G>, such that it is not a priori that they are coextensive even thought F = G. (At the very least, this will be the case for the concepts of the worlds <W> and <V> and the properties of being those worlds.) (Premise)
4. So, if (a), PI is false. (from 3 and PI)
5. If it is conceivable that Fx & ~Gx, it is not a priori that <F> is coextensive with <G>. (Premise)
6. So if (b), it is not a priori that <F> is coextensive with <G> even though F = G. (From 2 and 5)
7. So if (b) PI is false. (From 6 and PI)
8. So if PW is false PI is false. (From 1, 4, and 7)
   Therefore, PI entails PW. (From 8, Contraposition)

Since world-intensionalism entails property intensionalism, the former inherits the profligacy, the coherence concerns, and the whiff of anti-realism that taints the latter. World intensionalism can also be shown to have serious problems which therefore cast doubt on PI and property intensionalism. In particular, world intensionalism is self-refuting.[31] The first clause of PW is that if it is conceivable that Fx & ~Gx, it is possible that Fx & ~Gx. Why think this? The reason typically adduced—which is at the heart of metaphysical two-dimensionalism, is that the space of conceivable worlds does not outstrip the space of possible worlds. But consider:

(SN) The space of metaphysically possible worlds is more limited than the space of conceivable worlds.

SN seems conceivable. But this generates a problem. According to two-dimensionalism, if one can successfully conceive of the falsity of a statement, at the very least the primary intension of that statement is possibly false. But since SN is presumably a priori and necessary (if true at all) its

---

[31] I develop a version of this argument in Howell (2008a).

primary and secondary intensions coincide. So conceiving of SN does in fact deliver a world where SN is true. Since SN is necessarily true, if true, it's being possibly true means that it is actually true. If it is actually true then metaphysical two-dimensionalism is false, because if SN is true there is no longer any guarantee that there is a world answering to our primary intensions. Thus, on the assumption of metaphysical two-dimensionalism, metaphysical two-dimensionalism is false.[32]

The lesson of the reductio is that if possibility is tied too closely to conceivability, there is the risk that we can conceive of more things than can fit comfortably within a single logical space. In general, this is just a more pointed instance of the worry that individuating items epistemically makes it difficult to integrate those items into the objective order of things.[33]

In our response to the conceivability argument, we face the same sort of objection we faced when arguing against the presentation argument. In this case, it might be objected that I have been unfair to the world-intensionalist. In particular, the more sophisticated defenders of the conceivability argument—including Chalmers himself—do not accept PW as stated. Instead, they accept a version of PW formulated in terms of *ideal* reasoners and conceivers, such as:

(PWI) If it is conceivable by an ideal reasoner that Fx & $\sim Gx$, it is possible that Fx & $\sim Gx$, and for possible worlds W and V, if an ideal reasoner cannot establish a priori that $V = W$, then $V \neq W$.

PWI has the advantage that it does not tie possibility to the contingent abilities of reasoners like ourselves, who presumably have limited conceptual repertoires and imperfect reasoning capacities. Nothing at all follows, for example, from the fact that someone thinking quickly can conceive of a possibility, since he might have overlooked some incoherence in his conception. Similarly, nothing follows from my ability to conceive something if I am an impaired reasoner or a poor conceiver. It is only ideal conception that counts.

---

[32] Howell (2008a).

[33] One promising way out of this, I think, is to hold onto PW without claiming that in general conceivability entails possibility. In particular, one would want to distinguish between statements about the whole space of worlds and statements about what goes on within a particular world. Chalmers (2009) makes this move, but it is harder than it looks.

This idealization move affects my previous arguments in two ways. First, it might seem to deflect the charge that the world-intensionalist is committed to a form of anti-realism about possibilities. My charge might stick if possibilities were individuated in terms of the contingent abilities of fallible conceivers, but if possibilities are only tied to ideal conception it is substantially more plausible that such conceptions just pick out independently existing possibilities. The second effect of the idealization move is that my *reductio* might seem less plausible. Perhaps *I* can conceive that SN is true—or that PWI is false—but that is no more telling than my ability to conceive of the falsity of Fermat's theorem. I'm a poor mathematician and I haven't read Wiles' proof, so I can conceive of the theorem's being either true or false. Only conceivability by an ideal reasoner, someone much more like Andrew Wiles, would show anything about its possible (and in this case necessary) truth or falsity. The case seems analogous to my ability to conceive of the truth of SN. I might be a better philosopher than I am a mathematician, but an ideal reasoner I am not.

The idealization move is forceful, but I think it either winds up shifting the problem in a way that should significantly reduce the persuasiveness of the conceivability argument, or it does not go far enough to block my objections. The obvious question is how "ideal" conceivers and reasoners are being construed in PWI. A natural view is that an ideal reasoner is one who doesn't make any mistakes. In this case, however, this seems tantamount to saying an ideal reasoner is one whose reasoning tracks possibilities. This won't do, of course, as it makes the conceivability argument blatantly circular: whether or not zombies are conceivable, for example, just amounts to whether or not they are conceivable by someone whose conceptions track possibilities. Since the conclusion is supposed to be that zombies are possible, the argument would clearly beg the question.

There are other ways to analyze "ideal" in this context, and a survey of all the options deserves an investigation in its own right.[34] It seems, however, that if the question-begging deflationary reading is to be avoided, the notion of ideal reasoning needs to be thickened, perhaps by associating it with a type of reasoning that can be substantively defined. (I'll

---

[34] All the options face the question "Why think that our non-ideal conceivability is a good guide to ideal conceivability?" Since this is a sort of "ignorance theory response," which I classify as a type of hardline response, I flag it as a move to make but don't intend to pursue it; see Stoljar (2006).

suggest in the next chapter that it should be tied to deduction.) This can be done in one of two ways. It could be accomplished simply by reductively analyzing the notion of possibility in terms of that sort of reasoning. This route is independently implausible, but it risks either anti-realism about possibilities, or it begs the question by once again—though indirectly— identifying ideal reasoning as reasoning that gets possibilities right. The second way refuses to *analyze* possibility in terms of some system of reasoning, but only claims that the sort of reasoning in question is a perfect guide to possibility.

This last reading of PWI is more palatable, but it still seems troubled. If possibilities are not reductively explained in terms of some manner of reasoning, we have to ask why that manner of reasoning is such a perfect guide to them. It's not clear what the explanation could be: infallibilism and realism always make uncomfortable bedfellows. This fact lends new blood to the *reductio*: assuming realism about possibilities, it seems conceivable that PWI is false, simply because if there is a domain of truths that is independent of a method of reasoning it is conceivable that the method of reasoning can occasionally miss those truths. So what remains is a dilemma. Either two-dimensionalism is false by its own lights, or it is likely committed to a sort of anti-realism and threatens to introduce circularity into any argument that employs it.[35]

It seems far preferable to say that conceivability is a good but defeasible guide to an extensionally individuated set of possibilities. When should we suspect that conception is defeated? Well, an obvious case is when it leads us into contradictions—as it might when applied to necessary truths such as PW or Fermat's Theorem. (In such cases, the conceivability of both the truth and the falsity of these propositions that are either necessarily true or false would generate a contradiction if the inference from conceivability to possibility were infallible.) A more subtle case of defeat is suggested by the discussion of the exclusion problem as it applies to property intensionalism. Suppose that a case of inferring possibility from conceivability leads one to posit a type of property that does not integrate well into the causal structure of the world. Suppose one was forced to conclude that the

---

[35] Supposing that the two-dimensionalist doesn't think possibility can be analyzed in terms of conceivability in some form, it seems as though he is committed to the coincidence between conception and possibility being a sort of "strong-necessity" of the sort two-dimensionalism abhors. This would significantly weaken Chalmers' objection to "Type-B" materialisms to which subjective physicalism bears some resemblance.

"discovered" type of property lacked causal powers, such that it became mysterious how one knows about, refers to, or even thinks about properties of that type. Under these circumstances, it seems one's inference faces a significant defeater.

Subjective physicalism thus responds to the conceivability argument by embracing an extensionalist view of possible worlds. It is a corollary of this commitment that inferences from conceivability to possibility are defeasible. We should suspect that our conceptions have let us down when they commit us to properties that do not integrate into a coherent worldview and that seem fated to causal impotence. This, of course, is precisely what seems to be the case when it comes to property dualism.[36] We should thus side with subjective physicalism, concluding that this is one instance when our trust in conceivability should bow to our commitment to a coherent worldview.

This parallels the way we have responded to the presentation argument. The dualist arguments gain footing by grounding new appearances in new properties. It might often be the case that the inference behind that commitment is harmless. But an extensionalist about properties should be vigilant, looking for cases where intensionally individuated properties are being introduced. We should suspect that they have when the resultant properties have difficulty integrating into an objective worldview. In the case of phenomenal properties, that seems to be the case. Subjective physicalism requires that one reject the dualist's optional intentionalism, and embrace a more metaphysically robust picture of properties and possibilities. On this more robust picture, properties need extensional individuation conditions—so that, for example, properties are individuated by their causal profile—and properties must be modally independent—so that if F and G are such that necessarily x has F iff x has G, F = G. A lack of modal independence is indicative of a merely conceptual distinction, not one that carves nature at its joints. There are, perhaps, other marks of an intensionalist metaphysics, but these are the ones that most concern us in the anti-materialist arguments. Ultimately, the lesson is that the defender of physicalism must carefully monitor the seemingly innocent metaphysical moves of his opponent, lest the decisive moment in the trick go unnoticed.

---

[36] See Chalmers' own explanation of "The Paradox of Phenomenal Judgment" is in Chalmers (1996).

6

Deduction, Necessitation, and Acquaintance

In the last chapter, I argued that the anti-materialist arguments presuppose an intensional metaphysics of properties and possible worlds that the physicalist should reject. An important piece of the puzzle is still missing, however. For one thing, I have yet to say anything directly to the knowledge argument. Though I ultimately think the arguments in the last chapter cut against that argument as well, something is unsatisfying about leaving it at that. The physicalist needs to explain what exactly Mary learns, and why that knowledge in particular doesn't have dualistic implications. It is one thing to say the dualist takes advantage of a general metaphysical presupposition, but it is quite another to explain just why that generates such plausible arguments in the case of phenomenal knowledge *and apparently nowhere else*. What is so special about phenomenal knowledge that it makes these arguments, and their presuppositions, so attractive? In Chapter 3, I argued that except for hardline positions, any response to the knowledge argument must ultimately embrace acquaintance. So, it will surprise no one that my response to the knowledge argument, and the conceivability argument as well, ultimately involve acquaintance. Nevertheless, it must be shown just what role acquaintance plays, and whether or not it can be embraced by a physicalist.

Dualism and Deduction

The two most popular arguments against materialism can both be seen as two different ways of making the same grand argument which hinges upon a surprising and strong claim about the relationship between deduction and necessitation.[1] We have already seen in Chapter 3 that the knowledge argument is best construed as an argument about the deducibility of the phenomenal from the physical. Keeping Mary locked in her black and white room is simply a way to insure that she starts with only physical facts about seeing red. Giving Mary all the physical information about the world is meant to give her a complete physical base for her deductions, and making her logically infallible guarantees that she can come to know all of the truths logically derivable from the physical base. Claims that clever Mary can gain phenomenal knowledge within her room by shedding blood or stimulating her brain are beside the point when the argument is viewed in this way: it doesn't show the relevant deductive relations between the physical and the phenomenal.

It is perhaps less obvious that the conceivability argument is best viewed in terms of deducibility as well. As we saw in the last chapter, one of the difficulties facing that argument is that on some obvious conceptions of conceivability, there is no connection to possibility. After all, even the most numerate of us can in some sense conceive of the truth as well as the falsity of Goldbach's conjecture, but it is either necessarily true or necessarily false. So, the argument must involve conceivability in a stronger sense. There are many different proposals as to how conceivability should be construed, and the taxonomy of conceivabilities becomes Linnaean in scope.[2] It's not at all clear that this surfeit of notions of "conception" is an embarrassment of riches as opposed to a mere embarrassment. With every increase in the number of ways one can conceive, there is an increased risk that when we think we are conceiving in the right way, we are simply wrong.[3]

One recourse is to move to a positive notion of conceivability, tied more strongly to imaginability.[4] According to one such model, one cannot really positively imagine what it would be like for Goldbach's conjecture to be true. One could, of course, imagine what it would be like for the newspapers to report its truth or one could imagine hearing that a

---

[1] Chalmers (2009) also compares the conceivability argument and the knowledge argument, and agrees that there are ways to reduce one to the other. However, he is more inclined to construe the knowledge argument in terms of conceivability than he is to understand the conceivability argument in terms of deduction.

[2] Van Cleve (1983); Yablo (1993); Chalmers (2004b).

[3] See Stoljar's notion of modal error in Stoljar (2006, ch. 4).

[4] Chalmers (2004a).

Cambridge mathematician proved it, but those things—the newspaper's reporting and one's hearing the news—are in fact possible. Their possibility, however, does not imply that it is possible that Goldbach's conjecture is true. So perhaps moving to this more positive notion of conceivability can help the argument.

There are several problems with this notion of conceivability. Most importantly, it is difficult to tell what it actually involves. For my part, when I think of positive conceiving or imagination I tend towards the visual. When I imagine that pigs fly, I "picture" a pig with wings. But this might not be enough. How do I know it's not a fake pig, flying courtesy of Disney? Need imagination be so visual? It seems such imagistic imagination is simply inappropriate when it comes to theoretical conceptions, such as the sort we are asked to entertain in the case of zombies. If conception is not meant to be tied to imagination, then it might in fact seem too cheap.[5] Again, locating the right sense of conception will be a contentious matter simply because of the diversity of notions. Furthermore, something like positive imaginability seems too dependent upon psychological contingencies to be of much epistemic value. It's hard to see why it would be the case that our particular psychologies are good guides to modal facts, as opposed to either more "impoverished" or more limber imaginations.

Perhaps there is a notion of positive conceivability that will do the trick for the proponent of the conceivability argument, and perhaps it can avoid some of the dialectical complications suggested above. As a matter of fact, though, I don't think we need such a notion. We have a much more deflationary notion of conceivability that is robust, that makes the conceivability argument plausible, and that opens up a fruitful pathway for philosophical disagreement. According to this view, conceivability is closely tied to deducibility. If this is correct, one should rarely say that something is conceivable or inconceivable *simpliciter*. Instead, one should say that something is inconceivable *modulo* a certain set of facts—to say that p is inconceivable is always to say it is inconceivable given q, where q is either implicit or explicit.[6] The deflationary view holds, then, that p is

[5] See Fiocco (2007).

[6] In the case where someone says that something is inconceivable without specifying a set of facts with respect to which it is conceivable, one suspects that either the set of facts is contextually specified, or, in the extreme case, that the proposition or propositions are inconceivable modulo a set of propositions the speaker cannot doubt.

inconceivable given a set of truths T if and only if not-P is deducible from T, and p is conceivable given T if and only if not-P is not deducible from T. Given this, the conceivability argument ultimately doesn't depend upon the psychological vicissitudes of imagination, iconographic or otherwise. It ultimately amounts to deducibility. So, the point of the zombie argument becomes quite simple. Say that Q is the conjunction of the phenomenal truths that hold in our world, and P is the set of physical* truths. A zombie world is one where P and not-Q is true. A zombie world is conceivable on this account then, iff not-not Q is not deducible from P—that is Q is not deducible from P. Put more simply, a zombie world is conceivable iff one cannot deduce the phenomenal truths from the physical truths, and this is the way zombies threaten physicalism.[7]

If this is right, it seems as though the knowledge argument and the conceivability argument basically depend upon the following common core argument, which is a slight modification of the argument from Chapter 3:

1. There are phenomenal truths which are not deducible from a complete set of physical truths.
2. If one set of truths q is not deducible from another set of truths p, then p does not entail q.
3. If the physical truths do not entail the phenomenal truths, physicalism is false.
   Therefore: Physicalism is false.

As we have seen, premise two is simply a particular instance of a more general principle which many find quite contentious:

DN: P necessitates Q only if Q can be deduced from P.

In Chapter 2, we saw several ways that DN is resisted—namely by adducing a posteriori necessities or strong necessities of some other sort. These

---

[7] Although I think putting the argument in terms of deducibility is clearer than putting it in terms of conceivability, I am not necessarily committed to deducibility being a more fundamental notion. I find it much clearer to define conceivability in terms of deducibility, though one could perhaps do things the other way around. But judging from the voluminous literature about different ways to construe conceivability, and the many different questions that get raised about conceivability, deducibility seems more straightforward. For a sampling, see Gendlar and Hawthorne (2002). It might be, as an anonymous referee has suggested, that conceivability claims are often used as evidence that one thing is or is not deducible from another, but this does not show that conceivability is the more fundamental notion.

arguments were found wanting, however. There are other problems with DN, and with the argument as formulated, that must be addressed and will show a few openings that were previously masked.

Talk of truths invites ambiguity, as does the talk of propositions which is usually presupposed, and the ambiguity becomes problematic in the current context.[8] On the one hand, we are talking about truths being deduced from one another. This invokes the notion of truths as representational entities, the sort of thing we can actually employ in deductions and other cognitive processes. On the other hand, we are talking about truths necessitating one another. This, however, invokes the notion of truths as things that obtain in the world, like facts or states of affairs. When we talk about one thing T necessitating another U, we mean among other things that the existence of U is guaranteed by the existence of T. But if truths are propositions, and propositions are necessary, abstract, and eternal entities, every proposition trivially necessitates every other proposition—all the propositions exist necessarily. (They are not, of course, necessarily true on this view—they are true or false in or with respect to individual worlds.) When we are talking about necessitation, we are typically talking about connections between contingent things, and if so abstract propositions cannot be those things. Nor, though, can propositions considered as mental representations, since when we say one thing necessitates another, we are making no comment at all about whether thoughts of one thing come with thoughts of another. It is more proper to think of propositions, and thus truths, necessitating one another only indirectly, insofar as the states of affairs they represent necessitate one another. To avoid confusion, of course, we say instead that propositions or truths entail one another.[9]

In order to see how the knowledge argument can be avoided, we must not only strictly separate the metaphysical from the epistemological, as was encouraged in Chapter 5. We must also hold the representational apart from the things represented. DN clearly fails to do this, and to the extent

---

[8] John Heil has been influential in my thought about this, and Heil (2003) does a nice job teasing apart the ontological from the representational.

[9] It will forestall confusion if I am explicit that I am not here employing a Lewis/Stalnaker notion of propositions as sets of possible worlds. The notion I am employing is more traditionally Fregean, according to which propositions are structured objects of belief, composed of fine-grained intensionally individuated constituents. Though I have no fully developed theory of propositions, accounts of the sort developed by Bealer (1998) can serve my purpose, as can accounts by Chalmers (2011), though my two dimensionalism will differ from his in ways that are made clear in this and the previous chapter.

that the knowledge argument and the conceivability argument depend on DN, they do as well.

A careful restatement of the argument can avoid this issue.

1. There are propositions concerning phenomenal facts which cannot be deduced from the complete set of propositions concerning physical facts.
2. If proposition q is not deducible from a set of propositions p, then the set of facts represented by p does not necessitate the fact(s) represented by q.

   Therefore, the physical facts don't necessitate (at least some of) the phenomenal facts.

The restatement of this argument raises several new issues, most of which concern the second premise. Its plausibility, of course, depends on what counts as a proposition representing a fact. On at least one obvious reading, premise two is subject to clear counterexamples. Suppose, for example, that I name the set of propositions expressed by my physics book "Paul" and I name the set of propositions expressed in my chemistry book "Chuck." Now, consider the propositions "Paul is true" and "Chuck is true." If my books are good enough, the former proposition entails the latter proposition, but I certainly couldn't deduce the latter from the former.

There are two ways to respond to the Paul/Chuck counterexample. One would be to make a distinction between different types of propositions, insisting that premise two holds only for the most fine-grained sorts of propositions. That there are such propositions, and that they are the ones we are looking for, is intuitive. There is something physics is trying to express, and it's not Paul, since Paul would not convey any deep understanding of the world. (Compare: "The world is all that is the case.") At the very least, physics is looking to express a set of propositions which would constitute a complete representation of the physical facts such that all of the constituents of the fact, including the relations between them, get fully represented.[10]

Another possible response is that "Paul" expresses the same proposition (or set of propositions) as the physics text. There is no "Paul" proposition to be contrasted with a more fine-grained "physics-

---

[10] See Chalmers (2004b) on canonical representations, and Einstein, Podalsky and Rosen (1935).

text" proposition, though there is inequality in the expression of the propositions. How propositions are expressed obviously has a lot to do with what we can do with those propositions in any particular instance. Physics aims at conveying an understanding of the way the world works, so "Paul" is of very little interest to physicists. Nevertheless, proposition-ally at least, physics is trying to express "Paul."

If this second response is right, how does it affect the counterexample? Despite first appearances, I think it actually shows that the counterexample is not a counterexample at all. Chuck is deducible from Paul. It's just that under any normal circumstance no one could completely grasp the prop-ositions when they are expressed as "Chuck" and "Paul," and so no one could perform the deduction. If Paul and Chuck were expressed well enough, as they would have to be if they provided a complete picture of the world as required in Chapter 5—the sort we presumably hope physics will give—the deduction can be performed by a suitably sophisticated mind.

To accommodate the Paul/Chuck concern, and to keep the represen-tational distinct from the metaphysical, we can reformulate the principle at the basis of the knowledge and conceivability arguments as follows:[11]

DN*: A fact f necessitates a fact g only if there is a proposition q that represents g that is deducible from a proposition p that minimally represents f.

Where a proposition *minimally represents* f iff it represents f and only f.

As we saw earlier, there is a lot to be said for the non-deduciblity argument against physicalism. DN captures the important fact that in almost all cases necessary connections should be "epistemically transparent" once all the information is in. This transparency doesn't seem to exist in the case of consciousness and the physical; in this case there is a deductive gap. For the rest of the chapter, I will grant my anti-physicalist opponents that this is the case. In the end, viewing the explanatory gap as a deductive gap will open the way to a dissolution of the anti-physicalist's arguments.[12]

---

[11] There are complications with DN, some of which are noted by Block and Stalnaker (1999), which force the addition of a "that's all" fact and perhaps some indexical information in the "premises" of the deduction. Chalmers and Jackson (2001) make a good case that these additions are innocuous, and the main issues surrounding the plausiblity of DN are elsewhere, so I have simplified the principle here.

[12] There is another ostensible counterexample to DN that I will not discuss—the osten-sible failure of normative facts to be deducible from non-normative facts, despite the fact that

Deduction and Direct Reference: A False Start

We have seen in Part II that denying DN by appealing to strong a posteriori necessities is not particularly promising. I mentioned there that is another way DN might fail, however. DN would fail if some things stand in necessitation relations that cannot be fully represented propositionally. Perhaps with a little modification that strategy can be redeemed. The argument might go like this:

DN gains its plausibility from a certain Fregean picture of pure propositions, something like abstract versions of sentences, as the operands of deduction. But propositions need not be pure in this way: they can contain concrete individuals as well. We can agree with the Millian view that concrete individuals can figure in propositions, and we can follow Russell in thinking that this happens when we think about our sensations in a certain way. This is the type of proposition Mary learns when she leaves the room. Mary learns <★ is what it is like to see red>, where ★ is the sensation itself, imported into the proposition perhaps by some form of inner ostension or attention. This would explain why Mary has to have the experience in order to have her new knowledge. It also would explain why there are no deductive connections between Mary's physical knowledge and her new knowledge. One cannot deduce to a sensation any more than one can deduce to a rock. The textbook physical knowledge Mary gains from within the room is knowledge of pure propositions and, in general, one is not going to be able to deduce a Millian proposition from a proposition or set of propositions that are not Millian.[13] Despite the fact that these sensation-containing propositions do not stand in any important deduction relations to other, non-Millian propositions, sensations themselves stand in many necessitation relations. The necessitation relations are not reflected conceptually in the propositions because the key

the former appear to supervene on the latter. It would be interesting to explore the relationship between the is/ought gap and the DN principle, but it cannot be done here. An interesting line to pursue, and the one most consistent with the line I take in this paper, is that the is/ought gap is actually a result of the explanatory gap, perhaps because of the intimate connection between goods and pleasures and harms and pains. Thanks to Torin Alter for discussions about this.

[13]   There are exceptions to this. One can deduce the Millian proposition <★ is red> from the proposition <Everything is red.> Cases like this seem importantly different from the deductions we want Mary to perform, where the particular nature of the concrete constituent is playing a role in the correlative entailment.

component is not conceptual. The non-deducibility of phenomenal knowledge, which is knowledge that involves sensations of phenomenal states as constituents, is simply an instance of this more general phenomenon.

This general story has a great deal of initial plausibility, and something like it has attracted several philosophers.[14] I do not think it can be quite right, however. Nevertheless, its failure, and the reasons for its plausibility, are instructive.

This "semantic" account of Mary's plight cannot be right because we have known since Kripke that many things can be referred to directly, and so many individuals—not just sensations—can enter into propositional contents. Names, indexicals, and natural kind terms all plausibly refer directly if anything does, and this means that their referents constitute parts of propositions. If this is the case, Millian propositions and their deductive idiosyncrasies cannot explain what is unique about phenomenal knowledge, Mary's situation, and the conceivability of zombies. After all, Mary can baptize the sensation one gets when looking at red with the name "Bob" (perhaps by thinking "Bob is dthat sensation Jim is having right now) and can then come to think "Bob is what it's like to see red," and thus <* is what it's like to see red> all from within her room.[15]

The mistake this approach makes is that it explains the uniqueness of phenomenal knowledge in terms of semantics alone. But the explanation should not simply be in the way that sensations are referred to, or how they figure into content, it should have something to do with the particular way sensations are known. This point is muddied by the fact that belief content is historically construed in two different ways. On a purely semantic approach, belief content is simply meant to model the truth conditions of the thought. On a more epistemic approach, belief content is meant to indicate the cognitive significance of the thought—the role the thought plays in inferences, etc. It is well recognized that these two conceptions of content do not necessarily sit well together, and it is in fact direct reference and Millian propositions that make the divide clearest. (E.g. "Cicero is Tully" is cognitively significant, but the Millian

---

[14] Including Papineau (2002) and perhaps Balog (2012).

[15] In addition, if Mary's situation is simply that of not entertaining a Russellian proposition, we should have the sense that an explanatory gap arises in all cases of direct reference, but we have no such intuition.

proposition which involves the relevant individuals is <∗ = ∗> which is just as correctly expressed as the utterly insignificant "Cicero is Cicero." The Millian proposition doesn't, therefore, provide a model of cognitive significance.) What creates confusion is that knowledge is a propositional attitude, and philosophy of language tells us that many of these attitudes have directly referential elements, that is they have Millian propositions as objects. This makes it natural to say that we have "direct knowledge" of the objects of our propositions, which in turn makes it sound as though this knowledge involves an instance of epistemic directness or immediacy. But this last step involves a non-sequitor. The divorce of the semantic notion of content from cognitive significance should lead us to recognize that semantic directness, or direct reference, carries no guarantees of epistemic directness—even when the belief content in question is an object of knowledge. I can entertain, believe, or know a Millian proposition with, say, Cicero as a constituent but this by no means implies that my knowledge of Cicero is direct in any epistemically relevant sense, or even that it is conceptually unmediated.

Once it is recognized that semantic directness is consistent with conceptual or doxastic mediation, there is no longer any reason to believe that phenomenal knowledge is cognitively "isolated" because it involves Millian propositions. I could entertain as many Millian propositions as you please even though I am deploying concepts in a very traditional sense. If this is the case, the fact that my thought has Millian contents does not explain why I cannot come to have those thoughts by deductive or purely conceptual methods.

Deduction and Epistemic Two-dimensionalism

The Millian strategy failed because it tried to offer a purely semantic solution to the problem. The basic insight that fueled the strategy still seems worthwhile, however. In some way our thoughts about phenomenal states involve them directly in a way that our thoughts about other things do not. What we have learned is that the directness cannot be merely semantic: it must involve a unique epistemic element. But it doesn't seem correct to say that Mary doesn't learn something new, or that the thought about red she has after leaving the room is the same as the thought she had from within the room. In other words, it doesn't seem appealing to say that Mary's gain is entirely *non*-semantic so that she doesn't have thoughts with new contents when she leaves the room. But what other options are there?

Our options only seem constrained if we maintain that the purely semantic notion of content is the only notion of content. But this is neither mandatory nor advisable. We saw that there is a more epistemic notion of content that aims to model the cognitive significance of the thought. The Kripkean arguments for direct reference should perhaps convince us that this content is not the semantic content of our utterances, but there's no reason it should convince us that there is no such content. If we can resurrect an epistemic notion of content, we can better specify what Mary learns when she leaves the room.

Fortunately, something like this epistemic notion of content is already well developed by the anti-physicalists, among others.[16] As we saw in the previous chapter, Chalmers and others avail themselves of a two-dimensional semantics that is meant to capture not only the wider content of our thoughts, but also the content that is shared between me and my counterpart on twin earth. That two-dimensionalism faced difficulties (in particular, a possible *reductio*) but those difficulties arose not because it posited two layers of content but because the narrower layer—the layer involving the "primary intensions"—was cashed out in terms of metaphysically possible worlds. If we recognize that the narrow layer is epistemic, we can salvage many of the virtues of two-dimensionalism without being led to the dualism that seems to follow. This "epistemic two-dimensionalism" will allow us to acknowledge the intuitions of the dualists and agree that Mary learns something new. But it will also allow us to redeploy the Russellian intuition about phenomenal states, providing a counterexample to DN and an answer to the dualist arguments.[17]

This epistemic two-dimensionalism acknowledges that there is a level of content that corresponds to the semantic content. This "public content"

---

[16] Among others, one can find this apparatus developed in McGinn (1982); Chalmers (1996); and Jackson (1998).

[17] There will be those who urgently resist any sort of two-dimensionalism, such as Soames (2005). Dealing with these objections would require much more space than this chapter could allow, but it is worth noting that adopting a two-dimensionalist framework has independent dialectical appeal. If one can grant the most vocal anti-physicalists the lion's share of their apparatus (as well as most of the motivations for supporting DN) and show that physicalism can still be defended, the anti-physicalist arguments will be shown lacking on their own terms.

involves the Millian propositions that Kripke and others have taught us to expect.[18] These Millian propositions involve individuals introduced by proper names or demonstratives as in "Russell was a member of the House of Lords," or "That stuff fills my swimming pool," where Russell, the actual guy himself, is in the first proposition and H_2O is in the second. But though such propositions are the contents of many of our thoughts, they are never the only contents of our thoughts. There is a layer of content containing pure propositions—descriptive propositions composed of abstracta—which serves as a sort of mode of presentation of those contents.[19] So again, on this view of thought, there are two layers of thought content. One—we can call it the *cognitive content*—that is descriptive and that provides the cognitive significance of the thought, and one—we can call it the *public content*—that can be Millian, including properties and objects. So, for example, when one thinks "There is water in the bay," one's pre-scientific thought might have one layer that holds that there is a substance that flows at room temperature, is clear, freezes in the winter, etc. in the bay. This would, in other words, be the layer that me and my twin on twin earth have in common. There is, however, a second layer of content that is determined by the first layer plus certain contextual features having to do with one's causal history and one's linguistic community.[20] This layer might be that "$\star$ is in the bay" where water itself is part of the thought. Since the water that is part of the content of my thought would not be chemically the same as the stuff in my twin's thought content, this is a respect in which our thoughts are different.

Part of what it means for the cognitive layer of thought to account for cognitive significance is for it to be the layer that is active in inference. This is part of the reason why only pure propositions are typically allowed on this level—an object by itself cannot account for cognitive significance, because there are many ways one can think of any object, and the inferences licensed will depend on how one thinks of the object. I maintain, however, that pure propositions, with no concrete constituents, are not the only propositions on the cognitive level, even if they are

---

[18] This "public content" corresponds to Chalmers' (1996) secondary intensions, as discussed in the previous chapter.

[19] "Cognitive content" corresponds to Chalmers' (1996) primary intentions.

[20] How is it determined? At this point I'm reluctant to commit, but I think anyone's favorite externalist theory will do.

the paradigmatic cases. There is a necessary exception, and this is where the Russellian acquaintance insight and the Millian "directness" strategy kicks in.[21] Cognitive contents can include some individuals, namely occurrent phenomenal states. These can be imported into the cognitive propositions by means of a sort of attention to them—by a sort of inner demonstration or "this." It is this exception—and the fact that it is the only exception—that generates the answer to the argument from deducibility and explains why there are no knowledge or conceivability arguments for other objects or properties that figure in Millian contents.[22]

We can thus agree with part of the semantic Millian strategy outlined in the last section: DN fails in the case of phenomenal knowledge because the phenomenal states themselves enter the proposition known. But in this case the explanation is not merely semantic, because the only way that phenomenal states can enter the cognitive proposition is if they are known in a particularly direct way—by an inner act of attention or ostention. The sort of knowledge that Mary gains upon leaving the room can thus be properly called knowledge by acquaintance.[23]

With this picture of thought in mind, let's look back at the two ways that DN can fail. One way was if there were features of facts that could not be represented, and the other was if there could be necessitation relations between facts that cannot be deduced from complete descriptions of those facts. At first blush these paths didn't seem promising. On this view, however, they can be accepted in a way that is perhaps not so strange. The phenomenal states are not represented, in a sense—they are part of a representation, to be sure, but they are not there by proxy: they are there in person, as it were. Given that they are not descriptively represented in the propositions, it is possible that there are necessitation relations that hold between the facts represented by those propositions that are not descriptively represented.

So, we have the following account—phenomenal, "knowing what it's like" knowledge involves entertaining a proposition in the cognitive slot that contains a phenomenal state as a constituent. One can only come to

---

[21] This exception is necessary, because thoughts constructed purely from general terms could not succeed in achieving singular reference; see Chisholm (1976, p.31) and Brewer (1999, ch. 2) for arguments to a similar effect.

[22] There is, of course, something like the puzzles in the case of indexicals, as famously presented in Perry (1979), but the puzzles here are ultimately of a different sort.

[23] Compare Conee (1994).

entertain such propositions by importing the phenomenal constituents through acquaintance, which requires actually having the phenomenal states in question.[24] Crucially, phenomenal constituents do not get into the cognitive slot by deduction—not because one cannot deduce from pure to Millian propositions, but because unless constituents are imported by acquaintance there is no guarantee that the propositions containing them will accurately reflect cognitive significance. So, for example, say that one had as a cognitive proposition "Everything is shaped" and could deduce from this the Millian proposition <*The David* is shaped> where the David is a constituent of the proposition. Because one can think of the David in a number of ways without knowing that they are all ways of thinking of the same object, this Millian proposition does not determine the cognitive significance of the thought containing it. In other words, one is suddenly vulnerable to Frege puzzles if one can introduce Millian propositions into the cognitive slot by deduction. This holds for Millian propositions about phenomenal states no less than propositions about statues, and this is why deduction cannot deliver the sort of phenomenal knowledge that we feel Mary lacks.

This account has the advantage that it explains why the phenomenal facts are not deducible from the physical facts, and it explains it without making phenomenal facts non-physical. It explains it in terms of the special role they play in thought. Phenomenal properties are "ground zero" for many of our thoughts—they play essential roles in the way we perceive and think about the world.[25] As such, their role in thought is somewhat anomalous: they do not comfortably stand as objects of our thoughts.[26] They are more felicitously facilitators of thought. Despite appearances, this doesn't seem to be a mere contingency of our particular form of wiring. The point is, in a way, more Kantian than that. It would seem that any creature who enjoyed states which played the same role as our conscious states, that is any conscious creature, would find themselves in a similar

[24] As Alter (2008) points out, there are some exceptions to the claim that knowing what it's like requires actually having the experience, so officially this statement needs to be weakened. These exceptions don't threaten the argument I make here, however, and I deal with these exceptions in a later section.

[25] An anonymous referee raises the following question: Does my view imply that "zombies" would not be able to achieve singular reference, or even have thoughts at all? No, but my view does imply that they do not have singular reference like we do, with the same psycho-semantics, and it isn't unlikely that they don't have thoughts like we do either.

[26] I discuss this feature of phenomenal properties in Howell (2010).

bind to those of us trying to render our subjective states objectively explicable. The knowledge argument, the conceivability argument, and the argument from non-deducibility are to that extent endemic to our subjective point of view.

Acquaintance, Quotation, and Ineffability

Readers familiar with the literature will no doubt recognize similarities between my proposal and the suggestions of several different camps. My emphasis on acquaintance as the relation that imports a sensation into a cognitive proposition harkens back to the acquaintance solution of Earl Conee and others, while my claim that phenomenal states are contained in the cognitive propositions reminds one of the quotational model of phenomenal concepts developed by Papineau and others.[27] Finally, there is something that all of these models share with the "ineffability proposals" which maintain that the knowledge argument only shows that phenomenal experience is ineffable, not that it is non-physical.[28] It will clarify my position to situate it more clearly in relation to these views.

The fact is that there is more than a little truth in all of these views, and so I have little concern that there is overlap between my view and theirs. The concepts of acquaintance, containment, and ineffability should play a role, I think, in any theory on this matter. The key is in their integration and explication.

To take the ineffability theorists first, it seems quite correct to say that "phenomenal knowledge," the knowledge Mary gains when she leaves the room, is in some sense not fully expressible in language and involves ways of thinking that are peculiarly resistant to communication and description. My view, according to which phenomenal states enter non-descriptively into propositions, gives something close to this result as well. The primary problem with these views is that by focusing on ineffability they don't fully explain what needs to be explained, and they don't get at the source of the ineffability.[29] They also don't directly address the non-deducibility argument. If the only concern was to explain why it is that phenomenal knowledge is not conveyed to Mary through her textbooks

---

[27] Connee (1994); Papineau (2002); Balog (2012).
[28] Byrne (2004); Hellie (2004).
[29] I provide further objections against this view in Howell (2007).

and computer screens, ineffability would suffice. (If something can't be described, it can't be given to her in those formats either.) But as we've seen, it is misleading to focus on how Mary gets the information she gets. The real question is whether phenomenal information can be deduced from physical information. Ineffability doesn't speak to this.[30] More importantly, it seems crucial to get at the reasons behind the ineffability of phenomenal states. If such states are merely ineffable because of a contingent limitation of the grain of our concepts, for example, then at most this would explain why *we* could not gain phenomenal knowledge from physical description—it would not explain the strong intuition that even a perfect reasoner, with concepts as finely grained as you please, wouldn't be able to deduce to phenomenal facts.

Phenomenal knowledge would be ineffable, in a sense, if it actually required the instantiation of the property that it was knowledge of. This is part of the appeal of "Experience Required" views of phenomenal concepts, and "quotational" views in particular. There are many different ways to develop such a model, and not all of them will be physicalist.[31] It is important to recognize, however, that "experience required" views only explain part of the data. The knowledge argument does not get its main motivation from the fact that "what it's like" knowledge depends upon having the relevant qualitative experience.[32] The argument shares a common core with the conceivability arguments, and together these arguments draw attention to the fact that "what it's like knowledge" is not deducible from physical knowledge. The "experience required" views alone do not explain this. Suppose, for example, that one has a quotational view of phenomenal concepts according to which the tokening of the concept requires the tokening of the experience the concept is of. Depending on what else is true of the quotational concept, it is still an open question whether or not one can deduce to propositions that include it. It is possible, given these views, that with certain physical information one could reason in such a way that one tokened the relevant phenomenal concept, along with its constituent state. The intuition behind the thought

---

[30] Perhaps there is a principle according to which ineffable truths cannot be deduced from effable ones. To make this case, more needs to be said about the structure of effable vs. ineffable truths.

[31] Chalmers (2002); Levine (2007); Papineau (2007).

[32] Though, see Alter (2008).

experiments, though, is that one still wouldn't be *deducing* the nature of the experience from the physical facts. The view I am proposing explains this gap by the fact that phenomenal knowledge requires that propositions containing experiences be in a particular part of thought—the cognitive slot—and they can only get into this slot when the subject is acquainted with the experiences. This goes beyond the "experience required" intuition and provides a deeper explanation of intuitions behind the thought experiments.

The problem with the quotational model is that as it is usually presented it is a purely semantic explanation of the uniqueness of phenomenal knowledge.[33] This is the sort of explanation we found wanting a few sections back, in part because the relevant semantic features are not unique to phenomenal knowledge. For the quotational strategy to advance beyond this, we need to know how the relevant objects—in this case the phenomenal states—get into the quotes, and we need a story of why only those objects get into the quotes. Quotation is a very general phenomenon that applies to a lot more than conscious states. More paradigmatically, of course, it applies to words. If that is the case, then why isn't an explanatory gap generated in these cases? Take the sentence:

A: "Love" is a four letter word.

Suppose that one were suddenly unable to use quotation marks. Would one suddenly be unable to express A? No, of course not. One could type or utter:

B: The English word for love has four letters.

It lacks the Wildean cleverness, perhaps, but the same information is there. No explanatory gap.

Of course this objection might seem rather silly. Quotation was a metaphor after all—there was no insinuation by anyone that quotation marks themselves introduced an explanatory gap. But if only "mental quotation marks" generate the explanatory gap, the metaphor promises very little illumination. What is needed is an account of precisely how it is that phenomenal states become quoted. Experience is required, but it is not enough—the experiences of the people outside the room can be

---

[33] This is especially clear in Papineau (2007), see especially chapter 5 and the sections on the explanatory gap.

discussed, named and directly referred to by Mary, but that doesn't give her the knowledge she needs. We need something further, something epistemic, to take up the slack.[34]

It is natural to suggest that Mary needs acquaintance with the experience—"a maximally direct cognitive relation to the experience."[35] This seems to be on the right track, but it depends on how we understand acquaintance. According to Earl Conee, acquaintance is a third category of knowledge to be distinguished from factual knowledge ("knowledge-that") and ability knowledge ("knowledge-how").[36] Since it is distinct from factual knowledge, Mary's gaining this new knowledge doesn't show that she lacked any information. Like the quotational account, Conee's acquaintance account agrees with the spirit of the account I have offered. Again, however, the picture it paints is not quite complete. For one thing, though there is something different about phenomenal knowledge that makes it unlike the knowledge we can gain from studying physics lessons, it seems a stretch to say that it is non-factual or non-propositional. This seems evident in part because of the way we are inclined to articulate "what it's like" knowledge—"That is what it is like to see red." This is in contrast to the way we express knowledge-how, which doesn't seem to be propositional. More conclusive, though, is an objection adapted from Geach.[37] Suppose, correctly, that I have never tasted vegemite. Based on some poor conjectures, I might think vegemite will either taste like my old friend peanut butter or it will taste like stinky tofu, which is fortunately as foreign to my palette as vegemite. Upon eating the vegemite, I can perform the following reasoning, which though doubtfully sound, is deductive reasoning.

1. <That> is not what it is like to taste peanut butter.
2. If <that> is not what it is like to taste peanut butter, it must be what it is like to taste stinky tofu.
    Therefore, <that> is what it is like to taste stinky tofu.

Given that this reasoning is deductive, it appears to operate on propositions. But if that is the case, and premise 1 expresses "what it's like"

[34] Papineau is very clear that he does not buy into the epistemic directness of the sort that I maintain must supplement any semantic view; see Papineau (2007, p.105).
[35] Conee (1994, p.136).
[36] Conee (1994, p.136).
[37] Geach (1965).

knowledge, "what it's like" knowledge had better be propositional. On the acquaintance view, at least as Conee develops it, this doesn't seem to be possible. So, acquaintance alone cannot capture what is needed.

One way of looking at things is that the acquaintance model leaves out the semantic aspect of phenomenal knowledge, while the quotational model leaves out the epistemic aspect. The model I am proposing can be seen as combining elements of each theory. It is acquaintance that imports phenomenal states into the propositions of the cognitive slot, but the acquaintance itself is only a condition for the relevant sort of knowledge of the Millian proposition that has a phenomenal state as a constituent.

What Mary Knows

The account I am proposing relies upon acquaintance and a general psycho-semantics that involves two-tiers: one cognitive tier that grounds the cognitive significance for the thoughts, and a public tier that, among other things, accounts for the commonality in thought among similar but differently positioned thinkers, and that explains some of the modal properties of our thoughts.[38] There are no doubt many interesting things that could be said about acquaintance as well as the two-tiered semantics based upon it, but I won't pretend to develop full theories here. Nevertheless, more should be said, if only to hedge against confusion.[39]

Acquaintance has a long pedigree, and it has been associated with many interesting epistemic and metaphysical theses.[40] On some views, acquaintance is a metaphysically direct form of knowledge, such that a state of

[38] See Howell (2006) for a further explanation and application of the semantics. It should be said that a two-tiered account might not be necessary. If wide-scope can capture rigidity as suggested in Sosa (2001), but denied in Soames (2002), then a single-tier descriptivist account will suffice. The important thing is that conscious mental states play the appropriate role at some level of reference-fixing.

[39] The most discussed implementations of this semantics is presented by Jackson and Chalmers, though there are others. My own version, which is outlined Howell (2006), lacks some of the metaphysical commitments often associated with those models. In particular it does not embrace a possible worlds semantics, and doesn't have the problematic commitment to PWI discussed in the previous chapter. (Note, though, that Chalmers (2011) develops a version of two-dimensionalism which does not depend on a possible worlds interpretation. My own view is closer, then, to Chalmers' later view, and falls into a more general "two content" camp that includes McGinn (1982).)

[40] See Fumerton (1995) for the most developed used of acquaintance in the epistemology literature.

acquaintance actually includes the state one is acquainted with.[41] On some views, it is viewed as a source of knowledge other than knowledge-that. Conee held this view, as we have seen, but so did Russell and more recently it has been defended by Michael Tye.[42] On this view, acquaintance is a way of knowing something that doesn't involve knowing facts about it, and some might claim it involves a commitment to non-conceptual content.[43]

I have some sympathy with several of these commitments, but in my view they are not necessary for acquaintance to play the role we are asking of it. What is important is that acquaintance is a way of knowing one's own states that provides a grasp of those states which no other way of knowing can provide. This alone secures the non-deducibility thesis, since deduction would be another way of knowing. There is, of course, a sense in which knowledge by acquaintance is non-conceptual on my view, since acquaintance imports sensations themselves into the propositions known. But it is not clear to me at least that this is inconsistent with the claims of conceptualists like McDowell.[44] On at least one reading of this debate, conceptualism is just the claim that one's ability to have representations supervenes upon the concepts one is in a position to deploy.[45] This doesn't seem like something I am forced to deny. Perhaps on other definitions of the debate acquaintance entails non-conceptualism, but I strongly suspect that this would only be on certain notions of concepts and representation that are themselves optional. In any case, I don't take a side in the debate as it is typically framed.

I think we should take issue, however, with those who feel acquaintance is itself a case of non-propositional knowledge. Again this risks being terminological, but I'm inclined to distinguish between acquaintance as a non-propositional source of knowledge, and acquaintance as non-propositional knowledge. It might be that acquaintance is non-propositional in the sense that when a subject stands in a relation of acquaintance the subject is not thereby standing in a relation to a proposition. But this does not yet mean that acquaintance provides non-propositional knowledge.

[41] See Gertler (2001, 2011).

[42] Tye (2009, ch. 5).

[43] I'm not sure Tye thinks acquaintance is always non-conceptual, but in Tye (2009) he seems to think they go together.

[44] McDowell (1994). This is typically taken to be a debate with Evans (1982).

[45] See Chuard (2009, forthcoming).

Acquaintance can be, as Tye puts it, "epistemically enabling" in the sense that it is a source of knowledge without itself constituting knowledge. Acquaintance is epistemically enabling because it puts the subject in a position to entertain a certain proposition (in the cognitive slot.) Perhaps the thought it enables is simply of the sort we might express by saying "this is thus." But this is a proposition, and it has truth conditions and can justify other propositions by standing in rational relationships with them.[46] This seems more like what we want out of phenomenal knowledge.

Confusions are also apt to arise with the two-tiered semantics of thought. First, it's important to realize that this is a semantics of thought, not of language or of belief ascriptions. An account of the latter must eventually jibe with the former, but they needn't be the same thing. So while the view I am advancing does resist a certain extreme anti-individualism about thought, it needn't resist content externalism in general.[47] In fact, it is explicitly aimed at capturing some of the externalist intuitions by way of the public content slot. Only a view that maintained that an internalist level of thought was incoherent would conflict with the view I propose.

Contrary to Conee and others, phenomenal knowledge is knowledge-that. This raises the crucial question of what it is that Mary cannot know while still in her room. It might seem that she can know all she needs to know. For example, suppose that while in her room she comes to know that Megan is outside looking at a rose. Mary can then christen the visual sensation Megan is having "Bob." Now, Mary can certainly think the thought "Bob is what it is like to see red." So, in some important sense Mary knows what it is like to see red.[48] She is, on the assumption that names refer rigidly, thinking the very same proposition she will think (assuming she is relevantly like Megan) when she sees the rose herself and says "This is what it's like to see red." This is right, as far as it goes. But it is not the whole story.

---

[46] My position is motivated in part by the worries of Sellars (1963) and Davidson (2001).

[47] The view might resist extreme interpretations of Burge (1979) and the urgings of Stalnaker (2009) for example, but there is no need to resist the basic insights of Putnam (1975).

[48] This agrees with a Burgean line pushed by Ball (2009) and by Tye (2009). Though in some sense I am coming at things from the opposite direction, I can actually agree with much of their opposition to phenomenal concepts.

Despite the fact that Mary knows the same proposition before and after her release, she is having very different thoughts. The contents of those thoughts overlap. In particular, both thoughts have as part of their content "$\star$ is what it's like to see red" where "$\star$" stands in for the red sensation itself. When Mary is in the room, however, that proposition is entertained as the public content of her thought, while after she leaves the room it is entertained as the cognitive content of her thought. For Mary to entertain that proposition as a cognitive content, that thought must capture the cognitive significance of her thought, so she must be acquainted with the sensation that is a constituent of the thought. This is what she gains by leaving the room and seeing the rose. The cognitive content of Mary's "what it's like" thought before she leaves the room could be any number of things—one possibility is <dthat visual sensation Megan is having is what it is like to see red> where "dthat" is a Kaplanian rigidifying operator.[49] She does, by way of thinking this cognitive proposition, think the Millian proposition as a public content, but she still learns something when she leaves the room, among other things that dthat visual sensation Megan is having is $\star$.[50]

So although it is true that Mary learns something when she leaves the room, there is also a sense in which she already knew it. It is even possible that she knew the same propositions before leaving the room. Her new knowledge comes from having the Millian proposition in the cognitive content slot which requires that she actually have the sensation in question. To this extent, then, my proposal inherits an objection to "Experience Required" views that has led philosophers like Papineau away from the simple quotation model of phenomenal concepts.[51] After Mary looks away from her rose and comes to focus on the magnificent green of the grass, she still knows what it's like to see red even though she is not then having a red sensation. "Experience Required" accounts like mine don't seem to accommodate this fact.[52]

My view has the resources to provide answers to this puzzle.[53] There are several different ways one can think the "what it's like" thought, on

---

[49] See Kaplan (1975).

[50] This is one way to explain the notion of concept mastery invoked by Alter (forthcoming, a) in his response to Tye and Ball.

[51] Papineau (2007).

[52] Papineau (2007) considers this worry and attributes the objection to Scott Sturgeon.

[53] Part, but not all, of my solution can be used by the quotational theorists as well.

my view. One way, of course, is the way Mary thinks of it when looking at a rose. But Mary need not be having a red sensation in order to have that thought content. She can, lying in bed reflecting on the day, think of how delightful it was to have a reddish sensation—even if she is staring up at her white ceiling. In such cases it is plausible that even if Mary is not really seeing red, she is using her memory to conjure up a reddish sensation of the same type, and she is enjoying her thought with this "proxy" sensation as a part.[54] It's not plausible to say, however, that when Mary is obsessed with the greenness of the grass that she is doing this, however, and yet it is surely plausible to say that Mary still knows what it's like to see red.[55]

There are several possible answers to this objection. One simple answer is to repeat that this psycho-semantics is not necessarily an account of belief ascriptions. In other words, though it might be true to say of Mary that she knows what it's like to see red, it needn't be the case that at the time of the knowledge ascription Mary has any thought about redness or red sensations at all.[56] Some ascriptions of standing, non-occurrent beliefs are apt to be based on an agent's abilities, dispositions, or memories.[57] The claim that Mary knows what it's like to see red when she is lost in sensations of green is probably made true in this sort of way. This is the extent, it seems to me, to which the ability hypothesis captures "what it's like" knowledge.[58] After experiencing red, assuming nothing goes wrong, Mary has a new ability—the ability to remember and imagine her red experience, which puts her in a position to entertain a Millian thought involving a proxy sensation (or mental state) of the same type. The new ability does not account for what she learns without her gaining new information, but the ability she gains is part of what makes it true to say she knows what it's like to see red, even when she is not seeing or thinking about red.

This helps to subdue another version of the objection. Suppose Mary is actually thinking about what it's like to see red, but simply isn't having a red sensation or any other proxy sensation. She might, in fact, truly say "I know what it's like to see red, but I'm having no reddish sensation, nor

---

[54] Papineau (2002).

[55] Alter (2008) gives other examples and argues similarly.

[56] See Chalmers (2011) in which he gives an account of belief ascriptions assuming two-dimensional semantics. His account would be consistent with what I have said here.

[57] The analysis of standing beliefs is, in general, not trivial. It doesn't seem that this view has any more problems with providing an analysis than any other.

[58] Nemirow (1980); Lewis (1999b).

anything similar."[59] It might seem wrong to say in this case that she merely has a standing belief. She is actively reporting a belief, so presumably it is occurrent. Nevertheless, it seems likely that the standing, non-occurrent belief still plays a role in her occurrent thought. When Mary says she knows what it's like in this instance, it seems likely that she is *referring* to her standing belief, so that her occurrent belief is that she has such a standing belief, and this standing belief is itself to be explained in terms of dispositions and abilities.

It also helps dissipate the force of this objection that on my view Mary did, in some sense, know what it was like to see red even before her release: she knew the exact proposition <* is what it's like to see red>. She can know such a proposition without having, and without having had, any red experiences. It's just that the proposition isn't in the cognitive slot, so that her thought doesn't have the same cognitive significance for her as the thought she has when she finally sees red. It's possible that the same thing can be said of many thoughts she has after she has experienced red—many of those post-release thoughts might be essentially the same as her pre-release thoughts. They needn't be different just because she has experienced red— although she *can* have different sorts of thoughts after experiencing red.

This story seems to capture not only what it's like to gain phenomenal knowledge, but also what it's like to think about the knowledge and conceivability arguments themselves. At times these arguments are persuasive, and at other times they're not. They're at their most persuasive when we actively focus upon our sensations and wonder how we could ever reason our way to an understanding that they feel the way they do. In such cases, we are having the Millian thoughts directly, in the cognitive slot of content. In other cases, however, we can achieve distance from those sensations and think about them more indirectly, as Mary does when she thinks about Bob. In those cases, the puzzle is not apparent—unless we recall cases of our being puzzled previously, in which case we probably conjure up a Millian thought once again.

Keeping the Dualist at Bay

Two related arguments continue to threaten the account I have given, and risk reintroducing dualism through the side door. I have maintained that

---

[59] Papineau (2007).

phenomenal knowledge of the sort Mary lacks requires that she entertain a Millian proposition with the phenomenal state as a constituent imported by acquaintance. The first concern, which we alluded to before, is that acquaintance might not be a physicalistically acceptable relation. "Acquaintance" is not, of course, a relation that physicists will talk much about, and one wonders if it can receive a fully satisfying explanation in terms of the physical sciences. It is a cognitive relation which is "essentially first-personal" which is to say, basically, that if one has knowledge in this way of an object, that object must be an experience that one is undergoing. This might seem to push the mystery of consciousness away from the conscious states and towards the process by which we know them.[60]

In other words, it looks like the dualist's argument can be revived but this time against the acquaintance relation itself. There appear to be truths about acquaintance that cannot be deduced from the complete physical truth. Since acquaintance is not itself a phenomenal state, my strategy for blocking DN does not apply to these truths. So, unless there is another exception to DN, there are facts about acquaintance which are not necessitated by the physical facts.

This objection seems persuasive at first, but it is incomplete. For one thing, as we have already seen, there is a gap between something's being physical and its being fully explained by physics. Acquaintance might be one relation that is the former but not the latter. But what exactly are the truths about acquaintance that cannot be deduced from the physical truth? What is it that Mary comes to know about acquaintance when she leaves her room? One obvious candidate is that she comes to know "this is what it is like to be acquainted with red." But if this is the truth she learns, then it seems that the two-tiered strategy applies since part of that proposition— the part that is associated with "this"—will include the experience of red. This might not be exactly the same proposition as the one expressed by "that is what it is like to see red" but it is certainly close, and it seems just as dependent upon the inclusion of the actual sensation of seeing red in the proposition. If this is the case, then any argument which explained why one can't deduce one's way to phenomenal knowledge of red will also explain why one cannot deduce one's way to a full understanding of acquaintance. The original strategy will therefore apply. What other truths

---

[60] Chalmers (2006a), Levin (2007), and Levine (2007) all voice something like this worry.

are left out? Could it be left out that there is such a relation as acquaint-ance? Perhaps, but the account has the resources to explain that as well.[61] If it is left out, it is because one can only fully understand the acquaintance relationship by having it, and one can only have it by being acquainted with something. So, Mary would have to have entertained some propos-ition (in the private slot) with an experience as a constituent, but she is not in a position to do so.

Those with anti-physicalist intuitions will no doubt remain uneasy. They might be mollified by distinguishing between two different things that it and other objections like it might show. The general objection is that any move the physicalist makes (whether it is the move I make, or a more traditional phenomenal concepts strategy) will always fail to com-pletely explain the odd epistemic situation of Mary (and zombies) and so will thereby fail to fully explain first personal phenomenal knowledge.[62] This objection might be meant simply to show that because of phenom-enal knowledge, a full understanding of the world requires one to be embedded in it, actually having some experiences. Not only is this not an objection to my view, it is my view! The purpose of my account is not to dispel all the mystery surrounding conscious experience but to block the inference from mystery to metaphysics.[63] The second possible ambition of the objection is to establish this inference, but if I am correct this inference involves appeal to something like DN which fails for the reasons given above.[64]

A second, related objection is more particular to the psycho-semantics I have presented in this chapter. I have argued that only phenomenal states can be imported into cognitive propositions, but one might wonder why

---

[61] Of course, she would have been acquainted with some experiences, just not colors, so she would know there is such a thing as acquaintance. But this fact trades off of a limitation of the thought experiment and doesn't really answer the objection, since that knowledge would not be deducible from her physical knowledge.

[62] The best articulation of this objection is in Chalmers (2006a).

[63] An anonymous reviewer has suggested that the mystery inherent in my view might bring it close to a form of Russellian Monism. Since the mystery I acknowledge has an epistemic explanation, I don't see the pressure to move towards the metaphysical picture painted by neutral or Russellian monisms.

[64] This answer is related to the one given by Papineau (2007) though his proposal involves iteration of the phenomenal concepts strategy at higher orders—applying it to phenomenal concepts rather than phenomenal experiences—while I am arguing that the "first-order" strategy already blocks the next anti-physicalist move. While it might seem a regress threatens Papineau's strategy, such regresses don't seem to loom in my case.

only those states can be imported. It should not be ad hoc that there is this single exception to the "pure propositions only" rule that otherwise governs the cognitive slot. The problem is that one of the most compelling motivations for the phenomenal exception introduces another dualistic argument.

The most natural and most Russellian motivation for the phenomenal exception would be as follows: normal objects can't be a part of cognitive propositions because the propositions would then fail to capture the cognitive significance of the thoughts—normal objects have many sides. Phenomenal experiences aren't like this. We can grasp them in full, not just from a particular point of view. Phenomenal experiences don't generate Frege puzzles—at least when they are attended to in this way. The constituents of cognitive propositions have to be such that a rational individual would not deny true identities holding between those constituents. Phenomenal states seem like the only non-conceptual candidates for constituents of a cognitive proposition given this condition.[65]

This Russellian motivation, compelling though it is, generates a dilemma. If physicalism is true, then any particular phenomenal state is identical with some physical state.[66] This, of course, could not be known simply in virtue of having, or being acquainted with the phenomenal state. So, either the physical nature of the state is an unnoticed part of that state or it isn't. If it is, then the Russellian motivation fails, because it is no longer the case that phenomenal states are "grasped in full" in acquaintance. Like any other state they have many aspects, and so Frege puzzle's can be generated—one might entertain the thought "<That> experience is not physical state p?"[67] If the physical aspect is *not* really a part of the state, however, and acquaintance does in fact enable one to grasp the phenomenal state in full, then there is a new anti-physicalist argument in the offing:

1. Acquaintance gives complete knowledge of phenomenal states.
2. A perfectly rational subject can be acquainted with a phenomenal state without knowing that it is a physical state.

    Therefore, the phenomenal states known in acquaintance are not physical states.

---

[65] Russell (1914/1971); Ackerman (1987).

[66] This is not to say it is type identical. I am inclined towards type identity, but I do not think that commitment is necessary. A theory such a that of Shoemaker (2007) would not be inconsistent with the view presented here.

[67] Block (2007).

This argument, which is related to the presentation argument discussed in the previous chapter, doesn't seem to rely on DN, and the most promising way out of the argument is forestalled by the commitments of the Russellian view of acquaintance.[68]

As a matter of fact, this argument is not necessarily anti-physicalist. As we shall see in the next chapter, one possible move is to acknowledge that in acquaintance one is presented, in full, with a new property, one that isn't mentioned in physics, while maintaining that the property is physical nonetheless. Since the non-deducibility argument is defused, there is no argument that this property does not supervene upon the base physical properties, and so it can satisfy the notion of physicalism developed in Part I. Nevertheless, if the argument succeeds, it must be admitted that there is a sort of emergent phenomenal property that will not be described by the objective sciences.[69]

If this sort of emergence of the subjectively known physical is to be avoided, it must be denied that acquaintance involves a complete grasp of phenomenal properties. While this admittedly undermines one motivation behind the phenomenal exception, it doesn't make it completely ad hoc. There is still a way that we know our own conscious states that others cannot know them and which is enabled by our actually having those experiences. This is knowledge by acquaintance, and there is no reason why that has to be wedded to any notions of infallible or complete access. There are plenty of independent reasons, in fact, to deny such epistemic versions of acquaintance.[70] Nevertheless, acquaintance is a sort of direct cognitive access of a sort we don't enjoy to properties or objects in general, so it is fitting that objects of acquaintance can enter into cognitive propositions.

The worry is, however, that even if the phenomenal exception is not completely ad hoc, the perspectival nature of phenomenal states—their having a physical and a phenomenal aspect—precludes the cognitive proposition containing the phenomenal state from capturing the cognitive significance of the thought. If this is the case, then the motivations behind the entire proposal, not just the phenomenal exception, are undermined.

---

[68] The way out given in Block (2007) seems precluded, for example.

[69] This would be a version of exclusive subjective physicalism, which is discussed in the next chapter.

[70] See Fantl and Howell (2003), for example.

In fact, there is a simple answer to this worry. The worry only arises if some agent can rationally believe, in the cognitive slot, the proposition $<\!^{\star}$ is not $^{\star}\!>$. But so long as the only way that the phenomenal state can enter the cognitive slot is by acquaintance, a perfectly rational agent will not believe $<\!^{\star}$ is not $^{\star}\!>$ in the cognitive slot. That could only occur if * figured in the subject part of the proposition in one of its aspects, and in the predicate part in another aspect. (If, for example, the sensation was thought about phenomenally in one case, and theoretical/physically in another.) But if the sensation can only be imported into the cognitive slot by acquaintance, it is very implausible that this confusion could occur. Such confusion would require at once attending to a sensation and denying that it is itself. It's hard to see how a rational individual could get himself into that state.

This does mean that when a phenomenal state is part of a proposition, the proposition alone does not characterize the cognitive significance of the thought. But the proposition plus the fact that the proposition is in the cognitive slot, which has certain conditions for admission, does. So the phenomenal exception does not really undermine the model of thought, and it does not require a notion of acquaintance that invites the Black-style dualistic argument.

Conclusion

Although the two most influential anti-physicalist arguments do not in the end provide a reason to embrace non-physical properties, they do reflect something important about the structure of thought and the limits of reasoning. Reason can help us get from thoughts about things to other thoughts about things, but reasoning alone cannot get us to the things themselves. In the case of phenomenal states, thoughts not only can represent them, they can also include them as parts. This is possible because of the role phenomenal states play in getting us to think about other things—they ground our thoughts about the external world. This makes phenomenal states unique, but not necessarily ontologically different from any other physical states.

7

Assessing Subjective Physicalism

It's time to climb out of the trenches and assess the terrain. What ground has been gained? What battles are yet to be fought? And where does all the preceding discussion leave us with the problem of consciousness?

Looking Back

In Chapter 3, it was argued that phenomenal consciousness proved particularly recalcitrant to physicalistic explanation. There is something it is like to see red and to smell onions, and no amount of information provided in textbooks and physics lessons will communicate what it is like. There are many ways to acknowledge this much without giving up on physicalism, but I argued they all ultimately boil down to the same thing: there is a way one can know one's own states that provides a grasp of those states that no other way of knowing can provide. In other words, all plausible responses to the knowledge argument wind up relying on some notion of acquaintance. At the very least, this forces us to acknowledge that an objective picture of the world in in some sense incomplete. Some states must be entered in order to be fully grasped. Objectivism is therefore false.

It is extremely tempting to think that there is a quick move from the falsity of objectivism to the falsity of physicalism. After all, physicalism is thought to be committed to the completeness of physics and physics is an objective way of depicting the world. If no objective theory is complete, and physicalism requires that physics be complete, then physicalism must be false. I argue that this is too quick. Physicalism is an ontological doctrine on the nature of the world. Objectivism is a view about the way the world can be known—it is essentially an epistemological doctrine. So too is the doctrine that physics can provide a complete depiction of the world. My strategy is to embrace the ontological doctrine while rejecting the epistemological doctrine. This is the core motivation behind subjective physicalism.

This view is only plausible, however, if several things can be established. First, there must be a robust notion of physicalism that both properly demarcates the dialectical terrain while avoiding epistemic elements, such as reference to the science of physics. I provided such a definition in Part I. In Chapters 5 and 6, I argued that we can block the argument from the failure of the epistemic doctrine to the failure of the metaphysical doctrine. In Chapter 5, I argued that both the conceivability argument and the presentation argument embrace a form of intensionalism about properties and possible worlds. This ultimately has the effect of epistemically individuating properties and possible worlds. If a properly metaphysical notion of these ontological building blocks is maintained, however, the falsity of physicalism can no longer be inferred from the incompleteness of objective depictions of the world. It remains to be seen, however, just why arguments like this get off the ground. Why, for example, are we tempted to make the mistake of embracing epistemic methods of individuation in the case of consciousness? What is special about phenomenal states?

In Chapter 6, I provide my answer to this question by pointing to the common core of the knowledge and conceivability arguments and explaining how they can both be answered by appeal to acquaintance. Phenomenal states are unique because of how they are known, by the fundamental, first-personal type of knowledge that is knowledge by acquaintance. These states, and our acquaintance of them, play a particularly foundational role in our thoughts about the world, which is why they slip through the nets of our deductions and our theorizing about the world.

Subjective Physicalisms

With the spadework behind us, we can now take a look at the resulting picture of the relation between phenomenal consciousness and the physical world. The result is subjective physicalism, the view that the world is fully physical but that there are some states that must be occupied in order to be fully grasped. In fact, there are at least two ways to cash out the view, depending on how one cashes out the incompleteness of physics and objective depictions of the world. Subjective physicalism could involve either of the following two claims:

1. A full physical description of the world leaves nothing out. All properties can receive objective, physical descriptions. Nonetheless, there are some properties that cannot be grasped fully unless they are grasped subjectively, via conscious experiences, as well as by objective physical descriptions.

2. Some physical properties can be grasped only subjectively. The properties that underwrite conscious experiences (e.g. qualia) are physical, but they are not identical with any property mentioned in a completed physics.

Call a view that accepts 1 *inclusive subjective physicalism*, and a view that accepts 2 *exclusive subjective physicalism*. According to inclusive subjective physicalism, a complete physics will refer to every property and event that there is. There are simply ways of understanding those properties that will not be imparted by an understanding of the theoretical descriptions of physics. According to exclusive subjective physicalism, on the other hand, some properties simply will not be represented in a completed physics.

Despite the fact that exclusive subjective physicalism maintains that there are properties that a completed physics wouldn't even refer to, it can still count as a form of physicalism. As long as those overlooked properties supervene on the basic physical properties, they are physical. This view is, ultimately, a physicalist sort of emergentism. Whatever appeal such a view might have, it should really only tempt those who insist on individuating properties intensionally. If the arguments of Chapter 5 are correct, there is no need to multiply properties for every new mode of presentation, and there is really nothing else to recommend acceptance of the more profligate ontology of exclusive subjective physicalism.

Inclusive subjective physicalism might seem to leave a nagging itch unscratched: What, on this view, constitutes "what it's like" to have phenomenal states? Whatever it is, isn't it something that physics is leaving out? If Mary does come to know something she did not know before, mustn't that be a property that the world has that physical descriptions leave out? It seems we are back to the infelicitous choice that keeps nagging the physicalist. Either we must deny the reality of qualitative experience or we must let new properties, indescribable by physics, in the door.

There is a two-part response to this worry. One questions the demand for something ontological to explain the significance of Mary's know-ledge, the other maintains that to the extent that something ontological is required, the ontology of subjective physicalism offers a unique way through what is left of the dualist's dilemma.

Underlying the dualist's dilemma is the sense that if Mary's epistemic gain does not reflect her discovering the ontological incompleteness of her previous view of the world it cannot account for the significance of her pre-release ignorance. If all she gains is just a new path to the same old thing, then it seems her epistemic gain is no more significant than it would be if she learned the same old facts in Russian.[1] This argument assumes, however, that a subject's epistemic gain is only significant if it adds a new property or thing—considered extensionally—into her ken. This assump-tion is undermined—as is the Russian analogy—once it is realized that some ways of knowing things are clearly more valuable than others.

The nature and value of a subject's knowledge does not merely depend on what is known, but also upon the way that it is known. Knowing a physical state by experiencing it is a way of knowing that is of particular value to us. It is the way we first know about the physical states that underlie experiences, it is the way we most often identify those states, and it is in virtue of having that perspective on those states that we have the rich view of the world that we have. The subjective perspective is closely bound up with our conception of ourselves as agents and as thinking things.[2] Although we might be able to conceive of the existence of zombies, we clearly cannot conceive of *being* zombies. There is a sense in which zombies have a perspective on themselves and on the world but we can hardly imagine that being *our* perspective. Lacking that perspective on an important class of things, therefore, would be a considerable deficit even if it is not a handicap that stems from an incomplete catalogue of the world's ontology. This alone explains, I think, why the perspective Mary lacks seems of particular importance.

One might agree that Mary's knowledge is more valuable than the knowledge of the same old things in Russian while still thinking that this

---

[1] Lewis (1999c).   [2] See Siewert (1998).

does not really mark the importance of Mary's epistemic achievement. After exiting her room, Mary is in a position to rule out ways the world might be that she was not able to rule out before.[3] This might suggest that she is actually coming to know about new properties.

This way of reviving the dualist's dilemma makes assumptions that subjective physicalism rejects. It illicitly presupposes an intensionalist view of properties, and if it assumes that the relevant "way the world might be" is a metaphysical possibility, it is assuming an intensionalist view of possible worlds as well. Thinking that either Mary's "aha"-moment is purely psychological or she discovers a property that physics leaves out relies on a false dichotomy. In fact, Mary does not discover a new property, but she does learn about a property in such a way that it allows her to rule out a set of "scenarios" that seemed to her consistent with what she had already learned. This has ontological implications only if one is committed to all such "scenarios" being possible worlds as opposed to merely conceptual possibilities, and the existence of these conceptual, epistemic possibilities only has ontological implications if we tie properties to concepts in an illicit way.[4]

One way to describe what Mary learns, according to subjective physicalism, is to say that she comes to grasp an aspect of the property that she already knew about under its physical description. What, though, are these aspects? They are not themselves properties, but are instead part of the nature of properties that are not expressible by physical description.[5] But how can they be part of the nature of properties without themselves being properties?

---

[3] See Lewis (1999c), though he does not draw the ontological conclusions.

[4] Chalmers often talks in terms of such scenarios. These epistemic scenarios are in many ways the possible worlds analogues of the "aspects" of properties I introduce shortly.

[5] "Aspect" talk is not unheard of in this debate. See, for example, Block (2007) and White (2007). It is clear, however, that in the end they take aspects to basically be properties. Aspects of the sort I am talking about are not unheard of in the metaphysics of properties. John Heil and C. B. Martin seem to have something like this in mind when discussing the dispositional/categorical property distinction. I say this despite Heil's insistence that he is not talking about aspects, but I think this is because he presupposes that aspects of properties must be properties of properties. There is still a sense in which properties both have dispositional and categorical sides to them even if in some deeper sense they cannot be separated as "parts" of the property; see Martin (1997) and Heil (2003). Aspects of a similar sort might also be necessary to make sense of the possibility of simple tropes that bear relations in a trope-theory such as that in Campbell (1990).

Consider the following analogy.[6] According to the classical atomists, spatial atoms are the smallest parts of our world: they are the parts of our world that do not themselves have parts. One objection to this is that if these atoms are extended in space, then they have a front half and a back half. But if that is the case, then the halves seem to be parts that are themselves smaller than the atoms, contrary to the atomistic hypothesis. The atomistic hypothesis thus seems contradictory. The solution for the atomists was to distinguish between an atom's actually being divisible versus its being conceptually divisible, and between its having real parts and its having conceptual parts. Real parts are parts that can be separated spatially from one another.[7] Conceptual parts are parts that can be separated "in mind only": the mind can attend to them and distinguish between them, but in fact they constitute a basic physical unity. This does not mean that the spatial atoms don't really have front and back halves and that these halves are somehow in the mind. It just means that these halves are not parts in a purely extensional, metaphysical sense.[8]

Aspects are to properties as conceptual parts are to atoms. They are features of the properties that the mind can discern—and in the subjective case they are discernible only to the subject who possesses the relevant properties. They are not, however, separable from the whole of which they are a "part." In this case, separability obviously does not mean spatial separability. Instead, the subjective aspect cannot exist without the physical aspect and *vice versa*. This is one way in which aspects are distinct from properties.[9] Another way they are different is that aspects are intensionally individuated while properties are not. As merely conceptual parts of the properties, they do not have individuation conditions that are purely metaphysical. This

---

[6] If one resists the example of classical atoms either because there are no such things or because they cannot really be simples, consider instead the more recently discussed possibility of extended simples, as argued for by Simons (2004); Braddon-Mitchell and Miller (2006); McDaniel (2007), and Sider (2007). The analogy would proceed in the same fashion.

[7] The modality here is metaphysical, not nomological.

[8] Cf. Aristotle when he asks of two parts of the soul whether they are "two only in account, and inseparable by nature, as the convex and the concave are on a surface?" Cohen, Curd, and Reeve (2000, p.775). Other potential examples of aspects are equiangularity and equilaterality, colors and shapes, etc.

[9] If this is right, the aspect-theory part of subjective physicalism might be forced to deny that there are necessarily coextensive properties. This doesn't strike me as too much of a cost, and I would be willing to bite the bullet on this especially since such a view is independently supported by resemblance nominalism; see Rodriguez-Pereyra (2002) for this implication and for the rejection of some apparent counterexamples.

fits with the idea that "qualia" are somehow inextricably bound up with how they seem to a particular subject.

Subjective physicalism does not, therefore, recognize a distinct set of *properties* that correspond to qualia, unless those are taken to be the properties physics describes and Mary understands while still in her room. There are, to be sure, aspects of states and properties that are subjective, and these roughly correspond to qualia. It is in virtue of these aspects that Mary learns something when she leaves her room. But unlike qualia traditionally conceived, the subjective aspects of certain physical properties do not enjoy independent metaphysical status. They cannot be a source of difference between objects, and they cannot become detached from the property of which they are aspects. They are not, therefore, prey to Churchland's *just more stuff* objection. To add these aspects to the list of physical properties would, in fact, be redundant— much as adding "the first half of atom A" and "the second half of atom A" to a list would be unnecessary, according to the atomist, if that list already included atom A.

Despite the fact that inclusive and exclusive subjective physicalisms sound distinct, there are bound to be some questions as to how different these two views really are. Some will no doubt feel that they are merely terminological variants of one another and that not much is at issue in deciding between them. Although I prefer inclusive subjective physicalism, there is something to this complaint. According to both views there is something important physics cannot teach us, and in both cases what is left out is physical. What it comes down to is whether one decides to call what is left out a property, as opposed to an aspect of a property. In Chapter 5, I urged two conditions on properties: two distinct properties cannot be necessarily connected, and properties cannot be individuated intensionally. These conditions should be accepted, I maintained, in order to avoid a "mixed metaphysics" that combined intensional and extensional entities. Such a metaphysics risks incoherence and plausibly gives rise to problems of causal exclusion where none should arise. I am persuaded by those arguments, but as is often the case in philosophy such arguments can be resisted as long as there are alterations elsewhere in one's ontology. Should one prefer, "property" could be a term that embraces both what I call properties and what I call aspects. (It's likely, in fact, that this is more in keeping with common usage of the term.) One would simply need to remain attentive to important differences between properties—in particular between extensional properties and intensional properties, and properties that are and are not "modally independent." Only some of these properties, then, could fall into the domain of intuitive principles of recombination and causal or explanatory exclusion. As long as all of these things are kept in view, perhaps it doesn't much matter what gets called a "property."

The fact that one can classify aspects as properties does not mean that it is advisable. How one feels about this sort of thing will depend quite a bit on one's meta-metaphysics. If one feels that distinctions of this sort are meant to carve nature at its joints, it seems to me that there is a pretty good case for the claim that the aspect/property distinction locates a joint. The very fact that properties broadly considered fall into two distinct groups, and that important metaphysical principles apply to one of these groups and not another, suggests that there is a real distinction here. Even if one were skeptical of such a realist view, it remains the case that there might be good practical reasons for making the aspect/property distinction. It seems preferable to flag important differences than to let them remain hidden under a single term, and metaphysical principles that remain general seem to be easier to manage than principles that come with caveats and ceterus paribus clauses. It thus seems that whether one adopts a realist meta-metaphysics or a more pragmatic outlook, one should adopt the aspect/property distinction and inclusive subjective physicalism.

Subjective Physicalism in Contrast

How does subjective physicalism compare to other positions in the contemporary debate about conscious experience? In its broad brushstrokes it is similar to many of the positions on the table, but it is ultimately distinct in emphasis, motivation, and in most cases it has fewer ontological commitments. In general, what distinguishes subjective physicalism is precisely the emphasis upon the *subjective*; that is that in some cases it is only by grasping the states one instantiates that one can understand states like that in general. Rather, it insists that we have all the makings of conscious experience given our physical constitution, but that this fact is not fully objectively explicable. Subjective experience is not something that can be grasped, much less explained, from outside the machine.

It might be thought that subjective physicalism bears some similarity to views that assimilate conscious knowledge to indexical knowledge.[10] Though subjective physicalism might seem to have a great deal in common with the indexical-knowledge views of consciousness, in the end the similarities are superficial. Indexical knowledge is no doubt closely linked with some sense of "subjectivity," but it isn't the sense adduced in the necessary condition for theory objectivity. A point of view or a location in the world is necessary for indexical utterances to be true, and the same can be said for beliefs with indexical components. It does not follow, however, that indexical knowledge provides subjective knowledge in our sense, or that new indexical knowledge provides new phenomenal knowledge.[11] This is why we can suppose Mary has all the relevant indexical knowledge when she is in the room, yet still feel that she is missing something. She can think "I will see a rose at 3 p.m. today" and she can even point to a brain scan of someone seeing a rose and say "and when I see the rose I will have an experience like that." Nevertheless, she doesn't have the grasp of the state that she will later gain in virtue of occupying it. This and other criticisms of the indexical view were discussed in Chapter 3.[12] The upshot is that unless the relevant sort of indexical knowledge comes with acquaintance, or some sort of unique first-personal knowledge, the indexical view is inadequate. If it does, then it seems acquaintance—not some semantic idiosyncrasy of indexicals—is what is really doing the work. In the latter case the indexical theorist might resemble a subjective physicalist, but only at the cost of abandoning the heart of his position.[13]

Subjective physicalism is a version of the view Chalmers dubs "Type-B materialism" that Frank Jackson calls "a posteriori physicalism," and I call epistemicism.[14] These views hold that while the facts about conscious experience are necessitated by the physical facts (i.e. SVP is true), they

---

[10] See, for example, Perry (2001a).

[11] This point is made nicely by both Jackson (1986) and Mandik (2001).

[12] Also, see Chalmers (2003); Block (2007); and Howell (2007).

[13] It might be the case that an explanation of the full cognitive significance of indexicals must make reference to states that are subjective in my sense—as I argue in Howell (2006)—but if that is the case, the epistemic uniqueness of conscious states explains the uniqueness of indexical knowledge, not the other way around. If this is right, Perry and others are correct that there is a connection between indexicals and phenomenal knowledge, but they have things the wrong way round.

[14] See Chalmers (1999), for example, and Jackson (2005).

cannot be inferred a priori from those facts. Though subjective physicalism is a form of Type-B materialism, it is distinct from and more satisfying than any of the views currently in that camp.

Most Type-B physicalists employ what Stoljar calls "the phenomenal concept strategy." Subjective physicalism certainly allows that there could be phenomenal concepts that play an important role in phenomenal knowledge. Indeed, given that first-personal phenomenal knowledge is distinct from its more objective counterpart, and given that this knowledge is portable—it can be retained beyond the occasion of the known experiences, and the concepts involved can be employed in a variety of thoughts—everyone should acknowledge that there are phenomenal concepts. Subjective physicalism does not, however, accord the same explanatory role to phenomenal concepts as most Type-B views. According to subjective physicalism it is simply a fact that there is something that it is like to instantiate certain physical states, and that by instantiating those states one is acquainted with them, and that objective descriptions cannot fully capture this fact. The puzzling aspects of conscious experience are present before phenomenal concepts and discrete phenomenal beliefs enter the picture.[15]

Phenomenal concepts play a more significant role in explaining standing phenomenal beliefs. Phenomenal knowledge thus breaks into two related parts. The initial illumination which Mary gets upon leaving the room, and what we find most difficult to explain, is provided by acquaintance with the phenomenal state. Since one can only be acquainted with occurrent states, however, and phenomenal knowledge is retained past the moment of experience, this cannot be the whole story. This is where phenomenal concepts come in, and it is also where the insights of the ability hypothesis pay off. When one has phenomenal knowledge—of what it's like to see red, say—and one is not then having an appropriate experience, one's knowledge consists in the possession of a phenomenal concept. Having such a phenomenal concept, though, is a matter of having certain abilities which are grounded in a past act of acquaintance.

---

[15] This suggests a view to which I am independently attracted, namely that there is a type of privileged access we have to our conscious states that is not fully reflected in our beliefs about those states. This is a candidate for a sort of non-conceptual knowledge. One needn't accept this, however. The point here is not necessarily that there can be non-conceptual consciousness, it is just that the burden of explaining consciousness cannot be borne solely by phenomenal concepts.

These include the ability to imagine being acquainted with the state in question—which is itself likely to be a matter of being able to imagine the state in question and be acquainted with what one thereby imagines. So phenomenal concepts and abilities play important roles in phenomenal knowledge, on this story, but they ultimately play supporting roles for the more fundamental role of acquaintance.

Ironically, in the end the subjective physicalist's closest friend is perhaps the property dualist. They both feel that there is something that it is like to instantiate certain states, that this can only be fully grasped by instantiating those states, and that objective sciences like physics leave this out. They differ, however, on whether physicalism can consistently acknowledge all three of these facts, and this difference has its source in the darker wilds of ontology.

What is Gained?

Given that subjective physicalism bears certain similarities to property dualism, one might be excused for asking what has been gained by the various metaphysical moves that have led us to this point. Has everything been done simply for the pride of calling oneself a physicalist?

In fact, subjective physicalism does bring some substantial advantages despite the fact that it is more concessive than certain more hard-nosed physicalist views. But those advantages are not always easily located. Certainly physicalism enjoys a certain elegance and simplicity that is lost with dualism, and subjective physicalism would seem to inherit this virtue.[16]

Without a doubt, there is something deeply appealing about a world-view that has everything cut of the same basic cloth. Dualism seems to present us with a messy patchwork by comparison. Nevertheless, I do not find these sorts of considerations, at least by themselves, very persuasive. There is almost always something metaphorical in talk about theoretical simplicity, and the metaphors chosen are meant to appeal to a somewhat minimalist aesthetic. But other metaphors could be chosen. Property dualists should reject the patchwork quilt metaphor, for example, in favor of a story in which non-physical qualia dyes the threads of a perfectly

---

[16] This is the sort of consideration adduced by Smart (1959/1971).

woven sheet. Or perhaps they can be more concessive, admitting that the world is a nice cotton blend.

We must get beyond these metaphors if we are to find a compelling reason to prefer physicalism. And it had better not be the case that in the end the preference for physicalism is aesthetic. It would be somewhat absurd if all of the emphasis on keeping physicalism metaphysical were in the service of a virtue that is in the eye of the beholder.[17]

There are further reasons physicalists will adduce for preferring their doctrine. Some find an inductive inference persuasive which argues that physical science has succeeded in explaining most of the world's phenomena, so we should expect physical explanation to prevail in the the case of the conscious mind as well. Other philosophers argue that we should embrace physicalism so as to minimize unexplained and brute features of the world. The dualist, after all, has to posit a basic psycho-physical law to explain the fact that certain conscious states accompany certain brain states. The physicalist has no need of such laws because the conscious events are identical with brain events.[18] Perhaps there is something to these considerations, but for reasons that will become clear in the next section, I think the subjective physicalist should be careful about trumpeting them too loudly.

There is one consideration, however, which weighs strongly in the physicalist's favor and generates a substantial bounty for subjective physicalism: the subjective physicalist, unlike the dualist, can provide a tolerable answer to the problem of mental causation. Recall that the problem of mental causation is generated by the apparent inconsistency of the following theses:

1. *Mental distinctness*: The mental is not identical with the physical.
2. *Physical adequacy*: Physical events have sufficient physical causes if they are caused at all.

---

[17] There is much more to be said about the reasons to prefer physicalism, most importantly related to "explanatory" arguments of the sort adduced by Hill and McLaughlin (1999). See Kim (2005) for a good discussion of these issues.

[18] Chalmers (1996) argues that the Type-B physicalist will need psycho-physical laws just as much as the dualist since they both have a need of some brute connection between the phenomenal and the physical. But the dualist laws, connecting distinct entities as they do, are real additions to the ontological structure of the world. The subjective physicalist's laws are more like hueristics, epistemic guides to remind us what is what.

3. *Mental causation*: Some physical events are caused by mental events.

4. *Non-overdetermination*: Not every case of mental causation is a case of overdetermination.

The general worry, as articulated in the introduction, is that unless mental distinctness is denied we face either the causal isolation of phenomenal properties or a physical realm that is infected by either false causal claims or incompleteness. By providing a way to deny mental distinctness, subjective physicalism preserves the relevance of the mental domain without casting the physical sciences into doubt.

But not so fast. The problem of mental causation gains its force in part from the fact that no one feels comfortable making bets against the explanatory completeness of the physical. This is not a result of some abstract adoration of the physical. It is due to the explanatory success of the physical *sciences*. The explanatory and causal adequacy of the physical is credible in large part because of the apparent likelihood that the physically *describable* is explanatorily and causally adequate. The threat of epiphenomenalism seems to threaten subjective physicalism no less than property dualism, only instead of threatening the relevance of phenomenal properties it threatens the relevance of subjective aspects of physical properties. Everything from arm-raisings to "ouch"-mutterings will be explained by the properties physics describes.

While this revised exclusion argument shows that merely being called "physical" does not redeem consciousness from causal irrelevance, it is important to recall that subjective physicalism is not simply a commitment to an idiosyncratic nomenclature. "Subjective" aspects are called physical because they are necessitated by the physical, and they are called aspects instead of properties because they cannot come apart from the physically describable aspects. Therefore, the "objective" properties could not cause what they do without them because they could not exist without them. The phenomenal state does all of the pushing and pulling we think that it does, but without excluding the causal efficacy of the physical state because they are simply two ways of looking at the same state.

Still, can't we ask whether the state causes what it does in virtue of one aspect rather than another? No. Although it appears to be a sensible question, in this case the "in virtue of" question is illegitimate. The reason is that causal explanation is not fine-grained enough to distinguish between necessarily co-instantiated properties. One can ask which of two co-instantiated properties are causally responsible for an effect if they are contingently co-instantiated, but one cannot really ask which of two necessarily co-instantiated properties (or which of a property's aspects) cause a particular effect. As a result, the question of causal competition between the objective and subjective properties cannot properly be raised.

Appearances to the contrary arise in large part because whenever we have co-instantiated properties and are inclined to think of one as the *real* cause, it is because we can ask which property would be sufficient for the effect if the properties failed to occur together. When a red brick breaks a window, the redness and the mass are co-instantiated, but we can ask whether the brick, were it a different color, would break the window. Here the question of which property is really responsible gains traction because of the separability of the properties. This is also why we can ask the property dualist whether the physical property that accompanies pain, or the qualitative property of pain causes the "ouch." Even though it might be a matter of psycho-physical law that whenever there is one there is the other, the connection is not necessary and we can therefore ask about possibilities where the laws are different and the pain occurs without the physical state or *vice versa.*[19]

According to subjective physicalism, the subjectively discovered physical aspects are necessary features of certain scientifically discoverable physical properties. Thus there is no case where there is a pain without the neural state or vice versa. So how would we decide which aspect is responsible for pain-effects? It is not obvious that we can even make sense of the question once we really internalize the close relationship between the physical properties and their subjective aspects.

Much more needs to be said about this matter, and I can hardly pretend to have closed the case here. What does seem to be clear, though, is that when it comes to mental causation there is a way out for the subjective physicalist that is not open to the property dualist. Dualism, by its very nature, runs into trouble with exclusion arguments—the mental properties are independent of the physical properties and as such they are apt to compete with them for causal roles. Subjective physicalism is a monist position precisely because it denies this sort of independence. If property

---

[19] This argument is basically that of Bennett (2003).

independence is a condition for causal competition, therefore, subjective physicalism can avoid the problems of mental causation despite bearing some basic similarity to its more dualistic cousin.

What is Lost

It is important to understand the benefits of physicalism, but it is equally important to understand the price we have paid for those benefits. As long as the problem of consciousness is taken seriously, physicalism cannot come without a cost. In my opinion these costs are worth paying, but we must be honest about them. They should temper our excitement at remaining physicalists, and they should have significant effects for how we do philosophy in other, related domains.

Subjective physicalism is a epistemicist view that embraces an epistemic and explanatory gap in the case of consciousness while denying that there is a resulting metaphysical gap. These views preserve metaphysical unity, but at the cost of a sort of theoretical disunity. It is true that everything is made of the same stuff, but it is also true that in the case of conscious experience we lack a complete understanding of the relation between conscious experience and its physical description. The force of this is made clear by the way the subjective physicalist, and the consistent Type-B physicalist, must respond to Chalmers' dilemma in "Phenomenal Concepts and the Explanatory Gap."[20]

The epistemicist must posit some feature of humans which explains the existence of the epistemic gap. For phenomenal concept theorists, the feature is that humans have certain cognitively isolated, functionally idiosyncratic concepts. For the subjective physicalist, it is the existence of a first-personal relation of acquaintance that we can have to our own mental states. Whatever the feature, Chalmers argues that it must both be the case that this feature explains the existence of the explanatory gap while itself being physically explicable. If it doesn't do the first, then the physicalist loses his answer to the anti-materialist arguments, and if it doesn't do the latter one mystery has merely been replaced by another and we must doubt whether that feature is physical. Chalmers argues that the physicalist who seriously believes in an explanatory gap cannot do both.

---

[20] Chalmers (2006a).

I think Chalmers is almost completely correct. We should admit that acquaintance is not itself fully physically explicable, in the sense that a full understanding of acquaintance and its objects cannot be gained from the facts physically described. This is just what it means to say that there are some states that must be occupied in order to be fully understood, which is a basic commitment of subjective physicalism. If we could fully understand everything about those states objectively, zombies would not be conceivable and Mary would have nothing to learn upon leaving her room. But now, Chalmers thinks, we have a further problem:[21]

On this account, even if there is a sort of explanation of the explanatory gap in terms of [acquaintance], the explanatory gap recurs just as strongly in the explanation of [acquaintance itself]. Because of this, the strategy may make some progress in diagnosing the explanatory gap, but it will do little to deflate the gap.[22]

This seems exactly right, and as usual Chalmers has provided an astute characterization of our plight in the case of consciousness. The subjective physicalist has diagnosed the explanatory gap without deflating it. Can we remain physicalists without deflating the gap? Here's what Chalmers says:

Just as the original explanatory gap gave reason to think that consciousness is not wholly physical, the new explanatory gap gives reason to think that [acquaintance is] not wholly physical.

... the proponent needs independent grounds to reject the inference from an explanatory gap to an ontological gap. If the proponent has no such grounds, then the [acquaintance] strategy does nothing to provide them. An opponent will simply say that the explanatory gap between physical processes and [acquaintance] provides all the more reason to reject physicalism. If the proponent already has such grounds, on the other hand, then the [acquaintance] strategy is rendered redundant. Either way, the strategy will play no role in supporting type-B materialism against the anti-physicalist.[23]

I think we can again agree with Chalmers most of the way, and being clear about what he has and hasn't shown with this argument will help us see what subjective physicalism can and cannot do. I think we should agree with Chalmers that:

---

[21] I have substituted "acquaintance" for "phenomenal concepts" in the quoted passages to avoid confusion. Chalmers was initially writing about phenomenal concepts, but he would make the same argument against acquaintance.

[22] Chalmers (2006, p.180).

[23] Chalmers (2006, p.181).

(a) The appeal to acquaintance does not by itself show that physicalism is true.

(b) We should view acquaintance as just as recalcitrant to physicalistic explanation as phenomenal states, and so

(c) We therefore require independent support for the truth of physicalism.

I feel less inclined to agree with Chalmers about,

(d) We require independent reasons to reject an inference from an explanatory gap to an ontological gap.

And I definitely think we should reject,

(e) If (a) through (d) are true, then acquaintance is redundant with respect to answering the anti-materialist arguments.

To start with my disagreements, it is not clear to me that even after the acquaintance strategy is deployed, as it was in Chapter 4, we need independent reasons to reject the ontological inference. If we have independent reasons to believe that physicalism is true, and the arguments against physicalism require accepting something like DN (connecting deducibility to necessitation), then proving that DN can fail because of acquaintance should allow us to retain our independent support of physicalism. The fact that another argument using DN can be run against acquaintance is of little consequence if DN has already been undermined, and this is the case even if an appeal to acquaintance was made in undermining DN. There is a sort of circularity here, perhaps, but it is no more vicious than the circularity involved in any theory which relies upon its commitments to refute objections to those commitments.[24]

In any case, the subjective physicalist does have independent reasons to reject the ontological inference. These reasons are provided in Chapter 5, and consist in a motivated rejection of the intensionalist ontology presupposed by the ontological inference. Supposing we rely on those reasons, as

---

[24] It is instructive in this context to consider the charges of circularity levelled against epistemic externalists who claim, among other things, that a certain characteristic C makes a cognitive process P justification producing, and that subjects can discover both that C is such a characteristic and that P has C, all by using P. For a classical defense of this move, see Van Cleve (1979) and, for sophisticated further defenses, see Sosa (2009). The circularity in this debate seems defensible in the same manner.

opposed to the reasons related to DN and acquaintance, does that make the appeal to acquaintance otiose as Chalmers holds in (e) above? No. It is one thing to show that there are general reasons to be suspicious of an inference, but quite another to show why it fails in a particular case. Most philosophers believe conceivability is a generally good albeit defeasible guide to possibility. If that is one's stance, there needs to be a story about why and how it is defeated in a particular instance. Acquaintance provides that story.

That being said, I think we should agree with Chalmers about (a) through (c), and this is something that too few epistemicists are ready to admit. The subjective physicalist, and epistemicists in general, must acknowledge that there is a sort of mystery in the case of consciousness. Whether that mystery is in phenomenal states themselves or how we know about them, there is a mystery, and it marks an asymmetry between our understanding of consciousness and our understanding of the rest of the physical world. We will not have an explanation of the relationship between conscious states and their physical basis of the same tight kind that we have in the case of H_2O and water, or heat and mean molecular kinetic energy. This fact has at least three major consequences.

First, it means that certain inductive arguments for physicalism should not be terribly compelling to subjective physicalists. At their clearest, these arguments infer from the past successes of science to future successes. In other words, they maintain that the past successes in scientific explanation should lead to confidence that remaining enigmas will be cleared up by the same sort of scientific explanation. But the subjective physicalist denies this inference. The subjective physicalist, as an epistemicist, maintains that even when all the physical information is in there will remain a certain explanatory gap in the case of consciousness that doesn't exist in other cases. This is betting, in a sense, on the *failure* of objective scientific theorizing. Once one has taken this stance, it seems poorly motivated to bet that because everything but consciousness has been assimilated to the physical domain that consciousness will be. The explanatory anomaly provides a compelling defeater for that inductive inference.

This observation leads to a closely related consequence. The subjective physicalist's justification for believing in the physicality of conscious states will likely be different than his justification for believing in the physicality of all other states. Phenomenal states cannot receive the sort of physicalistic explication that is available for other states. If a state can receive a physicalistic explication, as heat can be explained in terms of molecular motion, that provides a very strong reason to believe it is physical. That reason is not available in the case of consciousness. Furthermore, Chalmers is correct: diagnosing the explanatory gap does not by itself give any reason whatsoever for believing consciousness is physical. At best such a diagnosis can forestall a concession to anti-physicalism. If the anti-materialist arguments are defused by positing a quirk in our cognitive processes that disrupts typical scientific explanation, the most natural result should be a sort of skepticism and ultimately agnosticism. In such a circumstance one might think we should withhold judgment about the truth of physicalism.

This highlights an often overlooked connection between the most popular response to the anti-materialist arguments and the frequently denigrated mysterian or "ignorance" position on consciousness.[25] The epistemicist rejects the anti-physicalist arguments by maintaining that our normal ways of determining things don't work in this case. The ignorance theorist agrees. The epistemicist believes that nevertheless, physicalism is probably true. The ignorance theorist again tends to agree. What then is the difference between the two?

There are different sorts of ignorance theorists. Among other differences between them, some are what we might call optimists and others are what we might call pessimists. The optimists believe that our susceptibility to anti-materialist arguments is temporary. We await a conceptual revolution, of the sort precipitated by Copernicus or Einstein, and once such a revolution occurs we will see our mistakes in conceiving of zombies and in thinking about Mary. The relationship between the physical and the conscious will become transparent. For the most part, these theorists are hardliners of a sort: they believe that when all the physical truths are in, we will be able to deduce facts about consciousness from physical facts.

The epistemicist, and the subjective physicalist, is much more akin to the pessimist. There is a sort of cognitive block that prevents us, and will always prevent us, from deducing conscious states from physical states. The difference between the epistemicist and the ignorance theorist strikes me as more attitudinal than theoretical. The epistemicist commits while the

---

[25] McGinn (1989); Stoljar (2006).

ignorance theorist does not. Perhaps this is due to a disagreement about the facts about consciousness, but I'm inclined to doubt it. Both are likely to agree that there is an incredibly tight correlation between conscious states and brain states of the sort that strongly points to not only correlation but identity. Both are likely to agree, at least on reflection, that the problems of mental causation provide a strong reason to believe that conscious states must ultimately be physical. It might be, somewhat surprisingly, that the difference between these two camps really isn't a difference in their stances towards the mind–body problem at all. It might be that their difference is in the domain of epistemology. Quite possibly they have different beliefs about what constitutes sufficient evidence for belief, knowledge, and assertion. The epistemicist physicalist thinks, while the ignorance theorist does not, that we have enough evidence to call the game in favor of physicalism, while the ignorance theorist thinks otherwise. They both agree, really, on the evidence. They just disagree about what we are licensed to do with it.

The subjective physicalist believes that conscious states are necessitated by the physical states. But why commit? Why not remain a pessimistic ignorance theorist? In responding to the anti-physicalist, he has admitted that the normal test for such a necessary connection, deducibility, comes up negative. He argues, of course, that this doesn't mean that the phenomenal is not necessitated by the physical, but what positive reason does he have for believing that there is necessitation in the absence of such a test? The reason is simply the conviction that phenomenal states make unique causal contributions to the world, and that the story science gives us about the rest of the world is largely correct. This is, in the end, a picture of the world to which we are pretty deeply wedded, and subjective physicalism provides a way of retaining that picture in the face of the unique nature of consciousness. Depending on our epistemology, however, we might have to admit that subjective physicalism is something we can believe but not know. This wouldn't involve infallibilism or impossibly high standards of knowledge. It could, in fact, involve standards that allow most scientific beliefs to count as knowledge. The subjective physicalist should admit that belief in his position falls short of such standards, however. The conclusion of this debate depends on issues far afield, but there is reason enough to believe, I think, that the subjective physicalist, like other epistemicists, is in no position to be an ideologue.

There is one final consequence of subjective physicalism, and epistemicist theories in general, that is under recognized and potentially quite troubling. Subjective physicalism concedes that the depiction of the world given by physics and the objective sciences is complete in the metaphysical sense, provided in Part I, but incomplete in another, provided by Part II: it doesn't give us a complete understanding of the world. Our conception of the world would, in fact, be quite impoverished if we only had the picture physics gives us. We tend to assume, though, that when one combines the knowledge given us by physics, and a suitably comprehensive range of sensory experiences, we have something close to a full understanding of the world. But why should we think this? Our view admits that the world contains nooks and crannies that are metaphysically accounted for but go unnoticed in some sense by physics. The relation of acquaintance provides one entree into some of these nooks, but why think it is the only one? If in fact there are certain illuminating relations that some physical things can have to other physical things (which may or may not be their own parts) why think we occupy even a fraction of them? Why not think that our worldview is only slightly less impoverished than Mary's?

It is often counted a strike against dualism that it has no good reason to deny that rocks or electrons have phenomenal states. If it's merely a matter of psycho-physical law that qualitative states are linked to physical states, and those qualitative states can be otherwise epiphenomenal, why think we can catch a glimpse into any but the laws that concern us? In fact, the subjective physicalist is in no better position. For even if he denies that there are psycho-physical laws connecting qualia to physical states, he does think that there are special ways of knowing some physical states that increase our understanding of them, and that wouldn't be suspected from a fully objective picture of the world. But then what basis does he have for saying that there aren't other ways of knowing that will deepen our understanding of rocks in a similar way? Again, the physicalist's advantages over the dualist are fewer than we often think.

The Road Forward

If the argument of this book is accepted, we should believe that everything is physical but that some states have to be experienced in order to be fully grasped. It is perhaps a relief that we have staved off a metaphysical rift in the world, but that comes at the cost of an epistemological rift. There is a sense in which we cannot fully grasp the physicality of conscious states. It is my view that this is a rather significant admission.

To the degree that we are interested in philosophy because it helps us understand ourselves and our place in the world, it appears that we will inevitably be frustrated if we approach the world only armed with the objective pictures provided by the sciences. Consciousness is not a marginal phenomenon in our lives. It relates deeply to issues surrounding the self, knowledge, perception, reference, and the good life. There is scarcely an area of philosophy that would look the same if the world were to lack consciousness. If it turns out that consciousness cannot be completely grasped using objective means of description and understanding, it will likewise turn out that philosophical problems will not yield the desired fruits if pursued solely from within an objective framework. For those who see no explanatory gap there is little to be concerned about, but those of us who cannot in good conscience hew that hard line would do well to remember the lesson we have learned from the hard problem of consciousness.

Bibliography

Ackerman, Felicia. (1987) "An Argument for a Modified Russellian Principle of Acquaintance," *Philosophical Perspectives*, 1: 501–12.

Alexander, Samuel. (1920) *Space Time and Deity*. London: Macmillan and Co.

Alter, Torin. (1998) "A Limited Defense of The Knowledge Argument," *Philosophical Studies*, 90: 35–56.

Alter, Torin. (2005) "The Knowledge Argument Against Physicalism," *Internet Encyclopedia of Philosophy* <http://www.iep.utm.edu/know-arg/#H4> last accessed November 6, 2012.

Alter, Torin. (2008) "Phenomenal Knowledge without Experience," in Edmund Wright (ed.), *The Case for Qualia*. Cambridge, MA: MIT Press.

Alter, Torin. (2009) "Does the Ignorance Hypothesis Undermine the Conceivability and Knowledge Arguments?" *Philosophy and Phenomenological Research*, 69 (3): 756–65.

Alter, Torin. (2011) "Tye's New Take on the Puzzles of Consciousness," *Analysis*, 71 (4): 765–75.)

Alter, Torin. (forthcoming, a) "Social Externalism and the Knowledge Argument," *Mind*.

Alter, Torin. (forthcoming, b) "Review of 'Consciousness and the Prospects of Physicalism' by Derk Pereboom," *Mind*.

Alter, Torin and Robert J. Howell. (2009) *A Dialogue on Consciousness*. New York: Oxford University Press.

Alter, T., and S. Walter (eds). (2007) *Phenomenal Concepts and Phenomenal Knowledge*. Oxford: Oxford University Press.

Austin, David. (1990) *What is the Meaning of "This"?* Ithaca: Cornell University Press.

Ball, Derek. (2009) "Why There Are No Phenomenal Concepts," *Mind*, 118 (47): 935–62.

Balog, Katalin. (1999) "Conceivability, Possibility and the Mind Body Problem," *The Philosophical Review*, 108 (4): 497–528.

Balog, Katalin. (2012) "Acquaintance and the Mind–Body Problem," in Christopher Hill and Simone Gozzano (eds), *New Perspectives on Type Identity: The Mental and the Physical*. Cambridge: Cambridge University Press, 16–43.

Bealer, George. (1998) "Propositions," *Mind*, 107: 1–32.

Bennett, Karen. (2003) "Why the Exclusion Problem Seems Intractable, and How, Just Maybe, To Tract It," *Nous* 37 (3): 471–97.

Bennett, Karen. (2004) "Global Supervenience with Dependence," *Philosophy and Phenomenological Research*, 68 (3): 501–29.

Blackburn, S. (1990). "Filling in Space," *Analysis*, 50: 62–5.

Blakemore, Susan. (2004) *Consciousness: An Introduction*. New York: Oxford University Press.

Block, Ned. (2007) "Max Black's Objection to Mind–Body Identity," in T. Alter and S. Walter (eds), *Phenomenal Concepts and Phenomenal Knowledge*. Oxford: Oxford University Press, 249–306.

Block, Ned and Robert Stalnaker. (1999) "Conceptual Analysis, Dualism and the Explanatory Gap," *Philosophical Review*, 108 (1): 1–46.

Block, Ned, Owen Flanagan, and Guven Guzeldere. (eds) (1997) *The Nature of Consciousness*. Cambridge, MA: MIT Press.

Braddon-Mitchell, David and Frank Jackson. (2006) *Philosophy of Mind and Cognition*. Malden: Blackwell.

Braddon-Mitchell, D. and K. Miller. (2006) "The Physics of Extended Simples," *Analysis*, 66: 222–6.

Brewer, Bill. (1999) *Perception and Reason*. Oxford: Clarendon Press.

Burge, Tyler. (1979) "Individualism and the Mental," *Midwest Studies in Philosophy*, 4: 73–122.

Byrne, Alex. (2004) "Something About Mary," *Grazer Philosophische Studien*, 63: 124–40.

Campbell, Keith. (1990) *Abstract Particulars*. Oxford: Blackwell.

Chalmers, David. (1996) *The Conscious Mind*. Oxford: Oxford University Press.

Chalmers, David. (1999) "Materialism and the Metaphysics of Modality," *Philosophy and Phenomenological Research*, 59: 473–93.

Chalmers, David. (2002) "The Content and Epistemology of Phenomenal Belief," in Quentin Smith and Aleksandev Jokic (eds), *Consciousness: New Philosophical Essays*. Oxford: Oxford University Press.

Chalmers, David. (2003) "Consciousness and its Place in Nature," in S. Stich and T. Warfield (eds), *Blackwell Guide to the Philosophy of Mind*. Oxford: Blackwell.

Chalmers, David. (2004a) "Imagination, Indexicality and Intensions," *Philosophy and Phenomenological Research*, XVIII (1): 182–90.

Chalmers, David. (2004b) "Does Conceivability entail Possibility?" in T. Gendler and J. Hawthorne (eds), *Conceivability and Possibility*. New York: Oxford University Press, 145–200.

Chalmers, David. (2004c) "Phenomenal Concepts and the Knowledge Argument," in P. Ludlow, Y. Nagasawa, and D. Stoljar (eds), *There's Something About Mary: Essays on Phenomenal Consciousness and Frank Jackson's Knowledge Argument*. Cambridge, MA: MIT Press.

Chalmers, David. (2006a) "Phenomenal Concepts and the Explanatory Gap," in T. Alter and S. Walter (eds), *Phenomenal Concepts and Phenomenal Knowledge*. Oxford: Oxford University Press.

Chalmers, David. (2006b) "The Foundations of Two-Dimensional Semantics," in Manuel Garcia-Carpintero and Josep Macia (eds), *Two Dimensional Semantics*. Oxford: Clarendon Press, 55–140.

Chalmers, David. (2009) "The Two-Dimensional Argument Against Materialism," in Brian McLaughlin (ed.), *Oxford Handbook of the Philosophy of Mind*. Oxford: Oxford University Press.

Chalmers, David. (2010) *The Character of Consciousness*. New York: Oxford University Press.

Chalmers, David. (2011) "Propositions and Attitudes: A Fregean Account," *Nous*, 45 (4): 595–639.

Chalmers, David. (2012) *Constructing the World*. Oxford: Oxford University Press.

Chalmers, David and Frank Jackson. (2001) "Conceptual Analysis and Reductive Explanation," *Philosophical Review*, 110 (3): 315–60.

Chisholm, Roderick M. (1976) *Person and Object*. LaSalle: Open Court Publishing.

Chomsky, Noam. (1968) *Language and Mind*. New York: Harcourt Brace and World.

Chomsky, Noam. (1995) "Language and Nature," *Mind*, 104 (413): 1–61.

Chuard, Philippe. (2009) "Non-conceptual Content," in Tim Bayne, Axel Cleeremans, Patrick Wilken (eds), *The Oxford Companion to Consciousness*, Oxford: Oxford University Press.

Chuard, Philippe. (unpublished) "Conceptual Content?"

Churchland, Paul M. (1985) "Reduction, Qualia, and the Direct Introspection of Brain States," *Journal of Philosophy,* 82 (1): 8–28.

Churchland, Paul M. (1988) *Language and Problems of Knowledge*. Cambridge, MA: MIT Press.

Cohen, Jonathan. (2009) *The Red and the Real*. Oxford: Oxford University Press.

Cohen, S. Marc, Patricia Curd, and C. D. C. Reeve. (eds) (2000) "The Nichomachean Ethics," trans. T. Irwin, in *Readings in Ancient Greek Philosophy*. Indianapolis: Hackett, 870–929.

Conee, Earl. (1994) "Phenomenal Knowledge," *Australasian Journal of Philosophy*, 72 (2): 136–50.

Crane, T. and D. H. Mellor. (1990) "There Is No Question of Physicalism," *Mind*, XC: 185–206.

Crook, Seth and Carl Gillett. (2001) "Why Physics Alone Cannot Define the 'Physical,'" *Canadian Journal of Philosophy*, 31: 333–60.

Davidson, Donald. (2001) "A Coherence Theory of Truth and Knowledge," *Subjective, Intersubjective, Objective*. Oxford: Clarendon Press.

Dennett, Daniel. (1992) *Consciousness Explained*. New York: Back Bay Books.

Dennett, Daniel (2007). "What Robo-Mary Knows," in T. Alter and S. Walter (eds), *Phenomenal Concepts and Phenomenal Knowledge*. Oxford: Oxford University Press, 15–31.

Descartes, Rene. (1642) *Meditations on First Philosophy*, in J. Cottingham, R. Stoothof, and D. Murdoch (eds), *The Philosophical Writings of Descartes*, Vol. II. Cambridge: Cambridge University Press.

Dowell, Janice. (2006) "The Physical: Empirical, not Metaphysical," *Philosophical Studies*, 131: 25–60.

Ehring, Douglas. (1996) "Mental Causation, Determinables, and Property Instances," *Nous*, 30: 4.

Einstein, A., B. Podolsky, and N. Rosen. (1935) "Can Quantum-Mechanical Description of Physical Reality Be Considered Complete?" *Physical Review*, 47: 777–80.

Evans, Gareth. (1982) *The Varieties of Reference*. Oxford: Oxford University Press.

Fantl, Jeremy and Robert Howell. (2003) "Sensations, Swatches and Speckled Hens," *Pacific Philosophical Quarterly*, 84: 4.

Feigl, Herbert. (1958) "The 'Mental' and the 'Physical'," in H. Feigl, M. Scriven, and G. Maxwell (eds), *Concepts, Theories and the Mind-Body Problem*. Minnesota Studies in the Philosophy of Science, Vol. 2. Minneapolis: University of Minnesota Press, 370–97.

Fine, Kit. (2002) "The Varieties of Necessity," in T. Gendler and J. Hawthorne (eds), *Conceivability and Possibility*. New York: Oxford University Press, 253–82.

Fiocco, M. Oreste. (2007) "Conceivability, Imagination and Modal Knowledge," *Philosophy and Phenomenological Research*, LXXIV (2): 364–80.

Fodor, Jerry. (1974) "Special Sciences, or the Disunity of Science as a Working Hypothesis," *Synthese*, 28: 97–115.

Fumerton, Richard. (1995) *Meta-epistemology and Skepticism*. Lanham: Rowman and Littlefield.

Geach, P. T. (1960) "Ascriptivism," *Philosophical Review*, 69: 221–5.

Geach, P. T. (1965) "Assertion," *Philosophical Review*, 74 (4): 449–65.

Gendler, T. and J. Hawthorne. (eds) (2002) *Conceivability and Possibility*. New York: Oxford University Press.

Gertler, Brie. (1999) "A Defense of the Knowledge Argument," *Philosophical Studies*, 93: 317–36.

Gertler, Brie. (2001) "Introspecting Phenomenal States," *Philosophy and Phenomenological Research*, 63: 305–28.

Gertler, Brie. (2011) *Self-Knowledge*. London: Routledge.

Gillett, Carl and Barry Loewer. (eds) (2001) *Physicalism and Its Discontents*. Cambridge: Cambridge University Press.

Greene, Brian. (1999) *The Elegant Universe*. New York: Norton.

Hawthorne, John. (2002) "Blocking Definitions of Materialism," *Philosophical Studies*, 110 (2): 103–13.

Heil, John. (2003) *From and Ontological Point of View*. New York: Oxford University Press.

Hellie, Benj. (2004) "Inexpressible Truths and the Allure of the Knowledge Argument," in P. Ludlow, Y. Nagasaka, and D. Stoljar (eds), *There's Something About Mary: Essays on Phenomenal Consciousness and Frank Jackson's Knowledge Argument*. Cambridge, MA: MIT Press.

Hempel, Carl G. (1965) "Studies in the Logic of Explanation," *Aspects of Scientific Explanation*. New York: The Free Press, 245–90.

Hempel, Carl. G. (1969) "Reduction: Ontological and Linguistic Facts," in Sidney Morganbesser, Patrick Suppes, and Morgan White (eds), *Philosophy, Science and Method: Essays in Honor of Ernest Nagel*. New York: St. Martin's.

Hempel, Carl. G. (1980) "Comments on Goodman's Ways of Worldmaking," *Synthese*, XLV (2): 193–9.

Hill, C. S. (1997) "Imaginability, Conceivability, Possibility and the Mind-Body Problem," *Philosophical Studies*, 87: 61–85.

Hill, C. S. and B. P. McLaughlin. (1999) "There are Fewer Things in Reality Than Are Dreamt of in Chalmers's Philosophy," *Philosophy and Phenomenological Research*, 59: 446–54.

Holton, Richard. (1999) "Dispositions All the Way Round," *Analysis*, 59 (1): 9–14.

Horgan, Terry. (1984) "Jackson on Physical Information and Qualia," *Philosophical Quarterly*, 34: 147–52.

Horgan, Terry and John Tienson. (2001) "Deconstructing New Wave Materialism," in Carl Gillett and Barry Loewer (eds), *Physicalism and Its Discontents*. Cambridge: Cambridge University Press, 307–18.

Howell, Robert J. (2006) "Self-Knowledge and Self-Reference," *Philosophy and Phenomenological Research*, 72 (1): 44–70.

Howell, Robert J. (2007) "The Knowledge Argument and Objectivity," *Philosophical Studies*, 135: 145–77.

Howell, Robert J. (2008a) "The Two-Dimensionalist Reductio," *Pacific Philosophical Quarterly*, 89: 348–58.

Howell, Robert J. (2008b) "Subjective Physicalism," in Edmund Wright (ed.), *The Case for Qualia*. Cambridge, MA: MIT Press.

Howell, Robert J. (2009) "Emergentism and Supervenience Physicalism," *Australasian Journal Philosophy*, 87 (1): 83–98.

Howell, Robert J. (2010) "Subjectivity and the Elusiveness of the Self," *Canadian Journal of Philosophy*, 40 (3): 459–84.

Hudson. J. J. et al. (2011) "Improved Measurement of the Shape of the Electron," *Nature*, 473: 493–6.

Israel, David and John Perry (1991) "Information and Architecture," in John Barwise, Jean Mark Gawron, Gordon Plotkin, and Syun Tutiya (eds), *Situation Theory and Its Applications*, Vol. 2. Stanford University: CSLI.

Jackson, Frank. (1982) "Epiphenomenal Qualia," *Philosophical Quarterly*, XXXII: 127.

Jackson, Frank. (1986) "What Mary Didn't Know," *The Journal of Philosophy*, LXXXIII: 5.

Jackson, Frank. (1994) "Finding the Mind in a Natural World," in R. Casati, B. Smith, and G. White (eds), *Philosophy and the Cognitive Sciences*. Vienna: Holder-Pichler-Tempsky.

Jackson, Frank. (1995) "Postscript," in Paul K. Moser and J. D. Trout (eds), *Contemporary Materialism*. London: Routledge, 184–9.

Jackson, Frank. (1998) *From Metaphysics to Ethics*. Oxford: Oxford University Press.

Jackson, Frank. (2005) "The Case for A priori Physicalism," in Christian Nimtz and Ansgar Beckermann (eds), *Philosophy–Science–Scientific Philosophy, Main Lectures and Colloquia of GAP 5, Fifth International Congress of the Society for Analytical Philosophy*, 2003. Paderborn: Mentis, 251–65.

Kaplan, David. (1975) "Dthat," in Peter Cole (ed.), *Syntax and Semantics*, Vol. 9. New York: Academic Press.

Kim, Jaegwon. (1993) *Supervenience and Mind*. Cambridge: Cambridge University Press.

Kim, Jaegwon. (1998) *Mind in a Physical World*. Cambridge, MA: MIT Press.

Kim, Jaegwon. (2000) "Making Sense of Emergence," *Philosophical Studies*, 95: 3–36.

Kim, Jaegwon. (2005) *Physicalism or Something Near Enough*. Princeton: Princeton University Press.

Kim, Jaegwon. (2011) "From Naturalism to Physicalism: Supervenience Redux," *Proceedings and Addresses of APA*, 85 (2): 109–34.

Kirk, Robert. (forthcoming) *The Conceptual Link from Physical to Mental*. Oxford: Oxford University Press.

Kripke, Saul. (1980) *Naming and Necessity*. Cambridge, MA: Harvard University Press.

Kryukov, Alexey. (2003) "On the Problem of Emergence of Classical Spacetime: The Quantum Mechanical Approach," <http://philsci-archive.pitt.edu/id/eprint/1141> last accessed October 24, 2012.

Leanhardt, Aaron. (2011) "Precision Measurement: A Search for Electrons that Do the Twist," *Nature*, 473: 459–60.

Leuenberger, Stephan. (2008) "Ceteris Absentibus Physicalism," in Dean Zimmerman (ed.), *Oxford Studies in Metaphysics*, Vol. 4. Oxford: Oxford University Press, 145–70.

Levin, Janet. (2007) "What is a Phenomenal Concept?" in T. Alter and S. Walter (eds), *Phenomenal Concepts and Phenomenal Knowledge*. Oxford: Oxford University Press.

Levine, Joseph. (2007) "Phenomenal Concepts and the Materialist Constraint," in T. Alter and S. Walter (eds), *Phenomenal Concepts and Phenomenal Knowledge*. Oxford: Oxford University Press.

Levine, Joseph and Kelly Trogden. (2009) "The Modal Status of Materialism," *Philosophical Studies*, 145: 351–62.

Lewis, David. (1979) "Attitudes De Dicto and De Se," *Philosophical Review*, 88 (4): 513–43.

Lewis, David. (1983) "New Work for a Theory of Universals," *Australasian Journal of Philosophy*, 61 (4): 343–77.

Lewis, David. (1999a). *Papers in Metaphysics and Epistemology,* Vol. 2. Cambridge: Cambridge University Press.

Lewis, David. (1999b) "New Work for a Theory of Universals," *Papers in Metaphysics and Epistemology,* Vol. 2. Cambridge: Cambridge University Press.

Lewis, David. (1999c) "What Experience Teaches," *Papers in Metaphysics and Epistemology,* Vol. 2. Cambridge: Cambridge University Press.

Libet, B., C. A. Gleason, E. W. Wright, and D. K. Pearl. (1983) "Time of Conscious Intention to Act in Relation to Onset of Cerebral Activity (Readiness-Potential): The Unconscious Initiation of a Freely Voluntary Act," *Brain*, 106 (3): 623–42.

Loar, Brian. (1997) "Phenomenal States," in Ned Block, Owen Flanagan, and Guven Guzeldere (eds), *The Nature of Consciousness*. Cambridge, MA: MIT Press.

McDaniel, Kris. (2007) "Extended Simples," *Philosophical Studies*, 133: 131–41.

McDowell, John. (1994) "The Content of Perceptual Experience," *Philosophical Quarterly*, 44: 190–205.

McGeer, Victoria. (2003) "The Trouble with Mary," *Pacific Philosophical Quarterly*, 84 (4): 384–93.

McGinn, Colin. (1982) "The Structure of Content," in Andrew Woodfield (ed.), *Thought and Object*. Oxford: Clarendon Press.

McGinn, Colin. (1989) "Can We Solve the Mind Body Problem?" *Mind*, 98: 349–66.

McGinn, Colin. (2004) *Consciousness and Its Objects*. New York: Oxford University Press.

McLaughlin, Brian P. (1992) "The Rise and Fall of British Emergentism," in A. Beckermen, H. Flohr, and J. Kim (eds), *Emergence or Reduction?* Berlin: De Gruyter, 49–93.

McLaughlin, Brian P. (1995) "Varieties of Supervenience," in Elias E. Savellos and Umit D. Yalcin (eds), *Supervenience: New Essays*. Cambridge: Cambridge University Press, 16–59.

McLaughlin, Brian P. (2005) "A Priori versus A Posteriori Physicalism," in Christian Nimtz and Ansgar Beckermann (eds), *Philosophy–Science–Scientific Philosophy, Main Lectures and Colloquia of GAP 5, Fifth International Congress of the Society for Analytical Philosophy, 2003*. Paderborn: Mentis, 267–85.

Mandik, Pete. (2001) "Mental Representation and the Subjectivity of Consciousness," *Philosophical Psychology*, 14 (2): 179–202.

Martin, C. B. (1997) "On the Need for Properties: The Road to Pythagoreanism and Back," *Synthese*, 112: 193–231.

Maudlin, Tim. (2007) "Completeness, Supervenience, and Ontology," *Journal of Physics A: Mathematical and Theoretical*, 40: 3151.

Maxwell, Grover. (1979) "Rigid-Designators and Mind-Brain Identity," *Minnesota Studies in the Philosophy of Science*, 9: 365–403.

Melnyk, Andrew. (1997) "How to Keep the 'Physical' in Physicalism," *Journal of Philosophy*, 94 (12): 622–37.

Melnyk, Andrew. (2003) *A Physicalist Manifesto*. Cambridge: Cambridge University Press.

Milner, David A. and Melvyn A. Goodale. (1995) *The Visual Brain in Action*. New York: Oxford University Press.

Montero, Barbara. (1999) "The Body Problem," *Nous*, 33 (2): 183–200.

Montero, Barbara. (2001) "Post-Physicalism," *Journal of Consciousness Studies*, 8 (2): 61–80.

Montero, Barbara. (2006) "Physicalism in an Infinitely Decomposable World," *Erkenntnis*, 64 (2): 177–91.

Nagasawa, Yujin. (2002) "The Knowledge Argument Against Dualism," *Theoria*, 68: 205–33.

Nagasawa, Yujin. (2008) *God and Phenomenal Consciousness*. New York: Cambridge University Press.

Nagel, Ernest. (1961) *The Structure of Science*. New York: Harcourt Brace.

Nagel, Thomas. (1979a) "What is it Like to be a Bat?" *Mortal Questions*. Cambridge: Cambridge University Press.

Nagel, Thomas. (1979b) "Subjective and Objective," *Mortal Questions*. Cambridge: Cambridge University Press.

Nagel, Thomas. (1986) *The View from Nowhere*. Oxford: Oxford University Press.

Nemirow, Laurence. (1980) "Review of Thomas Nagel, *Mortal Questions*." *Philosophical Review*, 89 (3): 473–77.

Nenay, Bence. (2009) "Imagining, Recognizing and Discriminating: Reconsidering the Ability Hypothesis," *Philosophy and Phenomenological Research*, LXXIX (3): 699–717.

Ney, Alyssa. (2006) "Physicalism as an Attitude," *Philosophical Studies*, 138: 1–15.

Ney, Alyssa. (2008) "Defining Physicalism," *Philosophy Compass*, 3 (5): 1033–48.

O'Connor, Timothy and Hong Yu Wong. (2005) "The Metaphysics of Emergence," *Nous*, 39 (4): 658–78.

Oppy, Graham. (2007) *Ontological Arguments and Belief in God*. Cambridge: Cambridge University Press.

Papineau, David. (2002) *Thinking About Consciousness*. Oxford: Oxford University Press.

Papineau, David. (2007) "Phenomenal and Perceptual Concepts," in T. Alter and S. Walter (eds), *Phenomenal Concepts and Phenomenal Knowledge*. Oxford: Oxford University Press.

Papineau, David and D. Spurrett. (1999) "A Note on the Completeness of Physics," *Analysis*, 59 (1): 25–9.

Paull, C. P. and Ted Sider. (1992) "In Defense of Global Supervenience," *Philosophy and Phenomenological Research*, 32: 830–45.

Pereboom, Derk. (2011) *Consciousness and the Prospects for Physicalism*. New York: Oxford University Press.

Perry, John. (1979) "The Problem of the Essential Indexical," *Nous*, 13: 13–21.

Perry, John. (2001a) *Knowledge, Possibility and Consciousness*. Cambridge, MA: MIT Press.

Perry, John. (2001b) *Reason and Reflexivity*. Stanford: CSLI.

Putnam, Hilary. (ed.) (1975) "The Meaning of 'Meaning,'" *Mind Language and Reality: Philosophical Papers*, Vol. 2. Cambridge: Cambridge University Press, 215–71.

Ramachandran, V. S. and Blakeslee, S. (1998) *Phantoms in the Brain: Probing the Mysteries of the Human Mind*, New York: William Morrow & Company.

Robinson, Howard M. (1993a) "Dennett on the Knowledge Argument," *Analysis*, 53 (3): 169–73.

Robinson, Howard M. (1993b) "The Anti-Materialist Strategy and the 'Knowledge Argument,'" in Howard M. Robinson, *Objections to Physicalism*. Oxford: Oxford University Press.

Rodriguez-Pereyra, Gonzalo. (2002) *Resemblance Nominalism*. Oxford: Clarendon Press.

Russell, Bertrand. (1912) *The Problems of Philosophy*. London: Oxford University Press.

Russell, Bertrand. (1914/1971) "On the Nature of Acquaintance," in Robert Marsh (ed.), *Logic and Knowledge*. New York: Capricorn Books, 125–74.

Russell, Bertrand. (1927) *The Analysis of Matter*. London: Kegan, Paul.

Salmon, Nathan. (1981) *Reference and Essence*. Princeton: Princeton University Press.

Salmon, Nathan. (1986) *Frege's Puzzle*. Atacadero, CA: Ridgeview Press.

Salmon, Nathan. (1989). "The Logic of What Might Have Been," *The Philosophical Review*, 98 (1): 3–34.

Schaffer, Jerome. (1961) "Could Mental States be Brain Processes?" *The Journal of Philosophy*, 58 (26): 813–22.

Schaffer, Jerome. (1963) "Mental Events and the Brain," *The Journal of Philosophy*, 60 (6): 160–6.

Schaffer, Jonathan. (2003) "Is There a Fundamental Level?" *Nous*, 37 (3): 498–517.

Seiberg, Nathan (2005) "Emergent Spacetime," Rapporteur talk at the 23rd Solvay Conference in Physics, December, <http://arxiv.org/pdf/hep-th/0601234v1>, last accessed October 24, 2012.

Sellars, Wilfred. (1963) "Empiricism and the Philosophy of Mind," *Science, Perception and Reality*. London: Routledge and Kegan Paul (reissued Atascadero, CA: Ridgeview, 1991), §1.

Shafer-Laundau, Russ. (2003) *Moral Realism*. Oxford: Oxford University Press.

Shoemaker, Sydney. (1988) "The Inverted Spectrum," *Journal of Philosophy*, 74: 357–81.

Shoemaker, Sydney. (2003) "Causality and Properties," *Identity, Cause and Mind*. Oxford: Oxford University Press, 206–33.

Shoemaker, Sydney. (2007) *Physical Realization*. Oxford: Oxford University Press.

Sider, Ted. (2007) "Parthood," *Philosophical Review*, 116: 51–91.

Siewert, Charles. (1998) *The Significance of Consciousness*. Princeton: Princeton University Press.

Simons, Peter. (2004) "Extended Simples," *The Monist*, 87 (3): 371–85.

Smart, J. J. C. (1959/1971) "Sensations and Brain Processes," in David M. Rosenthal (ed.), *Materialism and the Mind Body Problem*. Englewood Cliffs: Prentice Hall.

Smolin, Lee. (2006) *The Trouble with Physics*. Boston: Mariner.

Snowdon, P. (1989) "On Formulating Materialism and Dualism," in John Heil (ed.), *Cause, Mind and Reality*, Dordrecht: Kluwer Academic Press.

Soames, Scott. (2002) *Beyond Rigidity*. New York: Oxford University Press.

Soames, Scott. (2005) *Reference and Description*. Princeton: Princeton University Press.

Sosa, David. (2001) "Rigidity in the Scope of Russell's Theory," *Nous*, 35: 1–38.

Sosa, Ernest. (2009) *Reflective Knowledge: Apt Belief and Reflective Knowledge*, Vol. II. Oxford: Oxford University Press.

Stalnaker, Robert. (1981) "Indexical Belief," *Synthese*, 49: 129–51.

Stalnaker, Robert. (1984) *Inquiry*. Cambridge, MA: MIT Press.

Stalnaker, Robert. (1999) *Context and Content*. Oxford: Oxford University Press.

Stalnaker, Robert. (2003a) *Ways the World Might Be*. New York: Oxford University Press.

Stalnaker, Robert. (2003b) "Varieties of Supervenience," *Ways a World Might Be*. Oxford: Oxford University Press.

Stalnaker, Robert. (2008) *Our Knowledge of the Internal World*, New York: Oxford University Press.

Stitch, S. and T. Warfield. (eds) (2003) *Blackwell Guide to the Philosophy of Mind*. Oxford: Blackwell.

Stoljar, Daniel. (2001) "Two Conceptions of the Physical," *Philosophy and Phenomenological Research*, 62: 253–81.

Stoljar, Daniel. (2005) "Physicalism and Phenomenal Concepts," *Mind and Language*, 20: 296–302.

Stoljar, Daniel. (2006) *Ignorance and Imagination*. Oxford: Oxford University Press.

Stoljar, Daniel. (2010) *Physicalism*. New York: Routledge.

Strawson, Galen. (2003) "Real Materialism," in L. Antony and N. Hornstein (eds), *Chomsky and His Critics*. Oxford: Blackwell, 49–88.

Strawson, Galen. (2006) "Realistic Monism: Why Physicalism Entails Panpsychism," in A. Freeman (ed.), *Consciousness and Its Place in Nature*. Thorverton: Imprint Academic, 3–31.

Strawson, Galen. (2008) "Realistic Monism," *Real Materialism*. Oxford: Oxford University Press, 54–74.

Sturgeon, Scott. (2000) *Matters of Mind*. London: Routledge.

Tye, Michael. (1995) *Ten Problems of Consciousness*. Cambridge, MA: MIT Press.

Tye, Michael. (2009) *Consciousness Revisited*. Cambridge, MA: MIT Press.

Van Cleve, James. (1979) "Foundationalism, Epistemic Principles, and the Cartesian Circle," *Philosophical Review*, 88 (1): 55–91.

Van Cleve, James. (1983) "Conceivability and the Cartesian Argument for Dualism," *Pacific Philosophical Quarterly*, 64: 34–45.

Van Cleve, James. (1990) "Emergence vs. Panpsychism: Magic or Mind Dust?" in J. E. Tomberlin (ed.), *Philosophical Perspectives*, Vol. 4. Atascadero, CA: Ridgeview Publishing Company, 215–26.

Van Frassen, Bas. (2002) *The Empirical Stance*. New Haven: Yale University Press.

Vierkant, Tillmann. (2002) "Zombie-Mary and the Blue Banana: On the Compatibility of the 'Knowledge Argument' with the Argument from Modality," *Psyche: An Interdisciplinary Journal of Research on Consciousness*, 8 (19).

Wegner, Daniel. (2002) *The Illusion of Conscious Will*. Cambridge, MA: MIT Press.

White, Stephen. (2007) "Property Dualism, Phenomenal Concepts and the Semantic Premise," in T. Alter and S. Walter (eds), *Phenomenal Concepts and Phenomenal Knowledge*. Oxford: Oxford University Press, 210–48.

White, Stephen. (2010) "The Property Dualism Argument," in George Bealer and Robert Koons (eds), *The Waning of Materialism: New Essays*. New York: Oxford University Press.

Wilson, Jessica. (2002) "Causal Powers, Forces, and Superdupervenience," *Grazer Philosophische Studien*, 63: 53–78.

Wilson, Jessica. (2005) "Supervenience Formulations of Physicalism," *Nous*, 39: 426–59.

Wilson, Jessica. (2006) "On Characterizing the Physical," *Philosophical Studies*, 131: 61–99.

Wilson, Jessica. (2012) "Fundamental Determinables," *Philosophers Imprint*, 12 (4).

Wright, Crispin. (2003) *Saving the Differences*. Cambridge, MA: Harvard University Press.

Wright, Edmond. (2008) *The Case for Qualia*. Cambridge, MA: MIT Press.

Yablo, S. (1992) "Mental Causation," *Philosophical Review*, 101: 245–80.

Yablo, S. (1993) "Is Conceivability a Good Guide to Possibility?" *Philosophy and Phenomenological Research*, 53: 1–42.

Yablo, S. (1999) "Concepts and Consciousness," *Philosophy and Phenomenological Research*, 59: 455–63.

Name Index

Subject Index